MGI PhotoSuite® 4 For Dummies®

Available Editing Effects

Repair Brushes

Remove Red Eye: Adjusts the color value of the pixels to approximate the natural eye color of the subject

Remove Scratches: Averages the pixel color from the surrounding area to obscure scratches in the photo

Remove Blemishes: Averages the pixel color from the surrounding area to obscure blemishes and flaws in the photo

Invert: Takes the opposite of the actual pixel colors to make light areas dark and dark areas light (like a negative)

Enhancers

Lighten: Lightens the photo, to remedy underexposed areas

Darken: Darkens the photo, to remedy overexposed photos

Warm: Gives the object a "warm" or yellowish tint (use the slidebar on the screen to adjust the intensity of the tint)

Cool: Gives the object a "cool" or bluish tint (use the slidebar on the screen to adjust the intensity of the tint)

Soften: Creates halos around the color borders of the object; also makes the contrast sharper by darkening dark colors or lightening light colors adjacent to the border

Sharpen: Makes the contrast sharper by darkening dark colors and lightening light colors in small haloed areas adjacent to the border

Colorizers

Tint: Allows you to apply a tint to the existing colors in the photo so that the original colors appear as though they're being viewed through colored eyeglass lenses (see Chapter 10)

Colorize: Allows you to change the color of portions of the photo; you can also adjust the hue, saturation, and values and the red, green, and blue tones (see Chapter 10)

Sepia: Recasts your photo in a sort of rosy or, well — sepia — tone

Tan: Recasts your photo in tan and brown color tones

Moonlight: Romanticizes your subject by applying color tones that make it appear as though it were photographed under the light of the moon

MGI PhotoSuite® 4 For Dummies®

Available Editing Effects

Special Effects

Emboss: Makes your subjects look as though they're carved on a stone tablet

Gaussian Blur, Smart Blur: Gaussian Blur allows you to brush on a blurred effect to give a sense of motion or a sort of dreamy effect to the blurred object; Smart Blur selectively blurs areas other than your primary subject, to emphasize the primary subject

Glass, Smoked Glass, Crystallize: Makes your subjects appear as though they're photographed through a pane of glass or a crystal

Tile: Superimposes a mesh of black tile-like squares over your subject, making it look as though the area is composed of inlaid tiles

Splatter: Your subject appears as though you're viewing it through a rain-soaked lens

Fog, Snow, Wind: Makes your subject appear as though you were standing outside in adverse weather conditions to photograph it; wind is especially useful to give your subject the appearance of motion

Posterize: Reduces the number of colors and pixels in a picture so that you can create a poster that isn't grainy from being enlarged

Paintings: Changes color

Mosaic: Gives your photo the effect of being composed of numerous small squares of color

Randomize: Impressionism with a vengeance: Takes the pixels in your photo and randomly jumbles them

Cheat Sheet $2.95 value. Item 0749-4.
For more information about Hungry Minds, call 1-800-762-2974.

MGI PhotoSuite® 4 FOR DUMMIES®

by Jill Gilbert

Best-Selling Books • Digital Downloads • e-Books • Answer Networks • e-Newsletters • Branded Web Sites • e-Learning

New York, NY ◆ Cleveland, OH ◆ Indianapolis, IN

MGI PhotoSuite® 4 For Dummies

Published by
Hungry Minds, Inc.
909 Third Avenue
New York, NY 10022
www.hungryminds.com
www.dummies.com

Library of Congress Control Number: 00-103395

ISBN: 0-7645-0749-4

Printed in the United States of America

10 9 8 7 6 5 4 3 2

1O/QS/QY/QR/IN

Distributed in the United States by Hungry Minds, Inc.

Distributed by CDG Books Canada Inc. for Canada; by Transworld Publishers Limited in the United Kingdom; by IDG Norge Books for Norway; by IDG Sweden Books for Sweden; by IDG Books Australia Publishing Corporation Pty. Ltd. for Australia and New Zealand; by TransQuest Publishers Pte Ltd. for Singapore, Malaysia, Thailand, Indonesia, and Hong Kong; by Gotop Information Inc. for Taiwan; by ICG Muse, Inc. for Japan; by Intersoft for South Africa; by Eyrolles for France; by International Thomson Publishing for Germany, Austria and Switzerland; by Distribuidora Cuspide for Argentina; by LR International for Brazil; by Galileo Libros for Chile; by Ediciones ZETA S.C.R. Ltda. for Peru; by WS Computer Publishing Corporation, Inc., for the Philippines; by Contemporanea de Ediciones for Venezuela; by Express Computer Distributors for the Caribbean and West Indies; by Micronesia Media Distributor, Inc. for Micronesia; by Chips Computadoras S.A. de C.V. for Mexico; by Editorial Norma de Panama S.A. for Panama; by American Bookshops for Finland.

For general information on Hungry Minds' products and services please contact our Customer Care Department within the U.S. at 800-762-2974, outside the U.S. at 317-572-3993 or fax 317-572-4002.

For sales inquiries and reseller information, including discounts, premium and bulk quantity sales, and foreign-language translations, please contact our Customer Care Department at 800-434-3422, fax 317-572-4002, or write to Hungry Minds, Inc., Attn: Customer Care Department, 10475 Crosspoint Boulevard, Indianapolis, IN 46256.

For information on licensing foreign or domestic rights, please contact our Sub-Rights Customer Care Department at 212-884-5000.

For information on using Hungry Minds' products and services in the classroom or for ordering examination copies, please contact our Educational Sales Department at 800-434-2086 or fax 317-572-4005.

For press review copies, author interviews, or other publicity information, please contact our Public Relations Department at 317-572-3168 or fax 317-572-4168.

For authorization to photocopy items for corporate, personal, or educational use, please contact Copyright Clearance Center, 222 Rosewood Drive, Danvers, MA 01923, or fax 978-750-4470.

About the Author

Jill Gilbert has a law degree and a CPA, but quit her day job to pursue writing, computer technology, and amateur photography. She is currently completing requirements for the patent law bar certification, and in her spare time searches for photos and images that she can turn into new PhotoSuite editing projects. Her favorite photo subjects are her three kids, Tara, Julia, and Daniel.

Dedication

To amateur photographers everywhere, and their smiling subjects — especially Dan Welytok, Tara, Julia, and Daniel.

Author's Acknowledgments

Special thanks to MGI, and in particular Chris Taylor, Rick Speckeen, Anat Nulman, Bogdan Popescu, Hassan Khan, Jim MacMillan, Maria Huh, Raymond Shum, and Sora Choe for thoroughly editing the content of this book and sharing the creative resources of the company. And thanks, especially, for a terrific product that would inspire any author.

Special appreciation to Lila Sloan for assembling the perfect models for this book.

I'd also like to thank IDG editors Susan Christophersen, Ed Adams, and Carol Sheehan for getting this book on the shelves.

And thank you to David Fugate of Waterside Productions for showing a special interest in *MGI PhotoSuite 4 For Dummies*.

Publisher's Acknowledgments

We're proud of this book; please send us your comments through our Hungry Minds Online Registration Form located at www.dummies.com.

Some of the people who helped bring this book to market include the following:

Acquisitions, Editorial, and Media Development

Project Editor: Susan Christophersen

Acquisitions Editors: Ed Adams and Carol Sheehan

Technical Editors: Chris Taylor and the MGI Staff

Permissions Editor: Carmen Krikorian

Editorial Manager: Constance Carlisle

Production

Project Coordinator: Maridee Ennis

Layout and Graphics: Beth Brooks, Jill Piscitelli, Jacque Schneider, Jeremey Unger

Proofreaders: Valery Bourke, Arielle Carole Mennelle, Carl Pierce, Marianne J. Santy

Indexer: Maro Riofrancos

General and Administrative

Hungry Minds, Inc.: John Kilcullen, CEO; Bill Barry, President and COO; John Ball, Executive VP, Operations & Administration; John Harris, Executive VP and CFO

Hungry Minds Technology Publishing Group: Richard Swadley, Senior Vice President and Publisher; Mary Bednarek, Vice President and Publisher, Networking and Certification; Walter R. Bruce III, Vice President and Publisher, General User and Design Professional; Joseph Wikert, Vice President and Publisher, Programming; Mary C. Corder, Editorial Director, Branded Technology Editorial; Andy Cummings, Publishing Director, General User and Design Professional; Barry Pruett, Publishing Director, Visual

Hungry Minds Manufacturing: Ivor Parker, Vice President, Manufacturing

Hungry Minds Marketing: John Helmus, Assistant Vice President, Director of Marketing

Hungry Minds Production for Branded Press: Debbie Stailey, Production Director

Hungry Minds Sales: Michael Violano, Vice President, International Sales and Sub Rights

◆

The publisher would like to give special thanks to Patrick J. McGovern, without whom this book would not have been possible.

◆

Contents at a Glance

Cartoons at a Glance

By Rich Tennant

page 63

page 203

page 145

page 5

The 5th Wave

By Rich Tennant

"...and here's me with Cindy Crawford. And this is me with Madonna and Celine Dion..."

page 293

Fax: 978-546-7747

E-mail: richtennant@the5thwave.com

World Wide Web: www.the5thwave.com

Table of Contents

Introduction

Digital photography liberated us from film and made image editing a subject of awe and wonder. But until recently, editing those images has been the purview and privilege of professional photographers or serious hobbyists with time on their hands to master complicated digital editing programs.

Not any more! PhotoSuite 4 is a new, easy-to-use program whose developers aspire to put an image on every desktop. It's fun and easy to use, but don't let good design fool you into thinking that the program lacks sophistication or versatility. In fact, many professional photographers opt to use this state-of-the art program rather than the more cumbersome ones. This is because there are few editing tasks that are beyond PhotoSuite 4's capabilities.

Why a . . .For Dummies Book?

PhotoSuite 4 is hardly an intimidating program, and many loyal users of prior versions would argue that it's too simple to merit a book. Those users are right up to a point — you certainly don't need a book to start editing and creating with this user-loving program.

But you may want a road map to take you through the seemingly infinite features and capabilities of this program. This book is here to demonstrate things that you can do with this program and the quick steps to do them. It's much faster to flip through these pages and look at my finished projects and editing examples than to embark on a journey through two full CDs of features on your own. And, of course, you get more out of anything with the added perspective of a buddy.

This book is also here to provide you with background concepts if and when you want to know about them. It's certainly not necessary to master the nuances of hue, saturation, resolution, and lighting. But as you become more fascinated with PhotoSuite 4 and more serious about your own artistry, you may get curious. This book is here for you.

How This Book Is Organized

So many features, so little time. It's important to make the most of your PhotoSuite 4 moments and this companion book. Here's a quick rundown of where to look for whatever it is you may be routing around for in these pages.

Part I: The PhotoSuite 4 Phenomenon

This section of the book gives you an overview of the program's design philosophy. It helps you get a handle on what equipment you need — and more important, what outrageously expensive stuff you don't need — to get started. It also gives you a lesson in photo-science.

Part II: Lights! Camera! Action!

This section tells you how to import a photo into PhotoSuite 4 and how to position it on your screen after you do. It also tells you how to repair damaged photos and introduces you to the program's major editing features.

Part III: Step into the Drawing Room

This section is all about color. It introduces you to theoretical stuff such as what's a primary color, hue, and saturation. It gets you started drawing, painting, and playing.

Part IV: Being a PhotoSuite 4 Paparazzo

This is the section for advanced amateurs. It tells you how to share, send, and e-mail photos. You learn how to create animated Web pages (complete with sound) in thirty minutes or fewer, and how to stitch photos together to create interactive panoramas. You even get to create a stunning PhotoTapestry, in which the subject of your photo is depicted using hundreds of tiny, thumbnail-sized photos.

Part V: The Part of Tens

Don't start clicking without this information! This section provides tips for taking better photos and introduces you to ten file formats to save them to. It also gives you the top ten troubleshooting tips from MGI technical support.

How to Use This Book

The first rule of use for this book is to enjoy, enjoy. It's not a textbook and you won't be ridiculed for skipping over whatever doesn't interest you.

It's my egotistical hope that you'll see fit to read this book cover to cover. But research shows that you're more likely to zero in on sections on a need-to-know basis and then move on to what intrigues you. For this reason, I provide lots of cross references when you need to know how to use one feature before accessing another. I tell you right where to go in the book to get the related information.

Icons Used in This Book

Like other *...For Dummies* writers, I, too, resort to the use of icons. Here's what I'm trying to tell you when you see them:

Tells you a quick and easy way to do something or gives you useful, related information.

Reminds you of important information or a concept you should keep in mind.

Tells you more than you actually need to know but it may be something you'd like to know.

Read this or suffer dire consequences.

Foolish Assumptions

I assume that you're an amateur looking to get started and not a professional photographer who bought this book just to find flaws in my photos and write me letters about them.

Conventions

How I hate that word! I consider myself a nonconformist, but alas, a few conventions are in order.

PhotoSuite 4 is a sort of menuless program. The menu method of access is replaced largely by the Navigation bar at the top of every program screen. (I tell you more about this in Chapter 2, "Not Just a Pretty Interface.") Make sure that you know where the Navigation bar is (actually, you can't miss it) because I refer you to it frequently. I also refer to the area on your PhotoSuite 4 screen where your current photo of editing project is displayed in the Workspace.

Getting Started

This couldn't be easier. Just flip through the pages, look at the illustrations, and start reading whatever inspires you. And don't forget to check out the photos in the color insert pages. They're too cool to miss.

Part I

The PhotoSuite 4 Phenomenon

In this part . . .

This part gives you a whirlwind tour of PhotoSuite 4 and its lovely little interface. Chapter 1, "Touring the Suite," marvels at the rise of digital imaging but cautions you against flinging your film camera into the ocean at present. There are still some things that film-based cameras can do that the digital darlings cannot. Chapter 2, "Not Just a Pretty Interface," familiarizes you with the all-powerful PhotoSuite 4 Navigation bar and other program features. The remaining chapters in this part give you a lively lesson in basic photo-science.

Chapter 1

Touring the Suite

In This Chapter

- PhotoSuite 4 for the masses
- The nuts and bolts of PhotoSuite 4
- Electronic images: A pixel's worth a thousand words

Novice? Hobbyist? Pro?

It used to be that digital photography and image editing were high-tech, esoteric endeavors not to be attempted by the kind of klutz who owned an Instamatic (and was proud of it). But guess what? Even those of us with Instamatic-type intellects can master the basics of PhotoSuite 4 to edit, create, and display professional-looking work. (We just have to be careful not to drop our new digital cameras down the scenic ravine we're trying to photograph.)

You ask, how is this possible? What technology can compensate for an inability to center the subject of your photo? For the red-eye look you claim is a deliberate Andy Warhol sort of thing? For the washed-out lighting? For the blur of your thumb over the lens, or the coffee spilled on the *one* photograph that actually turned out?

PhotoSuite 4 provides the technology for dealing with each and every one of these debacles. The program provides you with dozens of photo-enhancing and image-editing features. You get more than 1,500 templates and props on your installation CD.

Think of PhotoSuite 4 as a digital-editing program for the masses that offers all the cool capabilities you'll find in a high-end, hard-to-master graphics program (such as PhotoShop). If you're a novice or a hobbyist, you'll be amazed by all that you can do and how easily you can do it. And if you're a pro, you may even decide to scrap your more temperamental software package and opt for the ease of PhotoSuite 4.

How PhotoSuite 4 Works

How exactly is it that you can take a really awful photograph obscured by the blur of your thumb across the lens and turn it into something professional looking?

It's so simple, you won't believe it!

PhotoSuite 4 takes an image that you provide and allows you to enhance it using the program's digital-image enhancement and editing features. If the image is not already in digital format, the software converts it. (Digital images are explained in the next section.)

All you need to do is feed PhotoSuite 4 an existing photograph or image from one of the following sources:

- **Your computer:** You can retrieve and edit a photo from your hard drive, a floppy disk, a CD-ROM, or a network.
- **The World Wide Web:** You can surf for images and import them into PhotoSuite 4 using the techniques I tell you about in Chapter 4.
- **Your scanner:** PhotoSuite 4 supports most scanners currently on the market and allows you to edit images you've scanned. (Chapter 3 tells you how to do this.)
- **An image you import from your digital camera:** Many cameras on the market have the capability of storing photographs directly on a floppy disk. Other cameras require you to make a connection to your computer and transfer the image. In Chapter 3, I explain how PhotoSuite 4 supports most cameras currently on the market.

After you've fed an image into PhotoSuite 4 using one or more of the technologies described in the preceding list, the program automatically lets you edit, repair, and enhance your little masterpiece

Getting on the TWAIN Train

Chances are good that you'll be climbing aboard, because TWAIN is the industry standard ensuring that scanners, cameras, and other digital equipment are compatible with your computer. Believe it or not, the acronym stands for "totally without an interesting name." (Isn't that the coolest?)

PhotoSuite 4 supports several brands of digital "directly." This support occurs through the camera's Application Programming Interface (API). The process is seamless to the user, who simply needs to select the correct camera model from the drop-down list. This means that the PhotoSuite 4 provides directions and drivers that you can install for that specific brand or model (A *driver* is software that makes the scanner or camera work with PhotoSuite 4.)

Because so many cameras are on the market and quantity and type are constantly multiplying and mutating like gerbils, PhotoSuite 4 can't keep up with them all. Not all cameras are directly supported by the software.

But don't worry if your camera isn't supported directly (that is, formally acknowledged on the list provided by PhotoSuite 4). PhotoSuite 4 includes an interface and simple-to-follow procedures for hooking up to all TWAIN-compatible equipment — which includes most products currently on the market.

Hooray for industry standards!

What Are Electronic Images?

The Art Institute of Chicago has on display a famous painting by the artist Georges Seurat that always intrigued me as child. It's called "A Sunday Afternoon on the Island of La Grande Jatte." It depicts a park scene using thousands of tiny colored dots that appear as a solid uninterrupted image from a few feet back.

This is pretty much the idea behind digital imaging.

Connecting the dots

Dots are the building blocks of digital imaging — thousands of tiny dots that form a single picture. The dots that make up the digital image are referred to as *pixels*.

Digital images, or *bitmaps*, as they're sometimes called, are made up of pixels. The images that appear on your computer monitor are rows and columns of pixels.

Computer monitors and all other types of digital images are evaluated according to their *resolution*. Resolution is the number of pixels per inch, and the greater the density of the pixels, the higher the quality of the image. I discuss resolution in a lot more "graphic" detail in Chapter 2.

Each pixel is assigned a color or shade, to contribute to the overall image. MGI PhotoSuite 4 undertakes the tasks of manipulating and rearranging the pixels to alter the picture you view. In other words, the entire program's editing and enhancement features rely on some variation of pixel manipulation. And that's how it all works!

Digital versus analog

Images taken with cameras that use film are called *analog*. All you really need to know about analog images is that PhotoSuite 4 must convert them to digital format before you can start editing them. Images taken by digital cameras are already in digital format.

You can convert analog images from any standard camera (for example, your $4.98 disposable) into digital format by scanning them. Think of your scanner as a sort of conversion tool that lets you convert pictures taken with good old-fashioned film to digital images that you can manipulate with PhotoSuite 4.

Because PhotoSuite 4 works with digital images, does this mean that you should run out and buy a brand-new, expensive, state-of-the-art digital camera to make the most of the program capabilities? Not necessarily. Read on for the pros and cons.

Definite digital advantages

You can do lots of things with a photo taken on a digital camera that you can't do with a standard analog shot. Consider the following:

- You can import an image from digital image into PhotoSuite 4 *directly* from your digital camera without having to convert them using your scanner.
- (Some digital cameras allow you to add effects, such as tints at the time you take the photo.
- In the viewfinder (if it has one) of your digital camera, you can see a photograph you've just taken and decide whether you want to keep it or delete it.
- Floppy disks and CDs are cheaper and more convenient to store than film.
- Although you can use a scanner to transform your photo into digital format, the scanning of an image can compromise the quality of the photos, depending on your equipment. However, a high-quality scanner is capable of capturing at a very high resolution (as high if not higher than most digital cameras).

Downsides to digital

It's true that you ultimately have to convert an image to digital format before you can do a heckuva lot with it using PhotoSuite 4. But before you swear off film and all cameras that use it, you may want to consider a couple of downsides of the digital variety.

First, digital cameras are still downright pricey. Unless you shell out the bucks for a *high-resolution* digital camera, you may find yourself less satisfied with the image you get than if you had opted to use your old analog device. In

Chapter 4, "Imaging Equipment for All Occasions," I discuss the different options available to you in purchasing a digital camera.

Second, if you're photographing children or other fast-moving objects, you might prefer using an analog camera to get the shot you want. Unless you're opting for a very expensive digital camera, you'll find that it takes several maddening seconds after you press the shutter button to store the image into memory. In contrast, your old film-guzzling analog camera allows you to take multiple shots and is more suited to quick action shots. Having to spend a few moments scanning an image to render a good action shot to digital format may be infinitely preferable to losing it altogether while your digital camera is saving the image into memory.

V-r-r-o-o-m! Starting PhotoSuite 4

Rev up your creative engines. PhotoSuite 4 is a breeze to install, and the interface is designed to accommodate users of all levels. You can cruise at a leisurely pace, mastering the basic menus and toolbars with the benefit of lots of clear direction and comprehensive Help features. Or, if you're an advanced user, you can step on the gas and access sophisticated program tools.

You don't have to be a mechanic

One of the reasons that PhotoSuite 4 is so simple to use, while providing a sophisticated array of graphics features, is that it operates on the principal of *encapsulation*. This means that it insulates you from features you don't need at the moment, showing you only the relevant features to each particular phase of the project as you're performing it. (Sort of like how your car or VCR works.)

Getting the key in the ignition

When you've installed PhotoSuite 4, you can launch it by selecting MGI PhotoSuite 4 from your start menu. Chapter 2, "Not Just a Pretty Interface," takes you on a tour of the PhotoSuite screens and features.

Chapter 2

Not Just a Pretty Interface

In this Chapter

- Getting anywhere you need to go with the Navigation bar
- Editing and enhancing your photos
- Special effects for every weird occasion
- Sharing photos via e-mail, Web sites, and slide shows
- Creating electronic albums
- Keeping current with the PhotoSuite 4 Web site
- Getting help from PhotoSuite 4

PhotoSuite 4 is designed with your comfort in mind. Its considerate interface shows you *only* the options you absolutely need for a particular phase of the project. You simply click a button to display one of the seven program screens representing different, logical phases of your editing project. This logic makes the sophisticated technology of digital editing simpler to master than an ordinary word processing program.

This chapter takes you on a cruise ship tour of the seven screens of the program. After you're aware of what's on each screen, you can revisit the features and explore them in depth.

The Face of PhotoSuite 4

The Workspace, located smack dab in the middle of your PhotoSuite 4 screen, displays the project you're currently working on. The project of the moment may be a photo, album, slide show, calendar, card, collage, or anything else you undertake. If you don't have a project in progress, the Workspace is predictably blank.

Your Workspace is surrounded by menus and bars that enable you to access all the program features to complete your masterpiece (see Figure 2-1) without ever having to lose sight of your work-in-progress for a single second. (In the next section of this chapter, I tell you how to use these menus and bars.)

The Library panel, located to the right of the screen, shows you all the photos, projects, albums, and slide shows you've opened during the current PhotoSuite session. It also has a drop-down menu that you can use to access any album. *Albums* are special files that PhotoSuite 4 uses to help you organize your photos. (Albums are discussed in Chapter 14, "Say 'Cheese!' Family Albums, Slide Shows, and Screen Savers.")

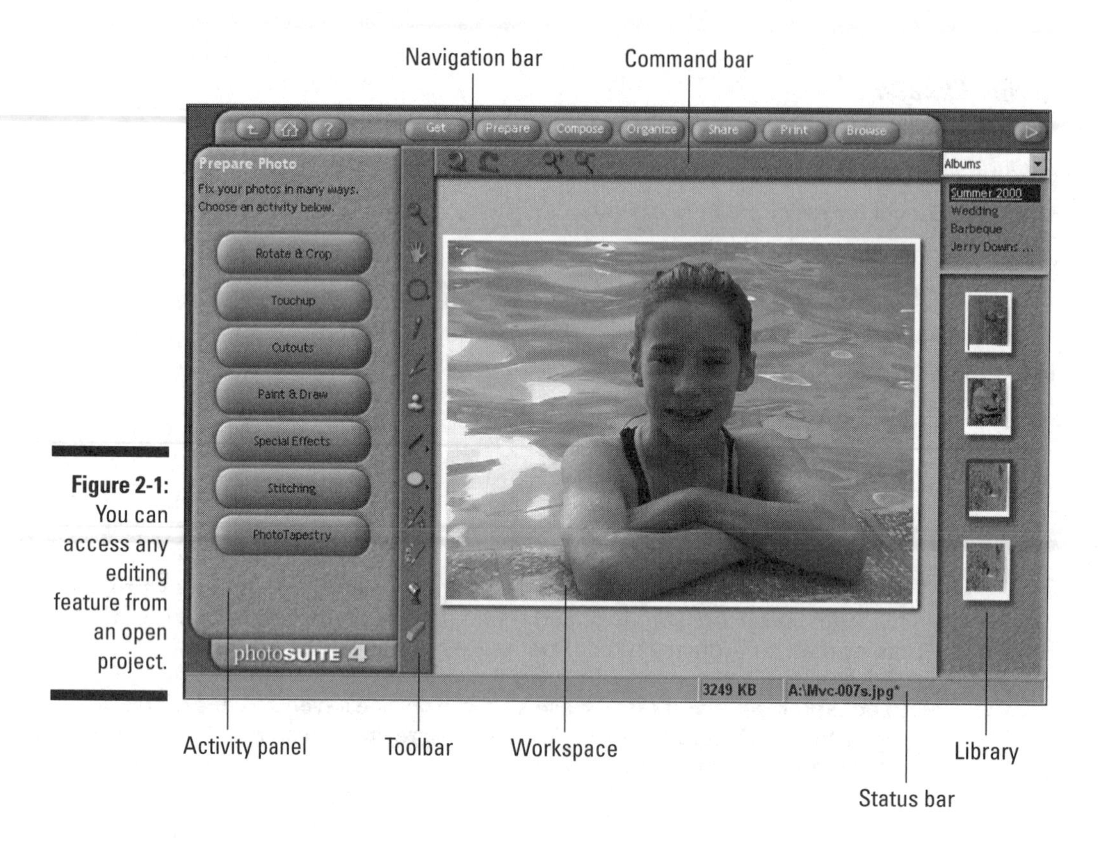

Figure 2-1: You can access any editing feature from an open project.

Bar Hopping

PhotoSuite 4 boasts five different types of button, menu, and status bars that allow you to access and track all the program features:

- **Navigation bar:** Allows you to access seven different program areas corresponding to logical phases of a project.
- **Activity panel:** Located on the left side of the screen, this panel lists and provides access to features available at each specific phase of a project.

- **Toolbar:** Located at the center of the screen, the toolbar provides access to more than a dozen photo editing functions.
- **Command bar:** Contains general application tools such as undo, redo and the Zoom feature.
- **Status bar:** Tells you the filename of the photo and how much space it's taking up on your computer. (Dimensions are shown only when cropping a photo.)

If you're not much of a barfly, you can still resort to the Windows standard menus (see Figure 2-1, shown previously). But for the most part, both PhotoSuite novices and veterans find the button bars fastest and most intuitive.

Negotiating the Navigation bar

The Navigation bar, shown in Figure 2-2, is visible at the top of every PhotoSuite 4 screen. It takes you to all the major screens of the program, allowing you to progress quickly through each logical phase of a project.

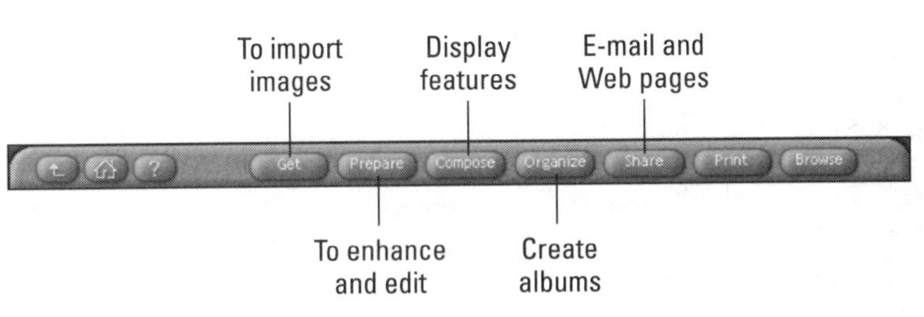

Figure 2-2: The Navigation bar enables you to quickly access program features.

The buttons on the Navigation bar are organized sort of chronologically, to correspond to each of seven possible phases of your project, as follows:

- **Get:** This button takes you directly to the options and features you need to import an image into PhotoSuite 4.
- **Prepare:** This button opens a screen that provides access to the major editing options and special effects.
- **Compose:** Click this button when you're ready to turn your photos into cards, tags, calendars, or comic books or to combine them into collages or add props.
- **Organize:** This button accesses features that help you create albums to arrange and display your newly edited and artistically enhanced images.

- **Share:** This button takes you to the screen you use to send e-mails, create Web pages and wallpaper, bore people with slide shows, and do just about any other sociable thing you can think of doing with photos.
- **Print:** This one's self explanatory, hey? This is the button you'll click to access all your printing options.
- **Browse:** Click this button to browse the World Wide Web and import photos from it into PhotoSuite 4.

PhotoSuite 4 has a surprisingly complete Help feature, just in case you hit an artistic roadblock. You can access it from the standard Windows menu located directly above the Navigation bar, or by clicking the Help icon (the question mark) on the Navigation bar.

Trying out the toolbar

The toolbar is visible only when you click the Prepare button on the Navigation bar to display the Prepare screen. The toolbar, shown in Figure 2-3, contains a dozen editing options.

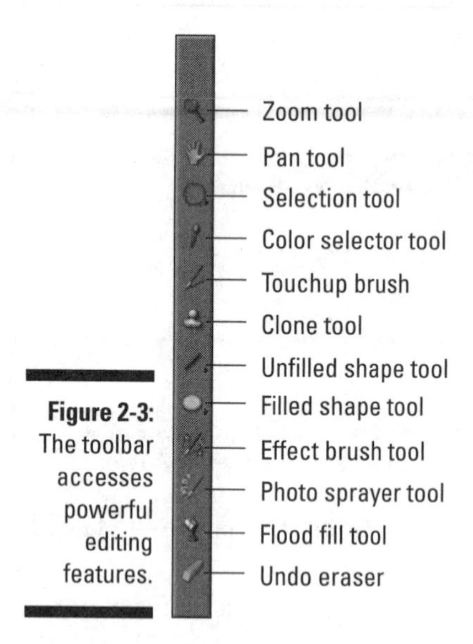

Figure 2-3: The toolbar accesses powerful editing features.

You can turn the toolbar on and off by doing the following:

1. **Click the Prepare button on the Navigation bar.**

   The Prepare window appears (see Figure 2-1).

2. **From the menu options at the top of the screen, go to View➪Tools.**

   If the toolbar is to appear on your screen, a check mark appears in front of the Tools option.

If you're a novice, begin working in the program with the Tools toolbar turned off and simply follow the step-by-step workflow. Also, when the toolbar is turned off, the preview image on your screen is about 20 percent larger, which makes it easier to edit.

Confronting the Command bar

The Command bar, which appears directly below the Navigation bar, contains a few little essentials that make the life of a wannabe graphic artist so much easier. By clicking the Command bar icons shown in Figure 2-4, you can avail yourself of the following:

- **An unlimited Undo feature:** This feature lets you remove special effects and edits you've added, one at a time. The feature is "unlimited" in the sense that it remembers however many features you add and allows you to peel them off one at a time, like the layers of an onion, to restore your original palette. (Note, however, that you cannot use the Undo feature after a photo or project has been saved.)
- **Redo feature:** This feature is especially convenient when used in conjunction with the Undo feature, because it allows you to apply features and take them off again until you decide you have just the effect you want. As with Undo, you can't make use of this feature after you've saved the project or photo.
- **Zoom tools:** This feature allows you to shrink or enlarge a photo in your work area so that you can work more easily editing a particular detail or get a perspective of the image as a whole.

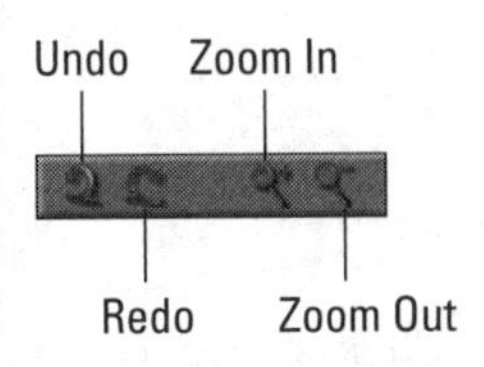

Figure 2-4: This little Command bar contains essential editing tools.

Tracking your photo activity in the Library

PhotoSuite 4 includes a Library, on the right side of the screen (available in any activity), which keeps track of all currently open photos, albums, projects, and slide shows. The Library displays these items as thumbnails, shown in Figure 2-5.

Thumbnails are miniature, postage-stamp sized versions of your photo.

Figure 2-5: The library icons give you instant access to all your open projects.

Get-ing Started

The editing process starts with the Get window. Click the Get button on the Navigation bar to access all the program features that allow you to import and open graphics files.

The Get window contains a column of buttons called the Activity panel. These buttons allow you to import images from different sources. For example, if you're accessing an image from one of the drives on your computer, you click the Computer button to display the Activity panel.

Chapter 5, "Where Do Little Images Come From?," tells you more about how to import images.

To have the Get window appear whenever you first start the computer, select the check box labeled Always start on this page.

Prepare-ing to Change the World

The options on the Prepare window don't really let you change the world, but they sure can make your pictures of it look better. After you've imported an image into PhotoSuite 4, you're limited only by your imagination.

Editing away your problems

You can access a wide array of editing options by clicking the Prepare button on the Navigation bar (refer to Figure 2-2).

Suppose that you have a compelling and revealing portrait of somebody famous and reclusive such as Bill Gates or Michael Jackson. The celebrity, whom you just happened to catch at an out of the way place, smiled obligingly into *your* camera and allowed you to capture his essence. The only problem is the big piece of spinach stuck to his teeth. You don't want *that* there, do you?

No problem for PhotoSuite 4, which provides just the ticket to allow you to edit out that disgusting little dental detail. Unfortunately, this example must remain in the hypothetical because I couldn't get anyone famous to pose with the spinach. I can, however, give you a feel for some of the editing capabilities that you'll find on the Prepare window:

- **The Bad Hair Day:** The model in Figure 2-6 shows you how PhotoSuite 4 provides an answer to the inevitable bad hair day. Photo Suite's clone features (covered in Chapter 7, "Eeek! Making Ugly Things Look Better") allows a quick redo of the hairdo, as shown in Figure 2-7.

Figure 2-6: A bad hair day.

Figure 2-7: PhotoSuite 4 resolves the bad hair day.

- **Get the red out:** What wanna-be photographer hasn't encountered that ghoulish red-eye look? Fortunately, you can use PhotoSuite 4 to get that red out. Color Plate 2-1 illustrates this PhotoSuite 4 capability by giving you a great before-and-after-the-red-eye shot of a crying kid.
- **Straighten Things Up:** I can never seem to scan a photo straight! I swear that the pictures move themselves after I close the lid on my scanner. But I can set things straight using Photo Suite's Rotate and Crop tools on the Prepare screen. I can rotate my photo to the left or to the right, flip it, or click a single button to straighten it. Chapter 6, "Getting that Slippery Photo Where You Want It," tells you how to use the Rotate and Crop tools.

Touch-up tools and tricks

Some of our best-loved subjects must be photographed under less-than-ideal circumstances.

Fortunately, you don't have to worry about as many small details with PhotoSuite 4, which means that you're less likely to miss an important moment. For example, you can confidently take that photo of your children at the beach with their sand castle, knowing that you can edit out the fat man in the tight bathing suit sitting in the background.

Here are a few more problems you can fix with the liberating features accessed from the PhotoSuite 4 Prepare window:

- **Less than perfect lighting?** The automatic Enhance feature allows you to increase the contrast and enrich the colors that appear in your photo. This feature is covered in Chapter 7.
- **Underexposed or overexposed photos.** PhotoSuite 4 includes a sophisticated array of touch-up brushes and filters that allow you to lighten, darken, tint, and colorize images that were originally under- or overexposed by the photographer. I tell you everything you need to use them like a pro in Chapter 7.
- **Scratched and damaged photos.** The Remove scratches feature allows you to get rid of the scratches that result from damaged negatives or photos. I talk about this tool in Chapter 8, "First Aid For Damaged Photos."

The tapestry effect

Another amazing special effect is the PhotoTapestry feature, illustrated in Color Plates 2-2 and 2-3. PhotoSuite 4 produces an ultra-artistic tapestry effect by replicating a photo consisting of many small thumbnail photos that are essentially woven together in a tapestry.

PhotoSuite 4 uses sophisticated technology to analyze your original photo's hue, color saturation, brightness, and other factors and then retrieves thumbnail images from an enormous database of images — either ones that are included on the installation CD-ROM or that you import yourself.

I cover the PhotoTapestry feature in Chapter 17.

Stitching photos

One of the most downright useful, as well as revolutionary, features of PhotoSuite 4 is the Stitching feature. Stitching allows you to put together a series of photos to form one continuous image (see Color Plate 2-4).

I tell you more about stitching features in Chapter 17.

For people who are really warped

This fun-house mirror effect seems to be everyone's favorite. You can use the pre-set warp feature to apply this effect to your whole photo, as shown in Figure 2-8. Or you can distort an image with some surprisingly artistic results, as shown in Figure 2-9 (see also Color Plate 2-5). In Chapter 12, "Walk on the Wild Side: Special Effects," I tell you how to really have some fun with this feature.

Figure 2-8: Here's an example of the PhotoSuite 4 Preset Warp feature.

Figure 2-9: You can really mess up someone's face with the Interactive Warp feature.

More creative outlets

PhotoSuite 4 provides you with lots of other creative outlets. Here are just a few examples you can find (discussed in Chapter 12):

- **Cartoonize.** Gives your photo subject a surreal appearance.
- **Paintings.** Use this effect to give your cheap, generic photo the appearance of an expensive oil painting or watercolor.
- **Ripple.** Gives your photo an underwater effect.
- **Splatter.** Gives your photo a spilled and splattered appearance by distorting portions of it in a random pattern.
- **Fog, snow, wind, and rain.** You can simulate any weather condition for your photo subject, such as a row of bikini-clad gals in a blizzard.

If none of the foregoing features impresses you or captures your imagination, that's okay. I've barely scratched the surface in this chapter in listing the special effects that PhotoSuite 4 offers, and I have not even touched upon the topic of combining several effects in one photo. Skim the table of contents of this book for more ideas.

Compose-ing a Photo-Symphony

You can use PhotoSuite 4 to create images of things that *don't* exist.

For example, did you ever wish that you could draw in one of those cartoon dialog balloons to show what a photo subject was really thinking? Or switch someone's head onto a cartoon body?

The Compose window contains all the tools you need to create weird and whimsical images. Here are just a few examples of things this book tells you how to do using the options on the Compose screen:

- **Add props and text.** PhotoSuite 4 comes with hundreds of ready-made props that you can drag, drop, and resize like the ones I've imported to be shown in Figure 2-10. You can also add captions and text to your photos, as I've done to the Word Balloon prop. Chapter 9, "Performing Photo-Surgery," tells you how.
- **Create collages.** You can add cutouts and combine multiple files and image files into a finished project using the Collage feature, discussed in Chapter 9.
- **Prepare photo layouts.** Select from hundreds of templates to create comic books, family trees, posters, paper photo albums, magazine covers, and posters.
- **Make calendars, cards and tags, and business items.** Select from still more templates to create the useful items I tell you about in Chapter 15, "Cheap Gifts and Chic Digital Accessories" and Chapter 16, "PhotoSuite 4 for Fun and Profit."

Organize-ing Photo Albums

Albums are the organizational data base tools of PhotoSuite 4. You can organize your photos into an album on your computer and then transfer the album on disk.

A master album is automatically created when you use this feature the very first time, and this album serves as a list for all of the subsequent albums you create. You can make as many copies of your albums as you have people who want to look at them. Chapter 14, "Say 'Cheese!' Family Albums, Slide Shows, and Screen Savers," covers the organization creation and structure of albums.

Figure 2-10: Revealing the subject's thoughts and adding a few props.

Share-ing the Fun

PhotoSuite 4 provides you with everything you need to throw a digital imaging party. You can socialize with a slide show by e-mail or on the Web. It costs you virtually nothing to keep in touch with friends and relatives on a visual basis:

- **Bore them with your vacation slides.** You can create the ultimate slide show to display on your monitor or use in a presentation. You can customize the order slides are displayed and even add a sound effect to each file for an extraordinary visual experience.
- **E-mail images everywhere.** The designers of PhotoSuite 4 realize how much of our daily lives we conduct by e-mail. Accordingly, they've included features that allow you to directly access your e-mail from the program. PhotoSuite 4 sends a generic message telling recipients they're receiving a digital photo and referencing the file sent in the message. You can add a personal greeting or let your picture say it all. You can read up on the PhotoSuite 4 e-mail features in Chapter 13, "Graphics on the Go."
- **Wallpaper the place.** PhotoSuite 4 allows you to create wallpaper for your computer desktop. You can select any photo you like as a background image for your workspace.

Print-ing Perfectly

The Print button on the Navigation bar gives you access to all the options you need to create a hard copy of the image on your computer screen. The Print Screen options are designed to work with a wide variety of printers and papers. But it may be that your printer doesn't produce the image quality you want, or doesn't work with the photo-quality papers that provide that finished, professional look.

PhotoSuite 4 gives you the option of using a *real* photo lab, not just your printer. You have the capability to use the Kodak PhotoNet online service to send your photos to the lab, using the PhotoNet Web site. After you're connected to the Web site, you're guided through a step-by-step process of submitting your digital images and ordering those high-quality prints you crave.

You can learn more about PhotoNet Online in Chapter 13.

Browse-ing the Great Beyond

You can access the PhotoSuite Web site or browse the World Wide Web for images to import into PhotoSuite 4 by clicking the Browse button on the Navigation bar. Chapter 5 tells you how you can drag an image from a Web page to your PhotoSuite 4 screen.

The PhotoSuite Web site provides you with access to tips, tricks, new downloads, and upgrades. For example, for Mothers' Day this year, I downloaded cards, frames, and clip art to spruce up the photos I sent to my mom. The PhotoSuite Web site also links you to dozens of photography-related Web pages.

If you envision a program innovation that isn't on the PhotoSuite Web site today, chances are good that you'll find it tomorrow.

Getting Help from PhotoSuite 4

Gee, PhotoSuite 4 has a lot of features.

I hope that, in this book, I anticipate every PhotoSuite 4 question you may ever have. But just in case I miss a few, it's a good idea to become familiar with the PhotoSuite 4 Help features.

You can access the PhotoSuite 4 Help menu by selecting Help⇨MGI PhotoSuite 4 Help from the menu at the top of the PhotoSuite 4 screen.

The comprehensive PhotoSuite 4 Help feature is structured similarly to that of most Windows-based programs. PhotoSuite 4 offers you the following three methods for finding an answer to your artistic dilemma:

- **Contents.** You can find the answer to your question by browsing through the table of contents of an on-screen Help manual.
- **Index.** You can scroll through an alphabetical index.
- **Search.** You can find the answer to your question by initiating a keyword search.

Chapter 3

Photo-Science: Fun with Chemicals and Computer Chips

In This Chapter

- Comparing digital and film-based pictures
- Discovering how chemicals and computer chips make pictures
- Viva la Resolution!
- Understanding pixels perfectly
- Finding out about lighting
- Understanding the science of color reception

The act of creating a photograph and capturing an image for eternity is nothing short of miraculous. And the process is simpler than you might think. Even if you're not generally intrigued by the chemistry and physics of day-to-day appliances, the science of creating a photograph is really pretty cool.

Digital versus Film-Eating Cameras

Does your brain go to static when it all gets too technical? If so, you can safely skip this section and move on. The information I give you is strictly a run-down of the differences between today's digital cameras and the film-based variety that captured your childhood memories.

Cookin' with film

Before the recent dawn of the digital camera, photographers everywhere relied almost exclusively on a process developed in 1850. This process hasn't changed a lot over the last 150 years. It has merely been refined to make it more convenient to use.

The basic recipe for predigital-era photography calls for a thin layer of light-sensitive silver particles and halide crystals suspended in a layer of gelatin, spread generously over the plastic roll of stuff you call film. (Yum!) When the halide crystals are exposed to light, they change chemically.

When the film is "developed," particles of silver bond to the halide chemical in proportion to the amount of light to which the halide was exposed. This process creates the negative. The negative gets exposed to a second type of developing process, which transfers the image to photo-quality paper and adds color tones. (I explain a bit more about this in the last section of this chapter, "A Touch of Color.")

The negative is a sort of picture in reverse — the dark and light areas of the negative are opposite of what they are in the finished photograph (hence, the term "negative"). The process of switching the tonal values around and adding colors or black-and-white gradations (called *grayscale)* is accomplished by transferring the images from the negatives onto photo-sensitive paper. Even today, many photography pros and hobbyists insist on processing their own negatives and using only traditional film-based cameras so that they can exercise better control over the tonal quality of their finished product.

Doing it digitally

Digital cameras use light-sensitive computer chips rather than film to produce an everlasting image. There are two types of chips: CCD and CMOS.

CCD stands for *charge-coupled device,* whereas CMOS is short for *complementary metal-oxide semi-conductor.* Both types of chips emit an electrical charge when they're struck by light. This charge is interpreted and processed by the digital camera to produce image data that's saved to the camera's memory or a removable floppy disk.

The chips register the color value of individual pixels, which are dots of color in the finished picture. When exposed to light, the chip stores and records the color value of each pixel so that the image can be reproduced. Each pixel receives a color value on a scale of 0–255, which indicates how intense the light was to which the pixel was exposed (I explain in greater detail how pixels are used to reproduce images in the next section of this chapter, "You Say You Want a Resolution . . . Well . . . .")

The digital chip captures only grayscale images. But the grayscale images are passed through various color filters.

The CCD chip is the more expensive, top-of-the-line variety, whereas CMOS is used in lesser-quality cameras. The CMOS chips introduce imperfections and distortions that are not present in CCD devices.

It's best to spring for a CCD camera, particularly because the cost difference is usually not significant.

You Say You Want a Resolution . . . Well . . .

Resolution is the key to image quality. Even if you're the most casual of hobbyists and are determined to avoid anything remotely technical, I suggest you read this particular section. Someday, you may fall hopelessly in love with an image and may want to do everything in your power to enhance its every detail.

What is resolution?

In Chapter 1, I tell you about one of my favorite paintings, *Sunday Afternoon on the Island of la Grande Jatte,* by Georges Seurat. The painting consists of hundreds of thousands of tiny dots of color that appear as a single, continuous image when viewed from a few feet back. The artistry of Georges Seurat aptly illustrates the technical concept of resolution. (I wonder whether anyone ever ran up behind him and yelled "Boo!" while he was doing all those dots.)

Resolution is the number of colored dots per inch that make up an image. Digital images are made up of tiny dots, each storing a distinct color or gradations of color. When viewed by the human eye, the effect of the pixels is to produce a smooth, continuous image. In a good-quality photograph, the gradations of the individual dots aren't usually apparent to the naked eye. As you can see in Figure 3-1 and Figure 3-2, I can use the PhotoSuite 4 Zoom feature (covered in Chapter 6, "Getting That Slippery Photo Where You Want It") to get a feel for this. I can zoom in to see the individual color gradations (although not each pixel) of the tooth of the monster fish at the amusement park.

Figure 3-1: When viewed normally, a digital photograph appears as a continuous image.

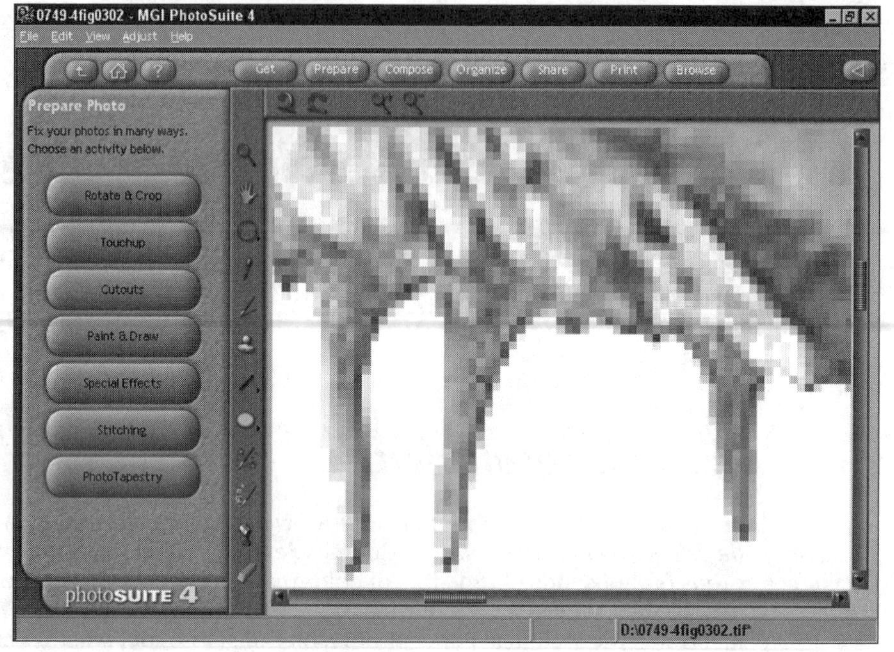

Figure 3-2: Here is the monster tooth magnified. See how the color gradations pop out at you?

Increasing the number of pixels for an image generally determines the quality of the image in the following ways:

- The more dots in the image, the more perfect the illusion of a continuous, uninterrupted picture.
- Because each pixel is a unique repository for storing color information, the more pixels you have, the more color information and variations you can depict. If you double the number of pixels in an image, you double the capacity to capture gradations of color in each individual dot.
- Increasing the number of pixels enhances the amount of detail for the shot.

Decoding information about pixels

Resolution, or quality, of an image is measured in terms of pixels per inch (ppi) It's based on the size of your photograph — you measure the number of pixels for each inch of your photograph.

The way pixels are measured is sort of confusing, because they're measured by *linear* inch and not by square inch, as you might expect. To complicate matters further, the pixels actually shrink and grow depending on the size of your photograph. Those little rascals actually expand and contract to fit within or fill the dimensions of your picture.

For example, say that my camera captures 1,280 pixels across and 960 pixels lengthwise. Suppose that I want to create a picture having a resolution of 300 ppi. To do so, I need to divide 1,280 by 300 to determine the maximum width my photo can have. Then I need to divide 960 by 300 to get the maximum length. In this case, I can have a photo 4.25 inches wide by 2.25 inches long to get the desired resolution.

Getting pixel-perfect pictures

Generally, the higher the resolution, the better the quality of the image, subject to the limitations of your printer and computer monitor.

Computer monitors, like cameras, have a pixel count. Scanners and printers use different measures of image quality. (See the section "Kosher pixels and other image condiments," later in this chapter.)

PhotoSuite 4 requires your computer system to operate at a minimum of 800 x 600 resolution.

The effect of increasing and decreasing resolution is usually perceptible but not always dramatic. Figures 3-3, 3-4, and 3-5 show three photographs of the same dimensions shot at different resolutions.

Figure 3-3 is reproduced at 1024 x 768 pixel count. This resolution allows you to see the baby's eyelids clearly, and the pudgy little hands are well defined against the baby's face. Figure 3-4 is produced at 800 x 600, and the loss of detail is negligible (although the file size is considerably less reduced, as I explain in the next section). By the time I get down to 640 by 480 pixels in Figure 3-5, those pudgy little hands are pretty blurry and the baby's left hand blends into his face.

I can get rid of that graininess, as shown in Figure 3-5, which was shot at the lowest resolution, by shrinking the dimensions of the photo so that there are more pixels per inch. This will not, however, improve the detail of the shot. (The baby's left hand will still blend into his face.)

Good quality prints should be about 300 ppi.

As a general rule, the higher the number of pixels, the higher the price tag on the camera. The manufacturers of PhotoSuite 4 advise that images shot at a resolution higher than your computer monitor and printer can accommodate may simply waste storage space. (See the section "Kosher pixels and other image condiments" for more information about coordinating the capabilities of your camera, computer monitor, and printer.

Figure 3-3: Reproduced at a resolution of 1024 x 768 pixels.

Figure 3-4: Reproduced at a resolution of 800 x 600 pixels.

Figure 3-5: Reproduced at a resolution of 640 x 480 pixels.

Pixels can be pigs

Now that you know that more pixels mean more detail and better image quality, does this mean that you should automatically set the equipment to capture the image at the highest resolution? Not necessarily. You can have too much of a good thing. It's a tradeoff between image quality and file space.

When it comes to file space, pixels can be downright piggy. For example, an image taken at 640 x 480 in True Color takes a whopping 936 kilobytes of storage space. A similar image shot with 320 x 240 resolution takes up only about 100 kilobytes. (The sidebar in Chapter 4 called "Calculating file size" tells you how to compute file size.)

Those space-hogging pixels can also be a real drain when it comes to viewing and editing the images. Large image files make gluttonous demands on your computer's processor and temporary memory (RAM) when you edit them. And they can really irritate your friends and relatives when they take hours to download and clog up their e-mail systems.

Resolving the resolution dilemma

So just how do you set about resolving the gut-wrenching dilemma between detailed images and reasonable demands on your computer's hard drive and memory?

A big factor should be what you actually intend to *do* with the image after you edit it. For example, if you intend to view it on your computer screen or as part of a slide show, lower resolution is fine. Most monitors don't have the capacity to view images at a resolution of greater than 73 to 96 ppi (or 1024 x 768). So anything above that is just wasted space as far as your audience is concerned.

If you plan on printing the image using a standard printer, be aware that too many pixels can actually degrade image quality if your printer isn't set up to handle them. Printer manufacturers disclose the dots per inch, or *dpi,* that can be produced by a printer. If you exceed the number of dpi your printer can handle, the effect can be smudgy or blurry.

Some people confuse pixels per inch (ppi) with dots per inch (dpi), used to measure printer quality, and try to match them. But ppi and dpi are *not* the same units of measure, so matching them doesn't do any good. Generally, the higher the resolution of the image, the more dots per inch you need to print all the detail. (Chapter 4, "Imaging Equipment for All Occasions," tells you what you need to know about purchasing the perfect printer.)

Kosher pixels and other image condiments

Your computer monitor, scanner and printer all have limitations when it comes to the amount of detail they can display — detail that is stored in the pixels of the image. You want to give some serious thought to the capabilities of your equipment so that you can save file space by storing only the amount of pixels that can actually be displayed or printed.

Some more pixel terminology

Whether you're shopping for equipment or fiddling with the settings on something you've just purchased, it helps to understand the lingo of pixels. Here are a few dotty little terms you'll hear bandied about from time to time:

- **VGA resolution:** Refers to a 640 x 480-pixel image
- **XGA resolution:** Captures an image at 1024 x 768 pixels
- **Megapixel:** Capable of producing an image having more than one million pixels

Printers measure dots, not pixels

Most printer manufacturers include information about the dpi, or number of dots per inch their printer can produce. It's important to remember that dpi refers to the number of dots of color a printer can produce per linear inch. This is *not* the same measure as pixels per inch.

Most printers use several dpi to produce a single pixel. So it isn't going to do you any good to compare dpi and ppi when shopping for a printer — it's oranges to apples. For example, a 300 ppi photograph may require a 1200 dpi device to print the image adequately.

What you *really* need to do is check your printer's manual or contact the manufacturer to find out the resolution (ppi) the printer is able to handle. Don't try to translate on your own.

Your monitor uses pixels

Your computer monitor displays images expressed in terms of pixels.

Your computer monitor probably allows you to choose from a variety of resolution settings, as shown in Figure 3-6. To view your options for setting the resolution on your computer monitor using Windows 2000, follow these steps:

1. **From the Start menu on your desktop, select Settings.**

   A pop-up menu appears.

2. **Select Control Panel.**

   A dialog box or screen showing several icons appears.

3. **Click the Display icon.**

   The dialog box shown in Figure 3-6 appears. The appearance of the dialog box may vary slightly depending on your version of the Windows program.

4. **Slide the Screen area control lever to set your computer monitor to the desired resolution.**

   Most monitors on the market today allow you to display at a maximum resolution of 1024 x 768 pixels.

Scanners convert samples to pixels

Scanner vendors often describe their product's capabilities in terms of *samples per inch,* or *spi.* A scanner takes a certain number of samples of the original image and translates them into a format that your computer can use to create pixels or dpi.

At the time of the writing of this book, most scanners are capable of capturing images of at least 800 x 600 spi. Sometimes you'll see hype about "interpolated" or "enhanced" scanner resolution. These terms refer to the capability of a scanner to improve the clarity of a low-resolution image by adding pixels. The scanner makes an educated guess about what the "missing" pixels would look like. With the addition of pixels, less space exists between the pixels, and the image appears smoother and more continuous. But because the scanner has to guess how the missing pixels should look, this isn't a great way to capture more detail or fine color gradations. It just makes the final image look less blurry.

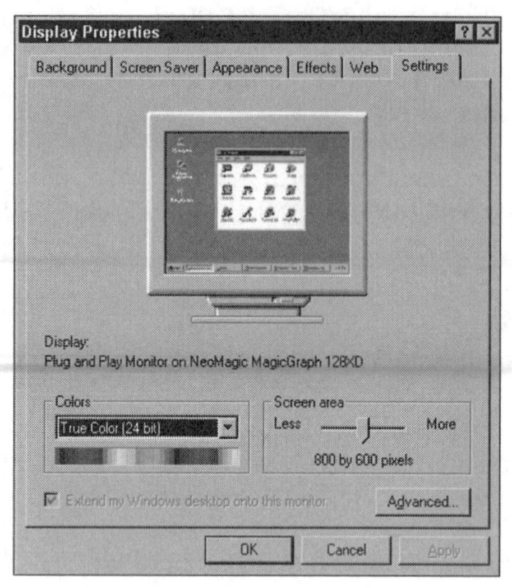

Figure 3-6: You can view and set the options for the resolution displayed by your computer monitor using a Windows dialog box identical or similar to this one.

Put your pictures on a diet

A good way to improve the appearance of a low-resolution image (one without a lot of pixels per inch) is to reduce the size of the photo. PhotoSuite 4 allows you to do this using the techniques I explain in Chapter 5, "Where Do Little Images Come From."

When you shrink the size of a picture, the number of pixels stays the same. But they all get scrunched up closer together. This gives you that smooth image effect.

A Summary of Pixel Pointers

Eyes crossing? Head spinning? Does all this talk about swirling dots merging into a single image make you motion sick?

To summarize, here are a few pointers for minding your pixels:

- For good image quality without unnecessary demands on your computer and printer, strive for about 300 ppi. (You can compute the dimensions of a picture that gives you this resolution, as I explain in a previous section, "Decoding information about pixels.")
- Reduce the size of your picture, whenever possible, to improve image quality.

- In resolving the trade-off between image quality and manageable file size, consider how you'll be viewing the picture. Most computer monitors don't allow you to view an image with a resolution greater than 1024 x 768, so why store all those extra space-hogging pixels?

On the Lighter Side

Understanding lighting is key to taking good photographs before setting to work on them with the PhotoSuite 4 editing tools. Although PhotoSuite 4 allows you to do a lot to correct crummy lighting (as I explain in Chapter 10, "In Color Living"), you'll get better overall results by paying attention to the lighting at the time you shoot your subject.

Many upscale digital cameras have adjustable light settings; others operate by automatically adjusting to the light without giving the photographer the ability to modify the settings. Even if you don't have a camera with adjustable light settings, you can exercise a lot of control by effective positioning of your camera and the subject you're photographing.

Growing digital pictures takes lots of light

Digital cameras need a lot more light than film-based cameras. Most digital cameras have an ISO number of 100. The ISO number tells you what sensitivity the digital chips have by comparing it to a rating on a roll of film. Film typically comes with ISO ratings of 100, 200, or 400.

An ISO rating of 100 is the least light-sensitive rating. Because most digital cameras have an ISO rating of 100 (the equivalent for film), you can see why you really need to brighten things up as much as possible.

Cameras that use traditional film rely on opening and closing a *shutter*, the device placed between the film end lens of the camera. When the shutter is open, it exposes the film to light. When it's closed, it blocks out light. The photographer controls the amount of light reaching the film by setting the camera to various shutter speeds.

Digital cameras use chips that are turned on and off for different periods of time to capture varying amounts of light, instead of opening and closing a shutter. In some digital cameras, the user can adjust the camera so that the chips respond more or less to a given amount of sunlight.

Where to get the light you need

Because digital photos are gluttons for light, you want to think about how and where to maximize the sources you have at your disposal. This section identifies the major sources of lighting and gives you a few pointers on how you can make them shine.

Flash dance

Digital cameras usually come with a built-in flash that has a range of about 10 feet. The trick to using the digital flash effectively is to get up close — but not too close. You want to bathe your subject in light, but not drown it.

Generally, with most digital cameras on the market, you want to shoot at a range of between 3 and 10 feet. You may find that the flash won't do a lot for you at a distance of 15 feet. At the other extreme, if you stand too close, your digital photos will be seriously overexposed to light. Figures 3-7, 3-8, and 3-9 illustrate the use of a flash at distances of 3, 10, and 15 feet.

It's a common misconception that flashes should be used only at night or indoors. In fact, you should use the flash on your camera any time the lighting is inadequate to illuminate the detail of your subject, even if it is 1:00 in the afternoon on a bright sunny day. Figure 3-10 was taken using a fill flash outdoors on an overcast day, to brighten and enhance the mood of the scene. The flash reflects off the metal of the motorcycle and illuminates details that would otherwise are hidden in the shadows, as they are in Figure 3-11, which was taken without the fill flash.

Many digital cameras have more than one flash setting. One setting may flash anytime you shoot a picture using your flash. The other setting may be an auto-flash mode that activates only if the lighting is too low to properly expose your picture.

A downside to using a flash is that it can turn your subjects into red-eyed monsters. Chapter 7, "Eeek! Making Ugly Stuff Look Better," tells you how you can correct red eye during the editing process using PhotoSuite 4.

Where the sun don't shine: Indoor lighting

The great news about indoor lighting is that it's almost as cheap as the natural kind. You don't need all kinds of fancy flashes and flairs — you can use plain-old house lamps to illuminate your subject.

You may have to experiment a bit, but lamps can give you all sorts of great effects. You can do the obvious — light up a dark room, for example. But you can also use a house lamp to create an effect.

Figure 3-7: This is an image shot at a distance of three feet at night with the built-in flash of my Sony Mavica digital camera.

Figure 3-8: Here's a similar image shot with a flash at a distance of 10 feet.

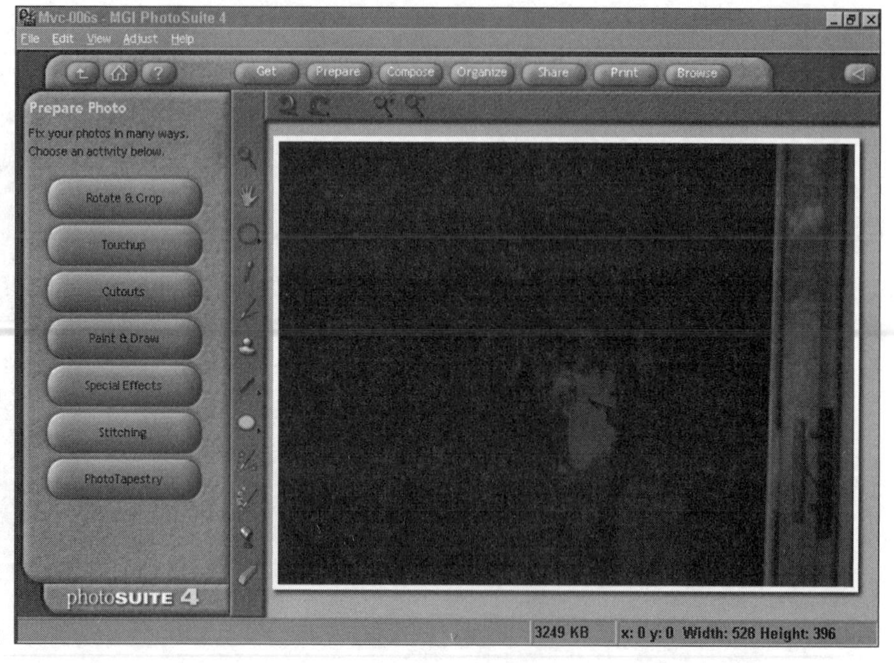

Figure 3-9: Here's the same image shot with a flash at a distance of 15 feet.

Figure 3-10: A fill flash helps create the mood in this outdoor shot on an overcast day.

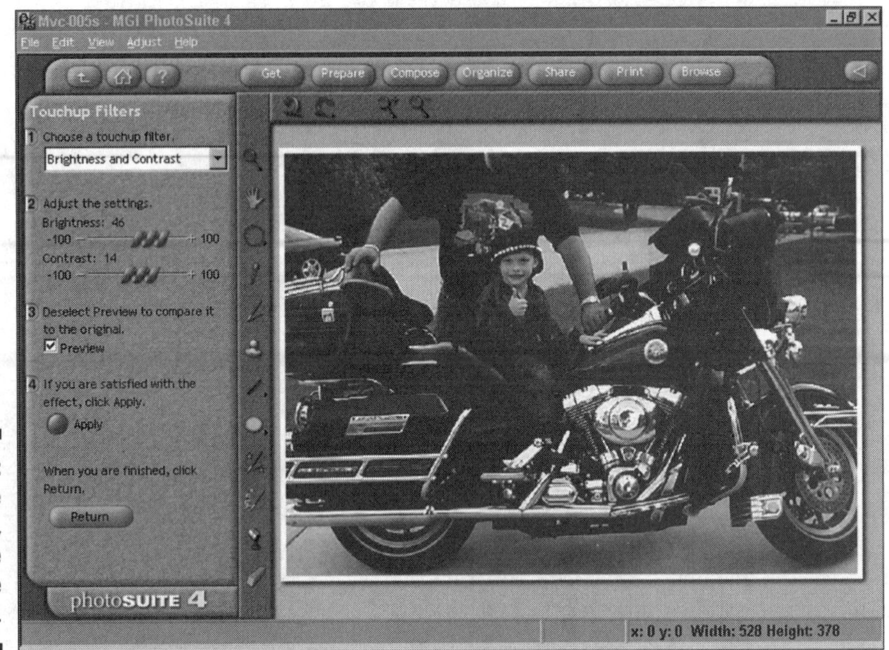

Figure 3-11: Without the fill flash, details are lost in the shadows.

A flash alone may not be enough to give you the effect you want (see Figure 3-12). Reflecting a lamp off a wall behind your subject can create contrast and brighten without a glare effect, as shown in Figure 3-13.

Outdoor lighting

Natural lighting can be a photographer's best friend, and produce poignant and dramatic results. But Mother Nature can also be temperamental when it comes to setting the scene. She just doesn't seem to shine that light when and where you want it.

And does it seem like your outdoor pictures look terrific in the viewfinder of your digital camera, but are really disappointing on your computer screen? Do you have under-exposed and over-exposed areas that weren't apparent in the camera's view finder?

These problems are common because a camera views a scene differently than the human eye. When you look at a sunset on the horizon, your eye adjusts to the brightly lit and dimly lit areas, and provides you with the illusion of an evenly lit scene. But this is only an illusion. The horizon is *not* evenly lit, and your digital camera, try as it may, can't even out the contrasts like the human eye. Instead, your camera uses *one* light setting for the whole scene — a sort of average. Since the camera cannot adjust the lighting for separate areas in the scene, some areas appear underexposed and others overexposed.

Figure 3-12: The light from the flash is adequate, but does little to enhance my subject.

So what's an amateur photographer supposed to do when it comes to the great outdoors? PhotoSuite 4 provides you with several tools to compensate for poor lighting at the time of your shot. I explain them in Chapter 10, "In Color Living."

Figure 3-13: Reflecting a lamp off the wall behind her creates more interesting contrast.

Here are a few additional pointers to keep in mind at the time you take your shot that so that you can get the best results using the PhotoSuite 4 editing tools:

- **Minimize contrast.** Try to photograph your subjects using scenes that minimize the contrasts in the lighting. This makes it easier for your digital camera to compensate for the lighting differentials. For example, don't include a lot of sunny sky in your photograph — your camera has to adjust for both that bright light and the lack of light emanating from your subject.

- **Overexpose rather than underexpose.** If you have the opportunity to adjust the exposure setting on your camera, adjust for the darkest areas. It's easier to correct overexposed (too light) photos using PhotoSuite 4 than underexposed photos (too dark).
- **Head for the shade.** It's a myth that you should *always* shoot photos with your back to the sun. You don't have the extreme light contrast of shooting into the sun, but you create other problems. If the sun is at your back, your subjects are probably all squinting because they have to look right into it. You're also likely to get weird, unflattering shadows across their faces.
- **Shoot when it's overcast.** Contrary to popular belief, midday sun is the *worst* kind of light in which to photograph a subject. It's harsh and creates contrasts that are difficult to compensate for. Much better to capture your scene using the more even and forgiving early morning or just-before-sunset lighting. Your subjects will be well illuminated, and you won't be going crazy trying to compensate for the contrast.
- **Make your own shade.** If you *must* shoot in the glaring light of midday try holding up a piece of poster board to create some artificial shade in which to shoot.

Night light

Unfortunately, digital cameras are a relatively poor choice for photographing in low light. Digital cameras need a lot of light, as I explained earlier in this section.

If you are after the best possible nighttime shots, take the shot using *film* having an ISO rating of 200 or 400. Then you can use your scanner to import them into PhotoSuite 4, as I explain in Chapter 5.

If you must do a night shot in digital, the best way to discern your camera's after dark capabilities is to experiment. Try taking pictures at varying ranges to see how much and how well your flash illuminates a particular scene.

A Touch of Color

Both digital and film cameras capture images by exposing light sensitive materials. The image is captured in black and white — lightness and darkness.

But these stark images contain a sort of color code — they store information about the color gradations that's decoded in the development process. The stark black and white image is decoded to produce a colorful masterpiece.

The way this works is fairly simple when you understand that the human eye has only three color receptors — red, green, and blue. Your red color receptor remembers the amount of red light, the green receptor measures green light, and so forth. Then your receptor combines all the information into a multicolored image inside your brain, with all the color detail and gradations that you normally associate with an image.

Each of the three color receptors — whether in a digital camera or inside your eyeball — has its own brightness value. The brightness value for each is stored in your digital camera using something called a *color channel*. The three different color channels are blended to create a satisfyingly realistic, full-color image. (Chapter 10 explains more about how this works and how to use the PhotoSuite 4 filters to separately adjust the different color channels.)

Chapter 4

Imaging Equipment for All Occasions

In This Chapter

- Deciding what you really need from your camera
- Getting your computer ready for PhotoSuite 4
- Being savvy about scanners
- Searching for the perfect printer

Stop! Don't buy a camera with the same mindset that prodded you to get that expensive exercise equipment that sits in the corner and gathers dust. The fact that you pay a lot of money for something doesn't mean you're going to get visible results.

Whatever you can do in PhotoSuite 4 with a top-of-the-line digital camera, you can do with the simplest of film-based cameras and a reasonably decent scanner. This chapter tells you how to be practical when buying a camera and how to coordinate it with the rest of your computer system.

Camera Consumerism

When it comes to cameras — especially digital cameras — it pays to be an educated consumer. Sure, you want to focus on the relative capabilities of the different types of cameras and look for a good sale. But if you're on a budget, you want to be realistic about whether you're better off with a low-end digital camera (as the technology continues to evolve), or a higher-end film camera for the same price.

Researching your options

Millions of cameras are sold every year, sometimes more than one to a customer. This is because people enjoy photography — and enjoy reading about it. This is great news for you, the savvy camera consumer, because it means that lots of publications and Web sites exist that are devoted to comparing and rating cameras.

One place to start is that old stand-by publication, *Consumer Reports*. This magazine rates both digital and film-based cameras on a one-to-five scale. It also gives you a thorough narrative on the pros and cons of the different models.

Also, of course, the Internet can be a photographer's best friend. especially if you're in search of a digital camera. In fact, the number of sites dedicated to photography equipment can be overwhelming. My favorite Web site is the comprehensive CNET Web site located at `http://hwreviews.netscape.com/hardware/0-1078.html?tag=st.co.1402664.dir1078`. The home page for this site contains links to reviews of specific models, cameras listed according to price range, and information about new models on the market.

Battle of the cameras: digital versus film

Don't be quick to jump on the digital bandwagon and disavow your faithful film-based camera. Our film friends can offer some advantages over the digital variety in several areas:

- **Image quality:** When it comes to building an heirloom photo album or having something really great to frame on your wall, consider this: The resolution of a Kodak disposable is roughly ten times that of my popular Sony MavicaFD83 mega-pixel camera.
- **Start-up cost:** A low-end digital camera costs much more than a relatively high-end film-based camera. The disposable camera mentioned in the preceding bullet cost $4.95, whereas my mega-pixel digital camera cost more than $600.
- **Distortion of color:** Digital cameras are prone to color distortion. The relatively new digital technology is playing catch-up since film related technology has been in existence and has been refined over 150 years.
- **Lighting:** Digital cameras require *lots* of light. If you plan to take a lot of shots indoors, a digital camera may give you problems.
- **Intricate detail:** Digital cameras do a crummy job when it comes to capturing lots of intricate detail because they have fewer pixels to do it with. For example, if you photograph a tree, you end up with about three pixels per leaf and a big blurry mess. Mega-pixel cameras in the 3.3 million range offer higher resolution but relatively unsophisticated color

technology compared to film cameras. It's best to stick with subjects with larger areas of uniform color and defined borders (such as close-up head and body shots) when doing digital.

- **Fast-moving objects:** A digital camera takes several seconds after you shoot a picture to save it into memory. This means that you can't take shots in rapid succession as you can with a film-based camera.

On the other hand, digital cameras are a blast! They offer the following advantages:

- **Instant gratification:** You don't have to wait to develop your photos.
- **Sending and saving to a disk:** Nothing beats a digital camera when it comes to sending and sharing photos over the Internet. You can pop out a disk (or download the photo using a cable) without having to take the time to scan it in.
- **Instant editing capability:** If you take digital photos, you get to skip the step of converting a photograph taken with film into a digital format.
- **No more film:** You don't have to buy film or develop it. You can simply delete the shots you don't want from your drive or disk without worrying about wasting film.
- **What you see is what you get:** You can preview a shot you've just taken in the viewfinder of the digital camera and decide whether it's a "keeper."

Buying a digital camera

When it comes to buying a digital camera, having the latest technological innovation is tempting but not necessarily more gratifying in the long run. Digital cameras are one area in which you can purchase technology that's slightly out of date and probably be no worse for it. For example, at the time of this writing, 3.3 million-pixel cameras have just made their debut in the market place. What does this mean to you?

Resolution revisited

Sure, you can spring for a 3.3 million-pixel camera (capable of producing pictures at a 2,048 x 1,536 resolution). Your friends will be impressed. But do you really need a 3 million-pixel or 6 million or 10 billion mega-pixel camera? Or is that sort of like loading your address book with names of people you don't know? Do you actually benefit from this added capability?

In fact, the word on the street is that 3.4-million-pixel quality gives sharp detail but doesn't improve the color quality of the shot over a 1 million-pixel camera. It also doesn't do any better in terms of lighting than much less expensive cameras on the market. So if you're looking at the big picture (no pun intended), you may be better off foregoing a million or so pixels and opting for a camera that's slightly out of date, in terms of resolution, but has a better flash capability.

Digital cameras need lots of light, more so than film-based camera. (See Chapter 3, "Photo-Science: Fun with Chemicals and Computer Chips.")

Shop the technological bargain basement

At the time of this writing, those cameras with a measly million pixels are precipitously dropping in price. You can get great bargains!

You can pick up some great cameras for $300.00 or less as a result of the mega-pixel mania. An 800 x 600 resolution capability is adequate for Photo Suite 4, and a 1024 x 768 resolution capability is about what most home computer systems and printers can comfortably handle.

If you sensibly decide not to opt for a higher pixel count than your computer system can handle, I advise you to be alert to sales.

Looking through the lens

A smart thing to do when you're buying a digital camera is to take it to the front of the store, look out the window, and try focusing on objects in the parking lot. As you focus on the distant and near objects, you can see how the lens adapts and what is included and excluded from your view. Ask yourself the following:

- What's the range of focus this lens can capture? If the camera has a zoom lens, try zooming in and out. Is the range adequate for your purposes?
- How long does it take the camera to re-focus between shots? Delays can cost you spontaneity because you have to make your subjects freeze their poses during the refocusing.
- Does the camera have an automatic-focus feature? Does it also allow you to focus manually? The latter adds to the versatility of the shots that you can successfully take. (See the sidebar "Lens lingo," in this chapter, for more information about this.)
- Does the camera allow you to change lenses (for example, use a telephoto or wide-angle lens, as discussed in the "Lens Lingo" sidebar)?
- Does the camera have a *focus lock* feature? If so, you don't have to wait for the camera to refocus after each picture. Yahoo!

Many of the lens issues that apply to digital cameras pertain to film-based cameras as well and are discussed in the sidebar.

Lens lingo

Focusing is not something that camera lenses just do. It's something that you need to do for them. One of the greatest innovations in camera history is the *auto-focus* lens. But contrary to its nomenclature, the process of focusing isn't truly mindless — allthough technology may someday get us to that point.

Here's a rundown of the lenses and features out there that offer photographers a range of control, convenience, and complexity:

- **Auto focus:** An auto-focus feature (sometimes referred to by manufacturers as point-and-shoot) is the easiest and most popular option for the weekend photographer. The most important fact that you need to know about an autofocus camera is that you have to *tell* it where to shoot.

  Viewfinders in most digital cameras have markings on them similar to the ones in the diagram shown in Figure 4-1. The center point is called the *focus point.*The camera automatically focuses on whatever part of the scene contains the focus point. Pretty simple, huh?

  But accidents do happen. For example, make sure, if you're photographing two or more subjects, as shown in Figure 4-2, that the focus point doesn't end up on a gap. If this happens, the camera may auto focus on some irrelevency in the distant backgound. Also, if you're deliberately placing a subject off center, be aware that your subject is *not* the focus point.
- **Focus free or fixed-focus cameras:** These are inexpensive cameras that you don't focus at all because the camera's focus is automatically set at the factory. You generally need to stand four to eight feet from your subject (look at the directions on your camera). If you're within the correct range, you can get a pretty decent shot with this type of camera.
- **Telephoto lenses:** These lenses allow you to take photographs of distant objects. They make objects look closer and they show less of a scene than a standard lens.
- **Wide-angle lenses:** With a wide-angle lense, you can photograph more of a scene than a normal lens would allow. The subjects of your photo appear smaller.
- **Zoom lenses:** Zoom lenses offer a convenient and economical alternative for those of us who are intimidated by the prospect of constantly switching lenses. They allow you to vary the range of your focus — for near or distant shots. Many cameras on the market come with some variation of a zoom lens.
- **Color filters:** Photographers use lenses with color tints to compensate for a variety of lighting conditions and to add special effects.
- **Focus lock:** A focus lock feature allows you to lock the focus on your camera so that you don't have to refocus between shots if you move around.

Figure 4-1: Point-and-shoot cameras have markings on the viewfinder that guide you to the focus point.

Figure 4-2: In the picture, the focus point is inadvertently set on the distant background.

Some other factors to consider

Digital cameras are a big investment, and you have lots of choices. There are currently more than a hundred models on the market. Here's a mix of high- and low-tech factors to consider in making your choice:

- **Durability:** This is a factor I *never* see mentioned in the consumer publications. I look for the availability of a good-fitting camera case, and a camera design with parts that don't protrude or bend from the camera in awkward ways that make them prone to breakage. I even opt for an extended warranty that covers the time period I hope to keep the camera and make sure that the contract provides that the camera will be repaired within a specific time frame (for example, 10 days) or replaced if it can't be fixed by then.
- **Battery life:** This can be a tough one to get information about because camera manufacturers don't always list the specifications of their batteries. It's an important cost factor, however, if you're going to need to buy an extra battery that costs in excess of $100. This expense can push you up into a whole different budget range.
- **Flash capability**: Most camera manufacturers also don't tell you how powerful their flash is. But because digital pictures need *so much* light, it's a good idea to test the flash capability in the store (bring your own floppy disk to check the test photo on your computer monitor back home).
- **Viewfinders:** Most digital cameras on the market have an LCD (liquid crystal diode) screen that you can view your shots on. During your in-store testing, take the camera in front of a sunny window and make sure that the viewfinder is easy to see and doesn't sort of fade in the light.

  Some digital cameras, such as the Epson PC 750, have a little switch that you can flip to adjust the lighting of the viewfinder to make looking into the viewfinder easier.
- **Downloading options:** Most digital cameras currently being introduced on the market allow you to use a removable floppy disk that you can insert right into your computer. This makes it really convenient to view, edit, and store your shots. Older digital models may have a cable that runs from your camera to your computer to transfer images.

  Removable disks are a definite improvement over the cable downloading option. Spring for the newer technology in this area and avoid succumbing to the great close-out price you may get on a cable model. The convenience of removable disks is well worth the added cost.
- **Memory:** Although the advent of removable floppy disks has made built-in memory less important, it's still a nice thing to have. On-board memory means that you don't have to change floppy disks every 6 or 8 shots. Manufacturers are constantly introducing and developing new devices on the high-end cameras that allow you to store images right in the camera. For example, IBM has introduced a mini hard drive having 340MB of storage capacity. Sony offers a removable "memory stick" with similar storage capabilities.

- **Speed and sensitivity:** Some cameras have ISO ratings (discussed in Chapter 3) that indicate how light sensitive the camera is. The more light sensitive the camera, the better the shot you can take when there is not a lot of lighting present. Common ISO ratings for digital cameras are 100 and 200. (The higher the ISO rating the better, so opt for the 200.)
- **Burst mode:** Ever notice how long it takes for a camera to save the image and refocus the camera after each shot? It can be really irritating when your trying to get multiple shots of a quick moving subject. To counteract this, some high-end cameras have a *burst mode* to enable you to take multiple shots in rapid succession.
- **Multimedia bells and whistles:** What discussion of digital cameras would be complete without a nod to wonders such as the capability to record a "movie" of 15 seconds or more complete with sound? Some cameras also have a *self timer*, which allows you to be both the photographer and the subject of your shot.

A tribute to film

Film-based cameras have been around for a long time and are highly refined at this point. They offer you the advantage of far better resolution, sharper color tones, and better results in less than perfect lighting than their digital counterparts. If fact, you may want to have both a digital and a film-based camera in your arsenal.

Here's a summary of the basic types of film-based cameras on the market:

- **Cartridge:** These cameras are lightweight and durable. They take film cartridges, which you just drop into the camera. They're also inexpensive. The downside is they offer you few options because most of the adjustments are automatic.
- **35-millimeter cameras:** There are dozens of 35-millimeter cameras on the market. These cameras take a standard roll of film. They range in user complexity from the simplest point-and-shoot models, which have automatic focus and unchangeable settings, to complicated models with lots of changeable lenses (see the sidebar, "Lens lingo," earlier in this chapter).
- **Single-lens reflex cameras:** A single-lens reflex camera allows you to see the scene in your viewfinder exactly as it will appear in your photograph. This feature allows photographers to make many sophisticated adjustments to control the scene by changing lenses and making an array of adjustments. Some of the most common adjustments are aperture and shutter speed. *Aperture* refers to the size of the opening in the camera through which the film is exposed to light, and *shutter speed* allows the photographer to exercise tremendous control over the time length of the exposure to light.

- **Disposable and special-use cameras:** Going on a raft trip or rock climbing? Don't rule out disposable and waterproof cameras that offer a surprising range of capabilities, such as telephoto lenses and automatic focus. The cameras are also surprisingly inexpensive, and you take them into the film developer just as you would a roll of film. I get some of my best shots with these cameras. In fact, they offer higher resolution than most digital cameras.

When using a disposable camera, pay close attention to the directions that tell you how close you should be from the subject. Many of these cameras don't allow you to adjust the focus to shoot at greater or lesser distances.

The right film

Film has traditionally been the magic stuff of which pictures are made. It's given an ISO rating, which is its sensitivity to light. The higher the ISO rating, the more light sensitive the film.

The ISO rating is sometimes called the film speed because the camera uses a higher shutter speed for more light-sensitive films. In reality, you're unlikely to routinely see a whole lot of difference in your pictures by using one film speed higher or lower. But when you enlarge the film, the films with the higher ISO ratings may appear "grainy." This is why films of different ratings are referred to as high or low grain.

But there are also times when you can dramatically improve your results by using the right film. Table 4-1 gives you a brief summary of the most common types.

Table 4-1 Film for All Occasions

Film Speed	*Characteristics*	*Best Types of Subjects and Lighting*
ISO 100	This is a low-grain film that captures lots of detail and works well for enlargements. Shots using this film can appear blurry.	Good for bright sunny days and close-range photos using a flash.
ISO 200	A medium-grain film, that requires slightly less light than ISO film. Also prone to blur.	Good for outdoor shots on overcast days and medium-range flash shots.

(continued)

Table 4-1 (continued)

Film Speed	*Characteristics*	*Best Types of Subjects and Lighting*
ISO 400	Considered an all-purpose medium-grain film that works well indoors or out, in a range of light conditions, with less chance of blur. Enlargements can appear grainy.	Use this film indoors or outdoors at a variety of ranges.
ISO 800	This is a higher-cost film and does not enlarge well.	Best choice for evening and low-light conditions. Also works well for long-range flash shots.

Is Your Computer Ready for PhotoSuite 4?

The manufacturers of PhotoSuite 4 have designed the program so that it can be used with most home computers. You shouldn't have to do any major upgrades if your computer is less than a few years old. This section tells you the minimum capabilities you need to start having fun with the program.

Bit depth

PhotoSuite 4 requires that your computer have an 800 x 600 resolution capability and 65,000 colors. The latter specification is called *color depth* or *bit depth.*

Your computer carries information about color in bits. Each bit is capable of producing or storing information about two colors. Bit depth is the number of colors your computer can read. Each time you increase your bit depth, you exponentially increase the number of colors your computer is capable of. To calculate bit depth, use 2 as the base number and the bit depth number as the exponent.

PhotoSuite 4 requires your system to have a minimum 16-bit depth capability. Photos at 16-bit capacity have 256 colors, which is fine for display on your monitor or the Internet but probably is not the quality you want for a printed photo. For that, you probably want a 24-bit, or 16.7-million, color capacity.

Here's a brain-teaser for you. If you shoot an image at 24 bit but your computer monitor or printer can reproduce only at an 8-bit color depth, what happens to the extra bits? The answer is that they're still stored in the image but just not printed out. If you were to upgrade your equipment, however, the extra bits of information would still available to contain information to enhance the image.

But when you print your picture using PhotoSuite 4, you don't want to store or try to transmit via modem all those extra bits of color data Those extra bits of color data greatly increase the file size with no discernible benefit to the viewer. File size is always a consideration because graphics take up so much more space than memory. The sidebar "Calculating file size" tells you how to calculate the size of a PhotoSuite 4 image.

Random access memory (RAM)

Another area in which file size is an issue is your computer's *random access memory,* or RAM. That's the memory used during the editing process, and it's released when you turn your computer off. The manufacturers of PhotoSuite 4 recommend that you have at least 32MB of RAM.

You should also be courteous with your friends when it comes to RAM, because sending them unnecessarily large files is a drain on their RAM when it comes to downloading and viewing the files.

Yo' monitor

Most systems come with a 15-inch monitor, which is kind of puny for digital imaging. A larger monitor has increased resolution capabilities.

Most standard-size monitors on the market are capable of displaying images at 1024 x 768 pixels. This is true even of Apple's iMac computer, which is designed with graphics in mind. If you'll be doing a lot of PhotoSuite 4 projects, you might want to spring for a larger monitor.

You also want to pay close attention to your monitor's refresh rate. The *refresh rate* is the number of times the screen is redrawn per second. This process should be imperceptible to you. The higher the resolution, the greater the refresh rate you need. A slow refresh rate can cause your screen to flicker and gyrate. As a rule, if your monitor is 17 inches or less, you can get by with a refresh rate of 75Hz. If your monitor is larger than that, it should have a refresh rate of 85Hz.

Calculating file size

Each digital image that you create with your camera or scanner takes up a certain amount of file space based on its size and color depth.

You can use the following formula to calculate the maximum size of a graphics file:

File Size = Pixels in Width x Pixels in Height x Color Depth

So if, for example, you take a 24-bit shot at 600 x 480 resolution, your maximum file size is 921,600 bytes (or just about a megabyte). This is the maximum file size because compression (discussed in Chapter 10, "Graphics on the Go," can alter your file size considerably.

Dealing the graphics card

The graphics card in your computer determines how large a monitor you can use and what bit depth it can see. PhotoSuite 4 requires that you have a graphics card with at least 8MB of video RAM (video RAM)), which is the memory used by your monitor. If you upgrade your monitor or have an older computer system, you may need to upgrade the graphics card as well. (This caught me by surprise when I upgraded my monitor.)

Storing your photos on a Zip drive

An ordinary floppy disk has a storage capacity of about 1.4MB . This means that it can hold about 6–8 images having a resolution of 800 x 600. (See the sidebar, "Calculating file size.") If you store many images on your hard drive, that can really eat into your file space, too.

Extra large floppy disk drives such as Zip disks provide a great way to store your images without running out of space on your computer. I recently purchased the popular Iomega Zip drive. It uses special Zip disks that look like an oversized version of the usual kind of floppy disk. They have a 100MB storage capacity (about eight times that of the usual floppy disk.) This is adequate for my needs. You can also get Zip drives and disks with a 250MB capacity.

Printers in a Nutshell

When it's time to show your friends and relatives pictures of your new baby, the fish you caught on your vacation or your prize-winning begonia, you don't want to have to boot up your computer. Those are the kind of "brag" shots you want to be able to pull out of your wallet.

When it comes to brag shots, your printer is your friend. You can print as many copies as you want, in any size you want. But the quality of those printed images can vary greatly, depending on the type of printer you choose. You want to carefully evaluate the speed, resolution, and cost of each model. (The Chapter 3 section "Kosher pixels and other image condiments" tells you how printer resolution is measured.)

Printers have come a long way in recent months, and manufacturers are working round the clock to develop ones that can capitalize on the digital craze. But as of the writing of this book, there is still not a printer on the market than can resize photos or produce them with the quality you get from a professional photo lab. Sorry!

For subjects and photos that warrant only the best reproductive technology, consider Kodak's PhotoNet Online service, covered in Chapter 13, "Graphics on the Go."

Here are the three frontrunners in terms of speed, resolution, and cost, listing in increasing order of sophistication and quality:

- **Ink jet printers:** Ink jet printers are really economical, and the newer models perform well with PhotoSuite 4 images. Ink jets start at less than $200. They work by spraying ink through tiny nozzles (called *jets)* onto your paper. As you might imagine, the more detailed your photo, the greater the possibility the ink won't stay where you spray it. Accordingly, ink jets aren't a good bet for high-resolution photos. Most ink jets print two or three pages a minute. If you opt for an ink jet printer, you'll probably get the best results using paper specially designed for it, although you can safely experiment with other types. Opt for this type of printer if you're on a budget or spot a sale.
- **Laser printers:** Lasers printers are faster, more accurate, and more expensive than the ink jet variety. They use a drum charged with electricity to pick up tiny amounts of colored toner and transfer them to the paper. You can also use a large variety of papers — experiment with all that glossy stuff. They're also really speedy, often delivering more than 15 pages a minute. Laser printers offer advantages in the areas of speed and cost, as well as versatility should you need to use them for word processing.
- **Dye sublimation printers:** These are currently every photographer's favorite! They deliver color, clarity, and sharpness for a price tags starting at around $250.00. They transfer color dyes onto the paper by a process called *thermal dye sublimation.* When the dye hits the paper, the heat makes it *sublimate*, or sink in. You do need to use special paper (which may not be available at your office supply store) and these printers are slower than laser printers. But the image quality and price tag make up for these minor inconveniences. You can pick up a good dye sublimation printer in the $500 range.

The more economical "dye-sub" models are fine for producing pictures taken with a mega-pixel camera, but if you're working with a camera shooting in 2 or 3 million-pixel resolution, you need to opt for a higher-end model.

Being Scanner Savvy

I love my scanner! My favorite thing about it is that I can use it to convert photos taken with an ordinary film-based camera to digital format. This means that I can edit *any* picture I want using PhotoSuite 4.

When you purchase a scanner, you probably want to ask for a *flatbed* scanner, as opposed to a *slide* scanner. Slide scanners are more expensive and are designed to copy slides and transparencies.

Here's a checklist of other information you'll want to track down:

- **Resolution:** Scanner resolution is measured in dots per inch (dpi), which is a whole different ball game than the pixels per inch (ppi) we talk about for cameras and monitors. Be sure to compare scanners based solely on their dpi and not their interpolated values, as explained in the Chapter 3 section "Kosher pixels and other image condiments."

  Interpolation is the process of adding pixels to an image. This is something the scanner's software does after the image has been scanned. Interpolation degrades the quality of an image, because it fills in pixels by guesswork. The guess is made by looking at the surrounding pixels, so no detail is added to the shot — only "filler" pixels.

- **Color depth:** Color depth (or bit depth) refers to how many colors your scanner can read. For working in PhotoSuite 4, you should spring for a scanner with at least a 24-bit color depth.
- **Software:** Your scanner won't print a single pixel without software to drive it. You can use the software that comes bundled with the scanner or you can purchase more sophisticated, software. Take a look at what the software offered along with your scanner does. What image features can you edit? What are your options for previewing the finished product?

Before you take home a scanner, ask to test drive it. It's a good idea to bring along a reasonably detailed "test pattern" with lots of fine lines, details, and contrasting colors. Check how clearly the patterns and colors of your test sheet are reproduced on the various scanners you're considering.

After you get your scanner home, it's a good idea to match the scanner resolution to the size of what you're scanning. The smaller the size of the image you're scanning, the lower the resolution you need to scan it at. For example, if you're scanning a wallet-size photo, you probably don't need to scan any higher than 300 dots per inch (dpi). If you scan at 600 dpi, you waste a lot of file space without any perceptible difference in quality.

Part II

Lights! Camera! Action!

"Remember, your Elvis should appear bald and slightly hunched-- nice Big Foot, Brad.-- Keep your two-headed animals in the shadows and your alien spacecrafts crisp and defined."

In this part . . .

If editing is your dream, PhotoSuite should be your scheme! (Yes, I actually get paid to write this stuff.) This part acquaints you with the wide range of repair and editing features. It tells you stuff such as how to take things out of one photo and put it into another — the old body switch trick.

Chapter 5

Where Do Little Images Come From?

In This Chapter

- Getting pictures into PhotoSuite 4
- Fetching photos from a disk or floppy
- Using successful scanning techniques
- Retrieving shots from your camera
- Downloading images from the Web

PhotoSuite 4 allows you to add your own dramatic artistry to a photo, or you can subtly express your perspective with a variety of image-editing tools that enhance but don't alter the image. But before you can do anything even slightly clever or artistic, you need to import a picture to work on.

This chapter tells you how to get a picture onto your PhotoSuite 4 desktop so that you can begin analyzing it, improving it, and making it your own.

Getting Images into PhotoSuite 4

Photographs are artistic fingerprints. Each one is unique, and the possibilities for creating them are infinite and complex. Fortunately, the ways of getting them into PhotoSuite 4 are *not* complex. You need only to learn how to import them from four different sources:

- **Copying images from a drive or disk**: You can open any compatible image file on a floppy disk or hard drive. (See Chapter 19, "Ten (Plus) Funky File Formats," for a complete list of file formats compatible with PhotoSuite 4.)
- **Importing a scanned image:** Scanners allow you to convert a paper copy of any photograph into digital format. Scanners are also great toys with features that enhance PhotoSuite 4's capabilities. So when PhotoSuite 4 meets your scanner, it's a real party.

- **Transferring images from your digital camera**: Older-model digital cameras may require you to hook up a cable to transfer images to your computer and begin editing them in PhotoSuite 4. But most newer cameras on the market allow you to pop out floppy disks, memory cards, or other storage devices containing the pictures you've taken.
- **Downloading images from the Internet**: You can import the World Wide Web into PhotoSuite 4! You can actually drag photos from the Internet right into the PhotoSuite 4 Library.

The Get screen, shown in Figure 5-1, is used to import an image into PhotoSuite 4 from any of the aforementioned sources. To access this screen, click the Get button on the Navigation bar. You can do this from any PhotoSuite 4 screen (see Figure 5-1).

Because the editing process usually begins by importing an image, you tell PhotoSuite 4 to display Get screen whenever you start the program. To do so, select the Always Start on This Page check box, as shown in Figure 5-1.

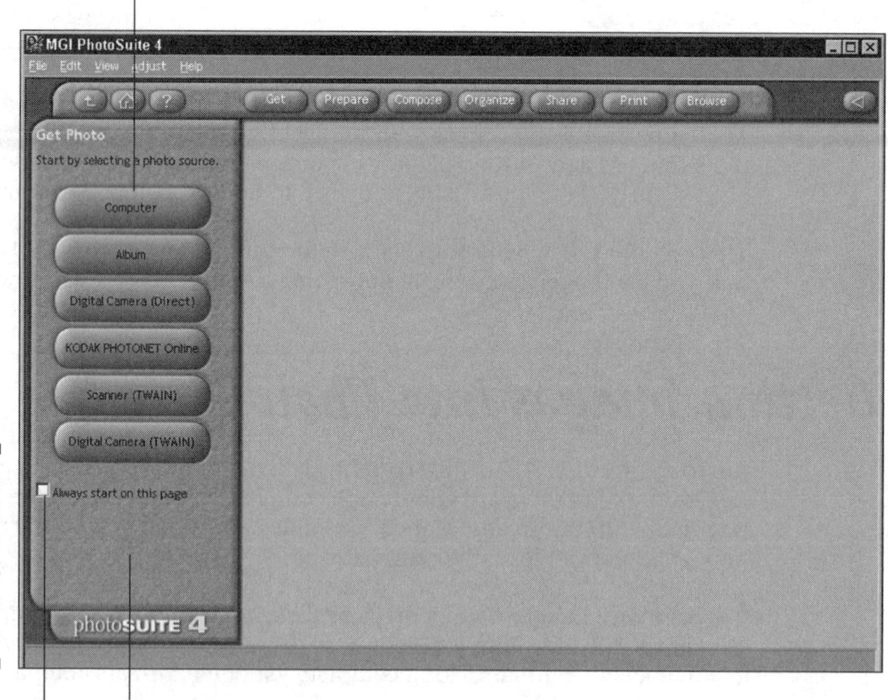

Figure 5-1: Import all images into PhotoSuite 4 using this screen.

Fetching Photos from Your Computer

You can retrieve a photo from anywhere on your computer within seconds, much the same way as you open a text document. The process is the same whether you set out to retrieve a photo from your hard drive, standard floppy disk, or extra-large floppy disk (such as a Zip) drive.

To access a photograph saved on one of your drives or disks, follow these steps:

1. **From the Get screen, click the button on the Activity panel labeled Computer (refer back to Figure 5-1) or select Open from the File menu.**

   The Open dialog box, shown in Figure 5-2, appears with a drop-down menu that displays all the drives and disks on your computer when you click the down arrow in the Look in field.

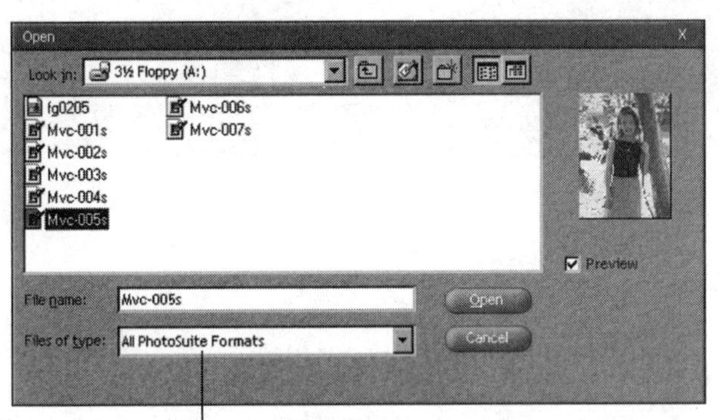

Figure 5-2: Use this dialog box to browse the image files on each drive of your computer.

Specify file formats here.

2. **Select the drive that you want to access from the drop-down menu.**

   An icon appears for each folder or file on the selected drive.

3. **Double-click the icon of the image file you want to open.**

   You don't have to open a file to preview it. Simply select the Preview check box in the Open dialog box to display its contents in the mini-preview window without opening it.

   The image appears on the Get screen, as shown in Figure 5-3, and you can begin your editing and printing activities.

Figure 5-3: When you open a file, the image appears in the Workspace.

The Scoop on Scanning

Scanning your first image can be really confusing because you're simultaneously working with both the PhotoSuite 4 software interface and the interface of your scanner's software. But maneuver the process once and then later you'll find that it's like riding a bicycle — you don't forget how.

A word about connecting your scanner

The hardest thing I found about scanning an image in PhotoSuite 4 was figuring out how to hook my scanner up to the computer. Unfortunately, I can't help you with this one! Besides the fact that I trip over my own cables when it comes to connecting peripherals, scanner specs differ from manufacturer to manufacturer. You need to check the instructions that come with your particular scanner model. Fortunately, PhotoSuite 4 supports all scanners that use the TWAIN industry specification — which is just about all of them.

TWAIN is an industry-wide standard for scanners, digital cameras, and other digital-imaging devices. It ensures compatibility among all the different digital-imaging devices and computers on the market. (TWAIN is discussed in more detail in Chapter 1 in the section called "Getting on the TWAIN Train.")

Scanning your first shot

Is your scanner up and running? Did you do the test scan recommended by the scanner's manufacturer? Did it work? Good! Now you're ready to import your first scanned image into PhotoSuite 4.

Here's how:

1. **From the Get screen, click the Scanner (TWAIN) button on the activity panel.**

   The Scanner Activity panel appears (see Figure 5-4).

2. **Make sure that the name of a scanner appears in the field labeled Choose a scanner (if you have more than one scanner connected, you can click the arrow in this field to choose one from the drop-down list).**

   If you leave this field blank, PhotoSuite 4's scanning capability is disabled.

3. **In the field labeled Enter file name prefix, indicate a prefix that you want to use for naming each scanned file.**

   Each scanned image is assigned a filename with the designated prefix in front of it (for example, Photo001, Photo002, and so on).

4. **Select or deselect the Open for editing check box.**

   If you select this check box, a thumbnail (miniature) image of each photo that you scan is added to the Photo library (discussed in the next section). This makes it convenient to retrieve the images. If you don't check this option, the file is saved to the folder C:\MyDocuments\MyPicures.

5. **Select or deselect the Add to an album check box.**

   If you select this check box, the photos are automatically added to the album shown in the field. You can use the drop-down menu to choose from among all the albums on your system. (I tell you all about creating and viewing albums in Chapter 14.)

6. **Click the Scan button to begin scanning your image.**

   The interface for your scanner's software should appear on your computer screen. (This is referred to as the *TWAIN interface.*)

7. **Using the specific TWAIN Interface for your scanner, scan the image.**

   For example, on the TWAIN interface for my scanner, I need to click the Preview, Scan, and Save buttons to complete the scanning process. Check the directions for your particular scanner.

8. **After the scanning process is done, close the TWAIN interface window by clicking the X in the upper right of the window.**

   Your image is now stored on your system, ready to be viewed and edited in PhotoSuite 4. If you selected the Open for editing check box (in the preceding Step 4), thumbnails of your images appear in the Library on the right side of the screen. (Be sure to also select the Photos option from the drop-down menu that appears above the thumbnail images.)

If your scanned photo is at the wrong angle or is crooked (like the one in Figure 5-4), high-tail it over to Chapter 6. That chapter tells you everything you need to know about rotating, flipping, and adjusting the position of scanned photos.

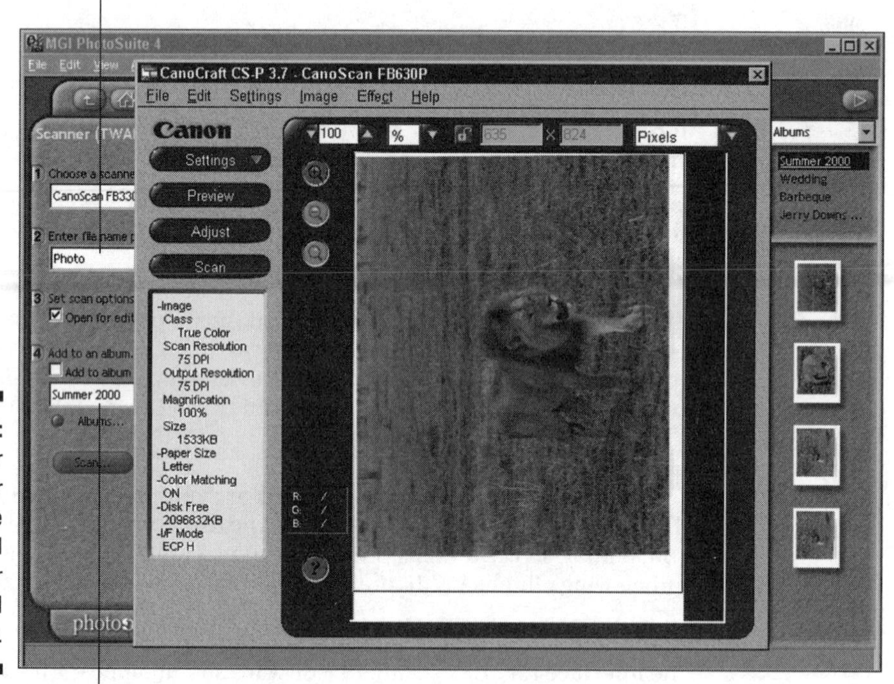

Figure 5-4: Select your scanner type, a file prefix and an album for scanned files.

Opening and editing those scanned babies

When you scan an image into your system, it's saved into a digital format that you've selected. You can retrieve the newly created digital image two different ways:

- **Drag and drop:** You can click your mouse on the thumbnail and drag it to the center of the PhotoSuite 4 screen from the PhotoSuite 4 Library that appears on the left side of the screen.
- **Use the File menu:** Go to the File menu and select Open to browse for the file.

Getting an Image from Your Camera

This is a topic that's declining in importance to most amateur photographers. Not because we don't get images from our cameras — but because it's becoming so simple that there's not much to write about the process.

Digital-camera technology is advancing and prices are declining so that most of us are opting for removable floppy disks that we can just pop out of our camera and into our computer. (I told you how to retrieve images from a disk earlier in this chapter, in the section "Fetching Photos from Your Computer.") If your camera uses floppy disks exclusively to store photos, you can skip this section altogether.

But you still may need to download photos directly from your camera through a cable running between your camera and the computer if:

- You have a high-end camera with on-board memory storage so that you don't have to constantly change floppy disks (as discussed in Chapter 4, "Imaging Equipment for All Occasions").
- You have an older-model camera that connects to your computer via the communications port.

To connect your camera, follow the manufacturer's directions. Most cameras have a TWAIN interface, as discussed in the previous section. PhotoSuite 4 supports all cameras with the TWAIN interface.

After you've connected the camera to the computer, follow these steps to download the images into PhotoSuite 4:

1. **From the Get screen, click the Activity Panel button labeled Digital Camera (Direct).**

   The screen shown in Figure 5-5 appears.

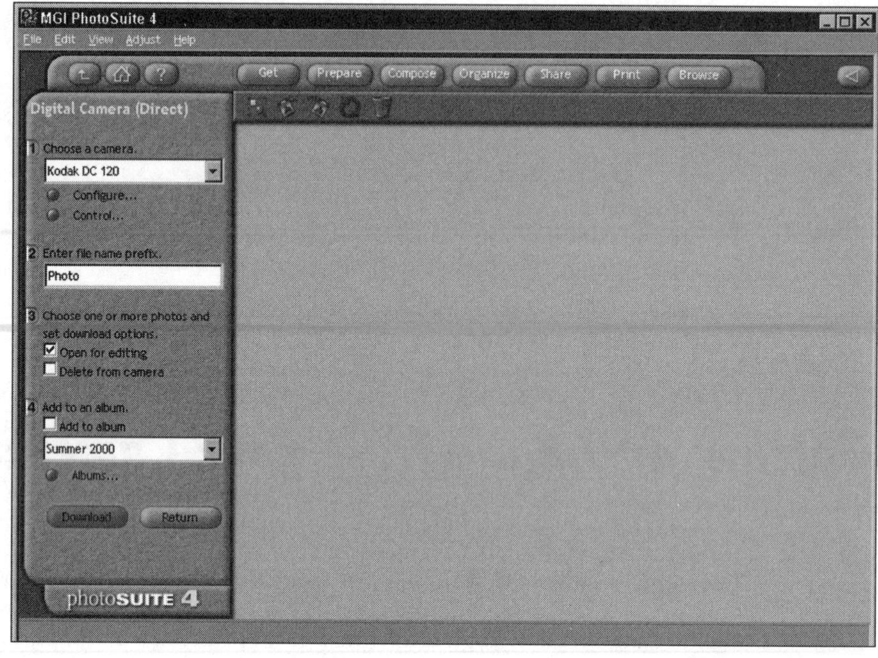

Figure 5-5: Use this screen to retrieve photos directly from a cable-connected camera.

2. **Select a camera from the drop-down list in the Choose a camera field.**

   Note: If your camera doesn't appear in the drop-down list, go back to the Get screen and click the Activity panel button Camera (Twain). If you've properly installed the driver software for your camera on your computer, the name of your camera appears in the drop-down list of *this* screen. If it doesn't appear, you need to install the camera driver before proceeding. The instructions for your digital camera tell you how to do this. After you've done so, proceed as though you're downloading images from a scanner, following Steps 2 through 8 under a previous section of this chapter, "Scanning Your First Shot."

3. **Click the Download button on the Activity Panel.**

   PhotoSuite 4 begins downloading the images stored in your camera.

4. **In the field labeled Enter file name prefix, indicate a prefix that you want to use for naming each scanned file.**

   Each scanned image is assigned a file name with the designated prefix in front of it (for example, Photo001, Photo002, and so on)

5. **Select or deselect the Open for editing check box.**

   If you select this check box, a thumbnail (miniature) image of each photo that you scan is added to the Photo library (discussed in the next section). This makes it convenient to retrieve the images. If you don't check this option, the file is saved to the folder C:\MyDocuments\MyPicures.

6. **Select or de-select the Delete from camera check box.**

   If you select this check box, the images are deleted from your camera after they're loaded into your computer.

7. **Select or deselect the Add to an album check box.**

   If you select this check box, the photos are automatically added to the album shown in the field. You can use the drop-down menu to choose from among all the albums on your system. (I tell you all about creating and viewing albums in Chapter 14.)

8. **Click the Download button to begin transferring the stored photos from your camera to your computer.**

   Your image is now stored on your system, ready to be viewed and edited in PhotoSuite 4. If you selected the Open for editing check box (in the preceding Step 5), thumbnails of your images appear on the right side of the screen. (If you want the thumbnails to appear, be sure you've also selected the Photos option from the drop-down menu above the thumbnails.)

9. **To view and select a photo, right-click your mouse on the thumbnail and drag it to the center of the PhotoSuite 4 screen, or go to the File menu and select Open to browse for the file.**

Editing on the World Wide Web

This is an area in which PhotoSuite 4 really shines. The program has astonishing Internet capabilities that literally bring all the imagery of the World Wide Web to your desktop. You can browse the Internet, spot a photo, that meets your needs, and import it into PhotoSuite 4 to edit to your heart's delight.

Importing an Internet photo

1. **From any screen in PhotoSuite 4, click the Browse button on the Navigation Bar.**

   The screen shown in Figure 5-6 appears.

2. **Type the address of the page you want to browse in the Address field (such as the home page for your browser software).**

   The page you've requested appears in your PhotoSuite 4 Workspace.

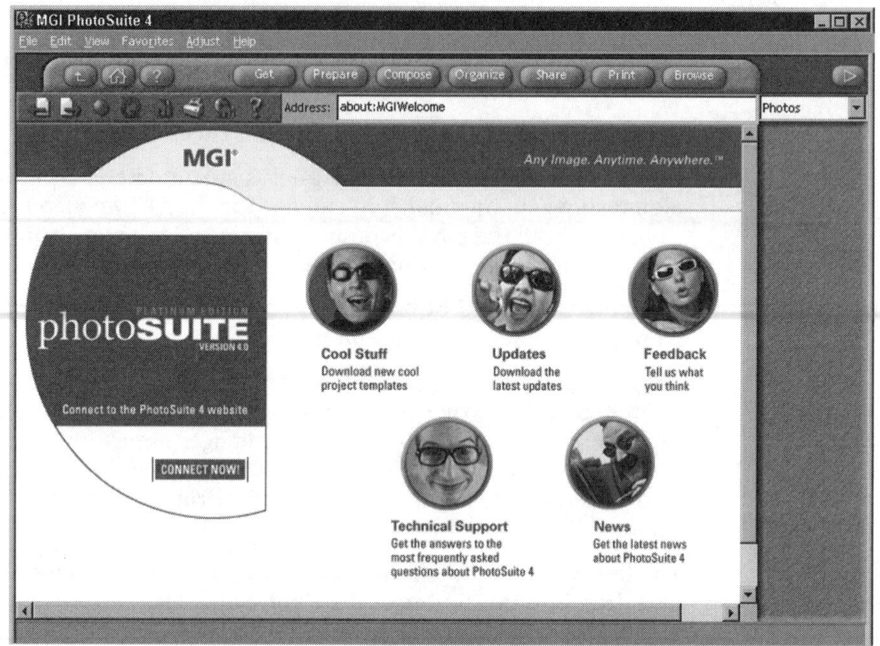

Figure 5-6: PhotoSuite 4 opens an Internet page in the Workspace.

3. **You can import most photos into PhotoSuite 4 by right-clicking the photo in the Browse window and dragging it to the Library. If this does not work, proceed to Step 4.**
4. **Right-click over the Internet photo you want to import.**

   A pop-up menu appears.
5. **Select Send Image to Photo Library. Double click the photo in the Library to open the image.**

Chapter 6

Getting That Slippery Photo Where You Want It

In This Chapter

- Using your editing palette
- Fixing upside down, crooked, and sideways photos
- Zooming in on your subject
- Cropping as opposed to chopping your photos

Each photo that makes its way onto your PhotoSuite 4 desktop provides you with a unique set of artistic opportunities from the minute you import it. This chapter deals with the preliminaries of positioning your photo on your screen and deciding how much of the "raw" photo you want to include within the borders of your finished product.

Your PhotoSuite 4 Canvas

The previous chapter told you the basics of how to import an image from a disk, camera, or scanner. But it didn't tell you what to with it after you've retrieved it. Figure 6-1 shows an image I've scanned into PhotoSuite 4 using the directions provided in Chapter 5, "Where Do Little Images Come From?" As you can see, I'm many steps away from having a suitable-for-onscreen-viewing product.

First and foremost, I need to correctly position my scanned image on the PhotoSuite 4 desktop. This most certainly involves rotating the picture so that it's no longer sideways. I also need to decide whether to enlarge or reduce my image and whether to eliminate portions of it by cropping.

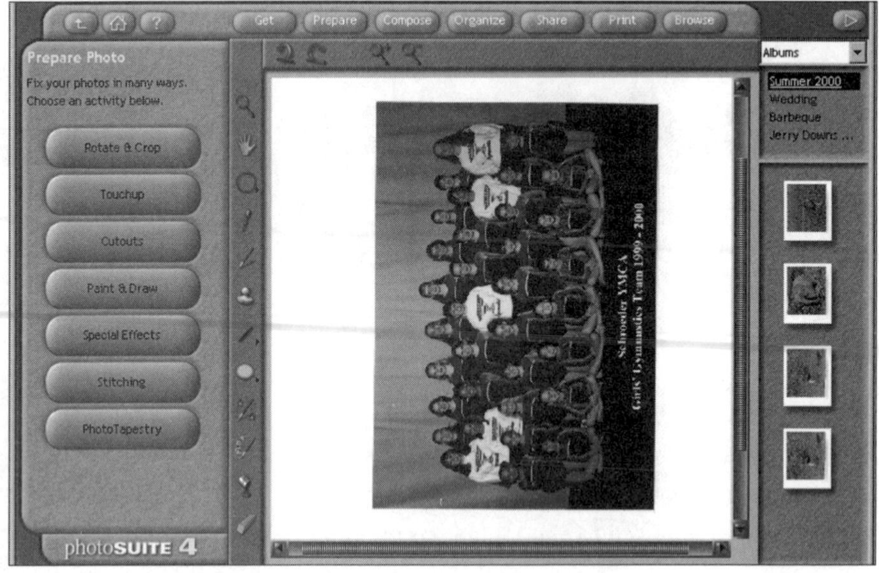

Figure 6-1: This scanned image hardly represents a finished on-screen work product.

Credit: VIP Photography

Decisions to change the size affect the overall quality of the image. I may not be able to enlarge my image as much as I'd like because doing so degrades the quality to an unacceptable level. Chapter 3, "Photo-Science: Fun with Chemicals and Computer Chips," tells you more about this.

Rotating a Photo

PhotoSuite 4 allows you to rotate a photo three different ways. You can

- Use a predefined 90- or 180-degree rotation angle
- Rotate the photo with your mouse using the freehand feature
- Define an angle of rotation and gradually increment it by a precise amount (for example, exactly 5 degrees)

At some time or another, you'll probably have reason to use all these features to realign your photos before you begin work on them.

Rotating by 90 or 180 degrees

Take a good look at the gymnastics team photo in Figure 6-1. If I were to rotate it 90 degrees, it would turn the photo halfway around. If I rotated it 180 degrees,

I would turn it all the way around. It's easier to actually see the effects of the 90- and 180-degree rotations by experimenting with the options.

To take the rotation features for a test drive:

1. **Click the Prepare button on the Navigation bar (you can do this from any screen).**
2. **Click the Rotate & Crop button on the Activity panel.**

   The Rotate & Crop Activity panel, shown in Figure 6-2, appears.

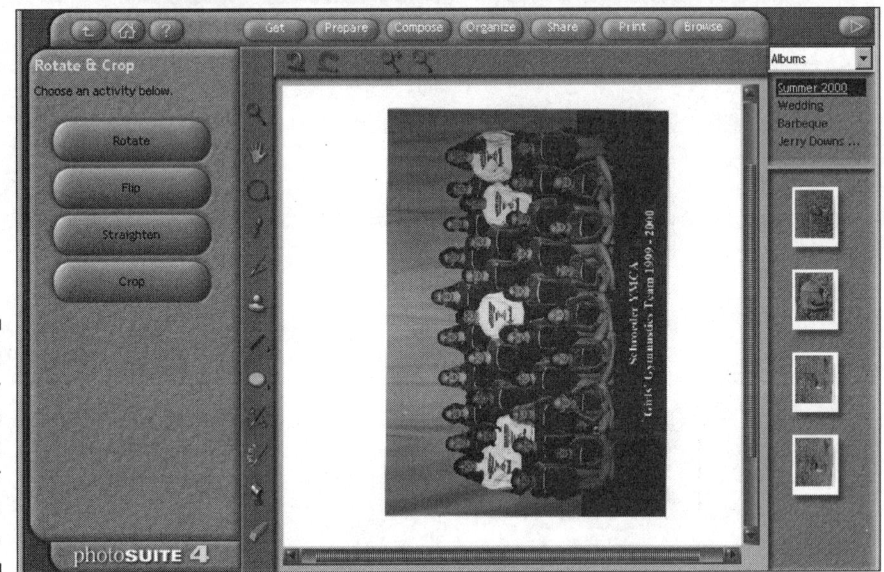

Figure 6-2: This Activity panel offers you several options for rotating a photo.

Credit: VIP Photography

3. **Click the Rotate button.**

   The Rotate Activity panel, shown in Figure 6-3, appears.
4. **Select one of the following options from the Rotate Activity panel:**
   - **No Rotation:** This gets your shot back to its original position after you've applied any of the other Rotate options.
   - **Rotate 90° left:** The effect of this option is shown in Figure 6-3.
   - **Rotate 90° right:** The effect of this option is shown in Figure 6-4.
   - **Rotate 180°:** This option turns your photo all the way around, as shown in Figure 6-5.

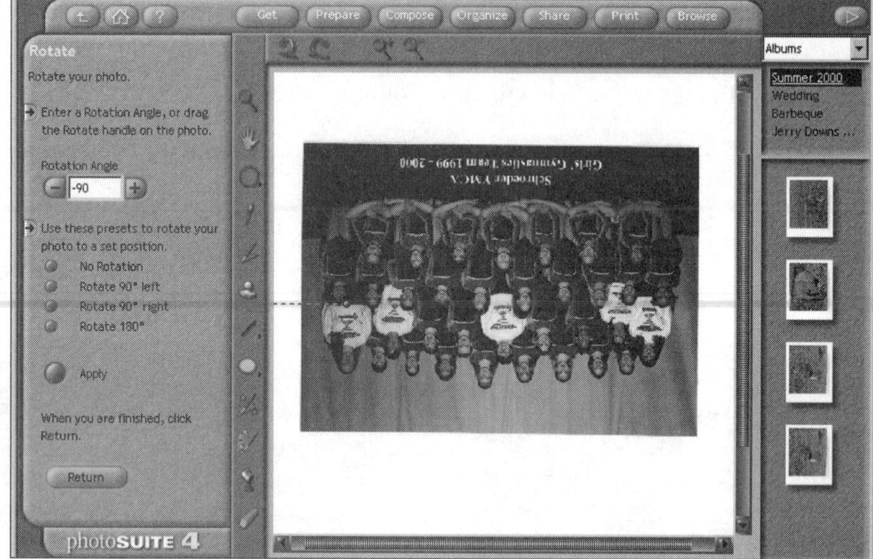

Figure 6-3: This is the shot in Figure 6-1 rotated 90 degrees to the left. Oops!

Credit: VIP Photography

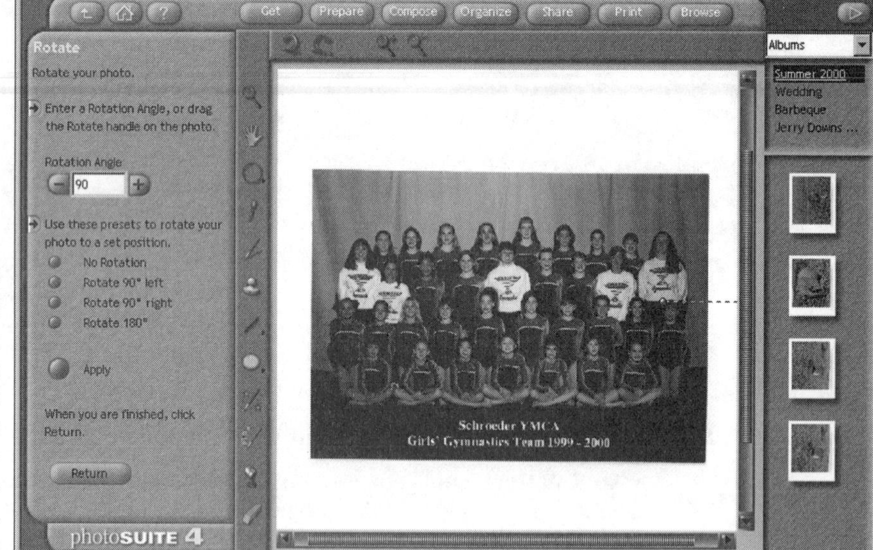

Figure 6-4: Here it is again rotated 90 degrees to the right — that's more like it.

Credit: VIP Photography

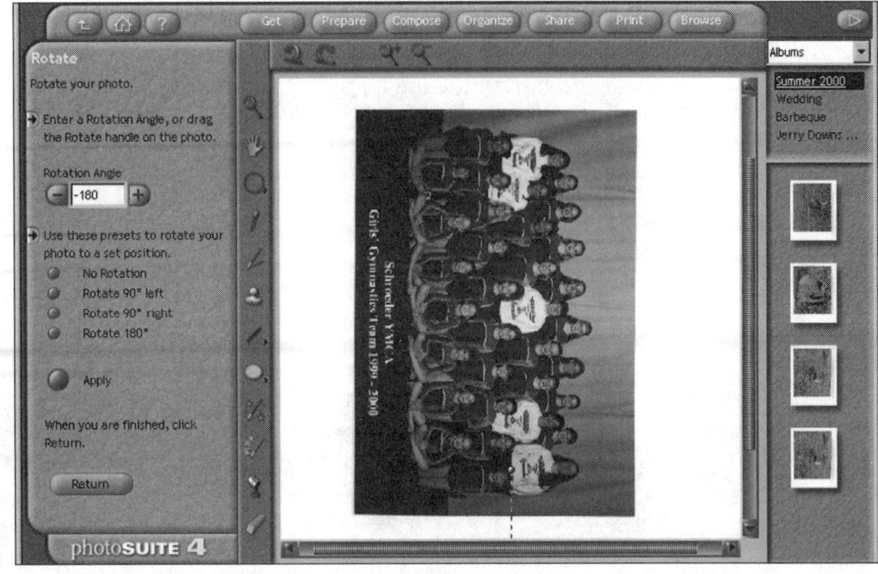

Figure 6-5: And here's that same photo from Figure 6-1 rotated 180 degrees.

Credit: VIP Photography

As you can see from Figures 6-3 through 6-5, the correct rotation is 90 degrees to the right. Rotation to the right correctly positions the photograph on the PhotoSuite 4 desktop.

Rotating a photo freehand (Wh-e-e-e-e!)

The freehand rotation feature allows you to exercise more control over the positioning of the photo. This works great when you *want* your photo displayed at an odd angle. (For example, if you want to do that Fred Astaire thing where it looks like someone is dancing on a wall.)

To use the freehand feature:

1. **Import a photo into PhotoSuite 4 as you normally would (using the directions from Chapter 5).**
2. **Click the Prepare button on the Navigation bar.**

   The Prepare screen and Activity panel appear.
3. **Click the Rotate & Crop button on the Activity panel.**

   A small blue ball called a rotation handle appears, connected by a dotted line to the top boundary of the photo.

4. **Position your mouse over the rotation handle and drag the photo to the position you want.**

   Vertical and horizontal lines appear around the photo as you drag it, as shown in Figure 6-6. These lines help you gauge the change in the angle and reposition the photo so that it's straight and even. The number of degrees you've rotated the photo appears in the Rotation Angle field.

5. **When you're satisfied with the rotation angle, click Apply to save the changes.**

   If you want to start over from the original angle of rotation after you've applied the changes, click Undo in the command bar.

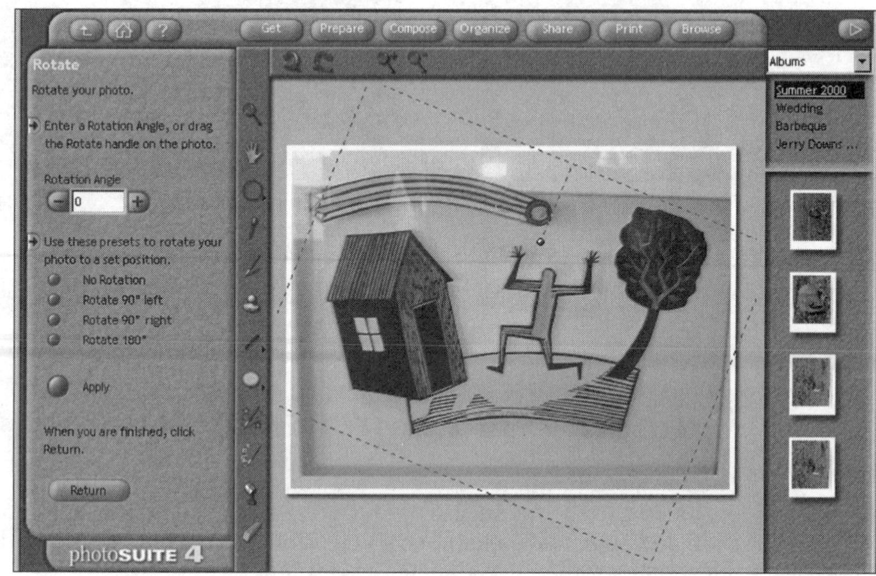

Figure 6-6: The guiding lines and patterns appear as you use the freehand feature to help you position your photo.

Credit: Marvin Hill

Defining your own rotation angle

Say that you want to rotate your photo by exactly 11 degrees to the right. PhotoSuite 4 not only lets you do this, it allows you to increase or decrease the angle of rotation five degrees at a time. To use these features:

1. **In the Rotation Angle field, enter the number of degrees to the right by which you want to rotate the photo.**

2. **Use the + and - buttons to increase or decrease the angle of rotation.**

   The photo rotates 5 degrees from its original position each time you click.

3. **When you're satisfied with the angle of rotation, click Apply to save your changes.**

   The new angle of rotation becomes the baseline, and the degrees in the Rotation Angle are set to zero.

Flipping Photos

The PhotoSuite 4 Flip tools are misunderstood and underrated creatures. Often, PhotoSuite 4 users think all they do is reposition the photo. But they actually do something far more sophisticated.

The Flip feature creates mirror images of your photos. You can start with an image such as the one shown in Figure 6-7, which is a shot of two middle-aged men named Dick and Dan stuffing hot dogs into their faces. (Hardly a glamorous shot, but professional male models weren't in my budget. Dan is the one in the short-sleeve shirt. Dick is wearing the tank top.)

Figure 6-7: Here's a photo of two guys named Dan and Dick shown before any of the Flip features are applied.

We can choose from the following photo Flip features (say *that* three times fast!) to reposition Dick and Dan in the shot:

- **Flip Horizontal:** Creates a mirror image of the photo vertically across the center line (sometimes called the *y*-axis). An example appears in Figure 6-8. Notice how Dick and Dan have switched places and their watches are now on the wrong wrists.

- **Flip Vertical:** Creates a mirror image of the photo across the horizontal centerline (called the *x*-axis). This is illustrated in Figure 6-9. Now Dick and Dan are upside down.
- **Flip Both Ways:** Creates a mirror image both vertically and horizontally. The result is a complete mirror image of the one displayed in Figure 6-8.

Now, surely you can use this feature more artistically than I have here in photographing men eating hot dogs. You can get some stunning artistic effects by displaying mirror images of things with interesting symmetrical patterns. Subjects in nature, such as foliage, offer interesting possibilities. For example, by repeating mirror images of individual plants and sections of growth, you can create an illusion of dense vegetation or a forest.

Figure 6-8: The Horizontal Flip option causes Dick and Dan to switch places.

To use the Flip feature:

1. **Click the Prepare Button on the Navigation bar.**

   The Prepare screen and Activity panel appear.

2. **Click Rotate & Crop on the Activity panel.**

   A second Activity panel with a Flip button appears.

3. **Click the Flip button.**

   Another Activity panel appears.

4. **Select one of the Flip options (horizontal, vertical, or both ways) and click Return when you're finished.**

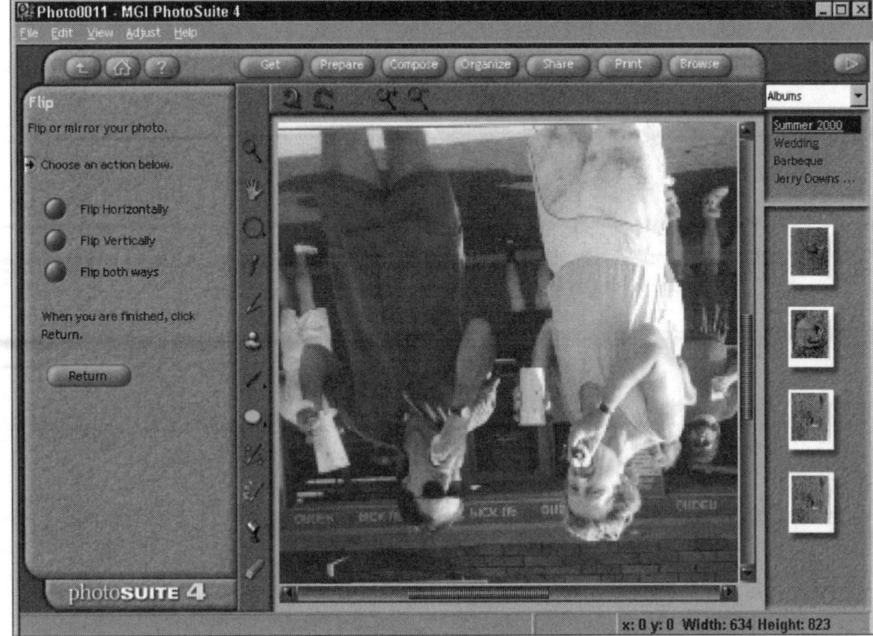

Figure 6-9: The Vertical Flip option creates a mirror image that makes the guys look as though they're upside down.

Zooming Right Along

The Zoom feature is another misunderstood tool. It allows you to temporarily resize an image on your desktop so that you can edit it more easily in the Workspace area. The image automatically reverts to its normal size before printing or saving.

If you want to *permanently* resize an image, you need to make this change using the Crop tool, which is discussed in the next section.

You can access the various Zoom options by clicking the Zoom tool (looks like a magnifying glass) located on the vertical toolbar on the Prepare screen. When you click this icon, the Zoom Activity panel (shown in Figure 6-10) appears on the left side of the screen. You can also zoom in or out using the buttons on the Command bar (see Figure 6-10).

You can select from the following Zoom options:

- **Zoom In:** This option allows you to double the size of a photo with a click of your mouse. You can use it repeatedly, as I've done to achieve the result shown in Figure 6-11.

- **Zoom Out:** This option reduces the size of your image by half each time you click it. You can also zoom out using the icon located on the Command bar (directly below the Navigation bar, as shown in Figure 6-10).
- **Zoom to Fit:** Click this option to automatically resize your image to correspond to the dimensions of your PhotoSuite 4 desktop.
- **Zoom to 100%:** Use this tool to restore the photo to its original size (that is, to the size it was before you applied one or more of the other Zoom tools).
- **Zoom by a Factor:** In this field, you can enter a Zoom factor, expressed as a percentage. For example, if you want the image to be resized to 90 percent of the original size, enter 90 in the field. You can then use the + or - buttons on the side of the field to increase or decrease the image by 10 percent of the Zoom factor each time you click. This is a good way to find the point at which the quality of an enlarged image degrades to an unacceptable level.

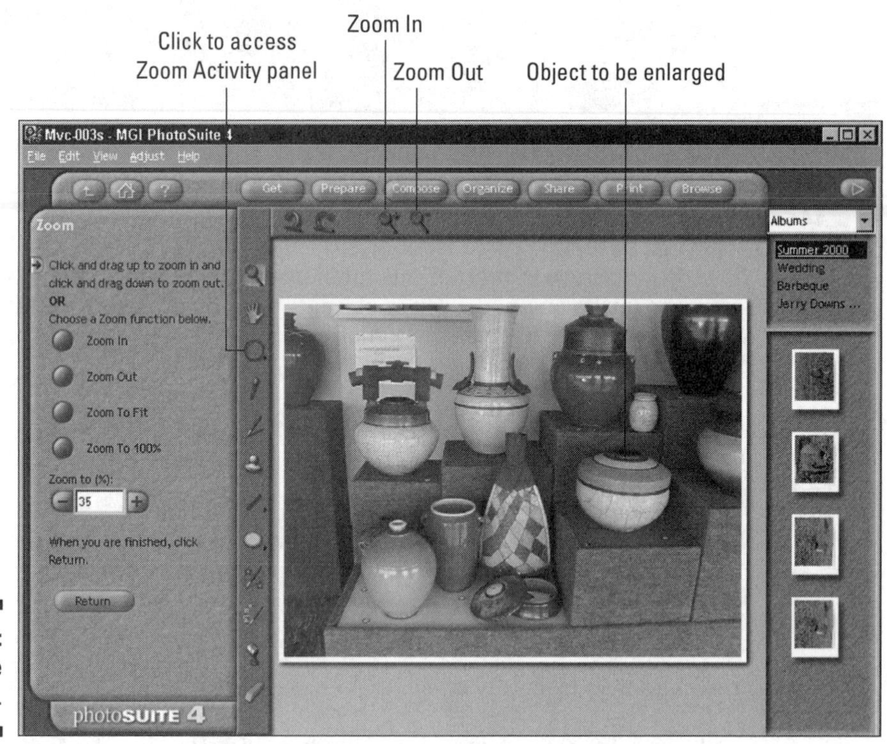

Figure 6-10: Access the Zoom tools.

Use the scroll arrows at the bottom and at the left side of the screen to center the resized image appropriately.

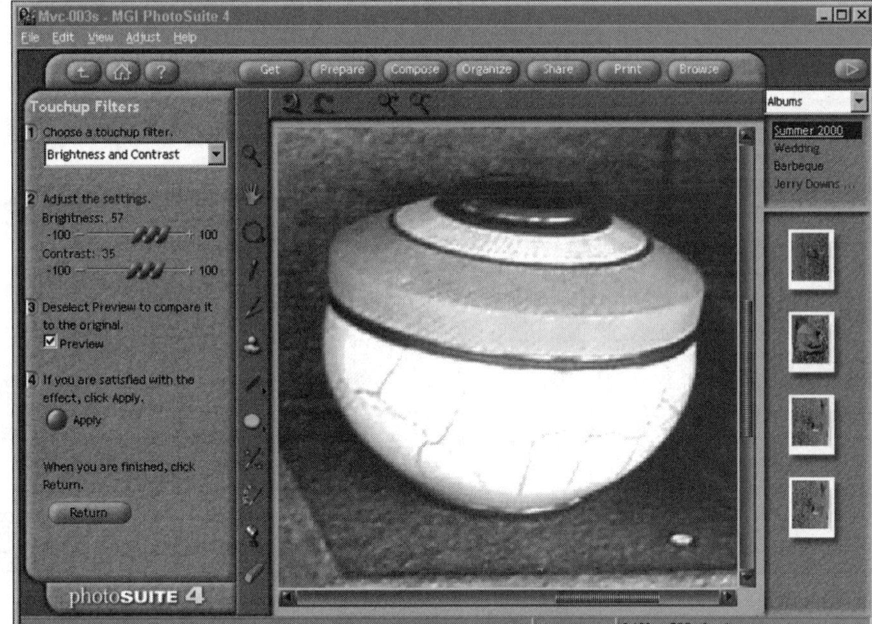

Figure 6-11: I can edit this object more easily now that I've zoomed in.

Cropping a Photo

The crop feature allows you to lop off portions of your photo and automatically enlarge the remaining portions to fit the new dimensions. Use this to get rid of stuff you *don't* want in your picture that's bordering the subject matter you *do* want.

To crop an image and enlarge the remaining portions to scale:

1. **Click the Prepare button on the Navigation bar.**

   The Prepare screen and Activity panel appear.

2. **Click the Rotate and Crop button on the Activity panel.**

   Another Activity panel appears.

3. **Click the Crop button.**

   The Activity panel shown in Figure 6-12 appears, and a broken line called a bounding box surrounds the photograph on your screen. Small blue spheres, called rotation handles, appear at various intervals along the sides of the bounding box.

4. **Click your mouse on a rotation handle and, while holding the mouse button down, drag the rotation handles until the bounding box surrounds the portion of the image you want to crop.**

   The blue spheres turn into hands as you drag the borders of the bounding box.

5. **When you're satisfied that the correct portion of the image is enclosed within the bounding box, click the Return button.**

   The newly cropped photo appears, full size, on your screen.

You can undo a cropping operation by clicking the Undo tool on the Command bar.

Figure 6-12: A bounding box allows you to redefine the boundaries of your photo.

Enlarging can compromise the quality of your image dramatically. This is because the pixels, or dots of color that make up the picture, grow and shrink to fit the resized dimensions, as explained in Chapter 3.

Chapter 7

Eeek! Making Ugly Stuff Look Better

In This Chapter

- Enhancing images
- Beautifying photos with the brush tools
- Clone-ing around
- Getting the red out of people's eyes

Sometimes it takes nerves of steel and guts of iron to be an amateur photographer. You wonder how the professionals endure it day after day, year after year. How do they cope with pictures that have *both* under- and overexposed areas in the same shot ? Do the pros ever click at the exact moment the subject is blinking or sneezing or a dead bird is falling from a tree? Or does anyone in a pro shot have glowing red eyes from the flash?

Of course they do! But professional photographers have tricks for salvaging photos after the fact. You can learn a few of them by breezing through the easy steps in this chapter.

I Could Have Enhanced All Night

Enhancing a photo gives me an adrenaline rush — as though I'd saved the lives of the people in the image. Or as though I'm an archeologist who has salvaged a relic.

Enhancing a photo means adjusting brightness, contrast, and other program settings to display the raw image data that you've captured with your camera to its best advantage. This is especially tricky for outdoor shots that often have both underexposed and overexposed areas (such as Figure 7-1).

Enhancing the automatic way

PhotoSuite 4 offers you a full range of enhancement tools for adjusting the brightness and contrast in your photo. But there's one you should try first, every time: the automatic Enhance tool. This feature simultaneously adjusts the brightness and contrast of the entire photo to display it at its best.

Figure 7-1 shows a photo before I used the automatic Enhance, and Figure 7-2 shows the same shot after I used the feature. Big improvement, huh?

Figure 7-1: Here is a photo that has not been enhanced.

Figure 7-2: The automatic Enhance feature improves the photo to this quality with a single mouse click.

The automatic Enhance feature uses data that the PhotoSuite 4 program covertly gathers about the image to make the adjustments. It tweaks the photo using a graph called a *histogram,* which plots all the brightness values of the pixels. It uses mathematical calculations to make bright ones brighter, and brings dark ones within an optimum range.

To use the automatic Enhance feature:

1. **Click the Prepare button on the Navigation bar.**

   The Prepare screen and Activity panel appear.

2. **Click the Touchup button on the Activity panel.**

   Another Activity panel appears.

3. **Click the Enhance button.**

   The photo is enhanced automatically, using the histogram technology described previously.

4. **Deselect the Preview option if you want to look at your original photo so that you can compare it to the enhanced version.**

   When you deselect the check box, the original photo appears on your screen.

5. **If you like the enhanced version of the photo better than the original, click Apply to save the changes.**

   The enhanced version of the image is saved in place of the original.

6. **Click Return when you're finished using this feature.**

Often you get dramatic results using the automatic enhancement feature. Other times, the change is imperceptible. Don't worry; your auto Enhance feature isn't on the blink when this happens. It just may not have a lot to do for a particular shot, if you've already photographed your subject in optimum lighting conditions.

Adjusting the whole photo manually

Most of the time you don't care about everything that happens to find its way into a photo. For example, you don't care about a littering of beer cans or the vagrant on the beach where you're photographing the sunset. But if you use the auto Enhance feature I tell you about in the previous section, the histogram gives you a sort of averaging of the best brightness and contrast settings for *everything* in your picture. Adjusting brightness and contrast settings for an entire photo manually gives you added control. This way, you can display a particular image in a photo to its best advantage. To adjust the brightness and contrast settings manually:

1. **Click the Prepare button on the Navigation bar.**

   The Prepare screen and Activity panel appear.

2. **Click the Touchup button.**

   Another Activity panel appears.

3. **Click the Touchup Filters button.**

   The Touchup Filters Activity Panel appears on the left side of your screen, as shown in Figure 7-3.

4. **Select Brightness and Contrast from the drop-down menu.**

5. **Use the sliders to adjust the brightness and contrast settings.**

   The sliders allow you to adjust the settings on a scale of -100 to +100, with 100 being the brightest or the highest level of contrast.

6. **Use the Preview box (which is selected by default) to preview the photo with the new settings, or deselect the box to see the original photo without the adjusted settings.**

   You can flip back and forth between the preview version and the original photo by putting the check mark in and taking it out of the check box.

7. **Click Apply to save the adjusted settings when you're satisfied; then click Return to exit the Touchup Filters Activity panel.**

In addition to using a Touchup filter on a whole photo, you can adjust individual sections. The section of this chapter called "Just a Touch Up, Dear" tells you how to use the Touchup brush tools to apply contrasts, filters, and special effects as selectively as if you were putting make-up on a face.

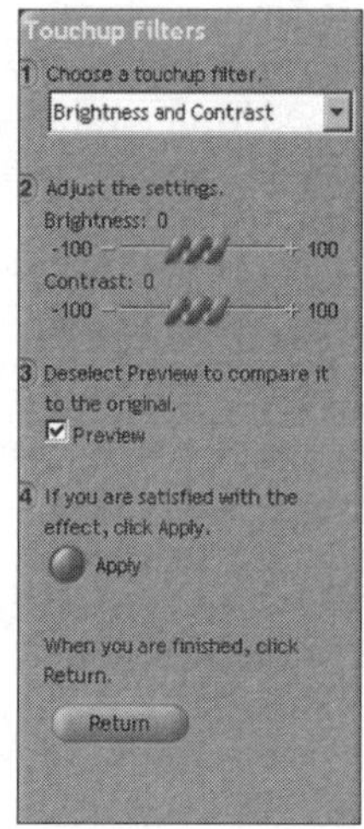

Figure 7-3: Use this Activity panel to adjust the brightness and contrast settings manually.

Just a Touchup, Dear

What amateur photographer hasn't had the sinking feeling of an almost perfect photo — with one fatal flaw? You have a shot that captures an event, emotion, or expression so perfectly, it makes you ache that it isn't a "keeper."

Touchup brushes and filters give you a leg up when it comes to correcting flaws such as over- or underexposed areas, blurriness, and unintended subjects. They can also help you create special effects, such as tints, moonlight, and weather conditions. PhotoSuite 4 includes surprisingly sophisticated retouching and airbrushing tools that allow you to exercise rigorous control over the editing process. This can, however, be a time-consuming and painstaking endeavor.

You can get many of the same effects using either Touchup brushes or Touchup filters. The difference between these two types of tools is *how* you use them. Brushes allow you to apply an effect selectively to portions of a photo. Filters apply the effect to the entire photo, with one click of your mouse.

Basic precautions for extensive touch-ups

You wouldn't dream of typing a lengthy Microsoft Word document without being very careful to save the text periodically. Otherwise, one power surge and your work product would be lost.

The same sad scenario can occur with your major editing projects if you don't take some basic steps along the way. Touching up a single shot can take you upwards of half an hour — and only seconds to save (or lose). And like any unique and creative work product, once it's lost it can never be precisely duplicated.

Here are some tips to avoid data loss and despair when undertaking major editing projects:

- **Save frequently:** Save images periodically, just as you would a text document. (Remember that the Undo/Redo feature works only up to the last save.)
- **Save before you close:** Remember that you must save an image before you close it. Don't be too quick to respond "duh" to this one. It's possible to make this error in PhotoSuite 4. Some editing dialog boxes require you to click only the Return button to save your changes. This is the case with the Touch up Brushes and Remove Red Eye dialog boxes. Other dialog boxes, such as the one for Touchup Filters, require you to first click the Apply button. If you forget, your changes are lost.

- **Make backup copies as needed:** Most editing screens in PhotoSuite 4 allow you to preview changes in some fashion before you apply them. But what if you apply changes and then like the original better after all, or you want to go back to a certain stage of the editing and try another approach? Backup copies (to which you assign different filenames) are great for this wishy-washiness. I create multiple backups and delete them when I'm truly satisfied with the end result.

  You can use the Undo/Redo feature until the pictures are actually saved to the file.

  Remember to delete all those "draft" files when you're satisfied with the finished product. Graphics files take up a lot of room (many of them close to 1MB).

- **Maximize your RAM:** The editing process takes massive amounts of RAM, as discussed in Chapter 4, "Imaging Equipment for All Occasions." PhotoSuite 4 recommends that you have a minimum of 32MB of RAM. But that's only a minimum. If you run short of RAM, your screen may freeze or display an error message telling you that the program can't proceed owing to a lack of memory. You can lose your current work product, or find that you can't save it.

Close all unused applications during the editing process to make the maximum amount of RAM available to PhotoSuite 4.

Brushing away the flaws

I used to wonder what people meant by centerfold models being airbrushed. Was it painful? Did it tickle? Then I realized that they were talking about the pictures — not the models.

Airbrushing is photo-editing technology that uses a software feature that simulates a paintbrush. You apply a color or special effect that you "brush over" the existing photo. Airbrushing also includes the cloning technique that I discuss later in this chapter, in "Send in the Clones."

Selecting the right brush

PhotoSuite 4 comes with all the brush tools described in Table 7-1. As you can see from the table, I've divided the brush tools into four categories based on what they actually do to your photo:

- **Repair brushes:** Help you fix something that's not quite right about a photo, such as an under- or overexposed area, blurriness, red eyes, or blemishes.

- **Enhancers:** Enhance an image *without* altering it or introducing colors not present in the original photo (for example, the soften and sharpen features, discussed later in this chapter, in "Softening and sharpening action shots").
- **Colorizers:** Allow you to introduce colors and tints not present in the original photo. These features are discussed in detail in Chapter 10, "In Color Living."
- **Special Effects:** These are the wild guys! Special effects allow you to turn your imagination loose. I discuss all of them and give you examples of their uses in Chapter 12, "Walk on the Wild Side: Special Effects."

Table 7-1 Summary of Available Editing Brush Tools

Repair Brushes	*Enhancers*	*Colorizers*	*Special Effects*
Remove Red Eye: Adjusts the color value of the pixels to approximate the natural eye color of the subject.	Lighten: Lightens the photo, to remedy under-exposed areas.	Tint: Allows you to apply a tint to the existing colors in the photo, so that the original colors appear as though they're being viewed through colored eyeglass lenses. I cover this feature in detail in Chapter 10.	Emboss: Makes your subjects look as though they're carved on a stone tablet.
Remove Scratches: Averages the pixel color from the surrounding area to obscure scratches in the photo.	Darken: Darkens the photo to remedy over-exposed photos.	Colorize: Allows you to change the color of portions of the photo. You can also adjust the hue, saturation, and values and the red, green, and blue tones. I cover these features in detail in Chapter 10.	Gaussian Blur, Smart Blur: The Gaussian Blur allows you to brush on a blurred effect to give a sense of motion or a sort of dreamy effect to the blurred object. The Smart Blur effect blurs only the background of a photo, to make the subject appear sharper.

(continued)

Table 7-1 *(continued)*

Repair Brushes	***Enhancers***	***Colorizers***	***Special Effects***
Remove Blemishes: Averages the pixel color from the surrounding area to obscure blemishes and flaws in the photo.	Warm: Gives the object "warm" or yellowish tint. (Use the slider on the screen to adjust the intensity of the tint.)	Sepia: Your photo is recast in a sort of rosy or, well — sepia — tone; traditionally used to give a photo an aged look.	Glass, Smoked Glass, Crystallize: Makes your subjects appear as though they were photographed though a pane of glass or a crystal.
Invert: Changes a photo to its negative.	Cool: Gives the object a "cool" or bluish tint. (Use the slider on the screen to adjust the intensity of the tint.)	Tan: Your photo is recast in tan and brown color tones.	Tile: Superimposes a mesh of black tile-like squares over your subject, making it look as though the area is composed of inlaid tiles.
	Soften: Creates halos around the color borders of the object and makes the contrast sharper by darkening dark colors or lightening light colors adjacent to the border.	Moonlight: Romanticizes your subject by applying color tones that make it appear as though it were photographed under the light of the moon.	Splatter: Your subject appears as though you're viewing it through a rain-soaked lens.
	Sharpen: Makes the contrast sharper by darkening dark colors and lightening light colors in small haloed areas adjacent to the border.		Fog, Snow, Wind: Makes your subject appear as though you were standing outside in adverse weather conditions to photograph it. Wind is really useful to give your subject the appearance of motion.

Repair Brushes	Enhancers	Colorizers	Special Effects
			Posterize: Reduces the number of colors and pixels in a picture so that you can create a poster that isn't grainy from being enlarged.
			Paintings: Changes a photo to look like an oil painting.
			Mosaic: Gives your photo the effect of being composed of numerous small squares of color.
			Randomize: This is impressionism with a vengeance. It takes the pixels in your photo and randomly jumbles them.

Softening and sharpening action shots

Sharpening and softening brushes and filters are useful if you photograph people who tend to move (as opposed to corpses).

When either the people in your picture or your camera moves during a shot, it can make the picture blurry. This is because cameras have different *shutter speeds.* The shutter speed is the amount of time that the film or computer chip is exposed to light. The faster your shutter speed, the better the ability of your camera to "freeze" fast-moving objects.

If your camera is a little slow on the draw, you can resort to PhotoSuite 4's sharpening brushes and filters to help correct the problem. These tools create the illusion of a sharper focus by adding small halos of light along the borders of the image. The darker side of the border gets a dark halo, the lighter side gets a light halo. The greater contrast along the borders gives the overall impression of a less blurred image.

On the other hand, there are times when you might actually want to add blurriness to a photo. Blurring the edges slightly gives the illusion of motion. This can be very effective for dynamic action shots. For example, in Figure 7-4, I've applied the soften brush to the feet, bat, and hair of the softball player to make her appear in motion while preserving the other details.

The blur feature is also useful to highlight and emphasize the primary subject of your photo. You can use the Smart blur feature to blur the background while leaving the primary subject in relatively sharp focus.

If you're using a film camera, fast action requires fast film! The higher the ISO rating of your film, the faster the moving object you're capable of capturing (ISO ratings and film are discussed in Chapter 3, "Photo-Science: Fun With Chemicals and Computer Chips").

Figure 7-4: Softening the runner's feet gives the appearance of motion.

Brushing basics

Working with touchup brushes is intuitive, because you use your mouse just like a paintbrush. Follow these steps to use your Touchup Brush tools:

1. **Click the Prepare button on the Navigation bar.**

   The Prepare screen appears.

2. **On the vertical Toolbar, click the Effect brush tool icon, as shown in Figure 7-5.**

   The Effect Brush Activity panel appears.

3. **Select the Touchup effect that you want to use from the drop-down menu (see Figure 7-5).**

   For a complete summary of available Touch-up effects, see Table 7-1, shown previously.

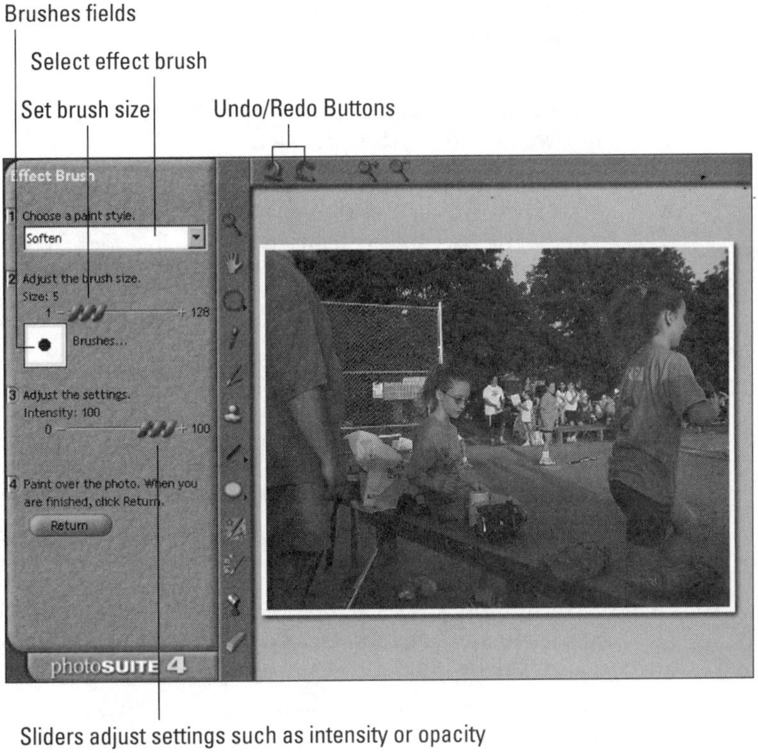

Brushes fields

Select effect brush

Set brush size

Undo/Redo Buttons

Sliders adjust settings such as intensity or opacity

Figure 7-5: The Effect Brush Activity panel.

4. **Adjust the size of your Touchup Brush using the slider (drag the bar to the right to increase the size of the brush; to the left to decrease it).**
5. **Double-click the field labeled Brushes.**

   An Activity panel appears, displaying a variety of different sizes and shapes of brush tools.
6. **Select from among the various brushes displayed in the Activity panel by first clicking the one you want and then clicking OK to exit the panel.**

   The brush type you've selected now appears in the field labeled Brushes in the Effect Brush Activity Panel.
7. **Depending on the Brush tool option you've selected in Step 4, the options in the dialog box vary. You may be presented with one or more of the following options:**
   - **Paint Color:** If you've selected the Colorize or Tint options, a Color swatch appears in the Activity panel. Click this field to display the Select Color dialog box to view a table of colors that you can use to paint or tint your photo, as shown in Figure 7-6. (This feature is covered in more detail in Chapter 10.)
   - **Adjust Intensity:** If you're working with options such as lightening or darkening, a slider appears in the Effect Brush Activity Panel to allow you to adjust the intensity.
   - **Adjust the Settings:** Some effects, such as tints and blurs, have a slider for you to adjust the opacity on a scale of 0 to 100. The more opacity, the less able you are to see the image through the effect or filter that you apply.
8. **Paint on the special effect by dragging the Brush over an area with your mouse.**

   The special effect you've chosen is applied to the areas over which you move your mouse.

   Clicking the left mouse and holding while moving over an area will apply an even coat, whereas repeated clicks will have an additive effect.)
9. **Click Return when you're finished to leave the Effect Brush Activity panel.**
10. **To save your photo, click File⇨Save to save over the old image, or File⇨Save As to store the image as a different file so that you don't have to alter the original.**

Use the Undo and Redo icons located just under the Navigation bar in the Command bar (see Figure 7-5, shown previously) to help you experiment with the Brush effects. The Undo icon allows you to get rid of whatever effect was last applied. You can click it successively to go back, undoing one action at a time.

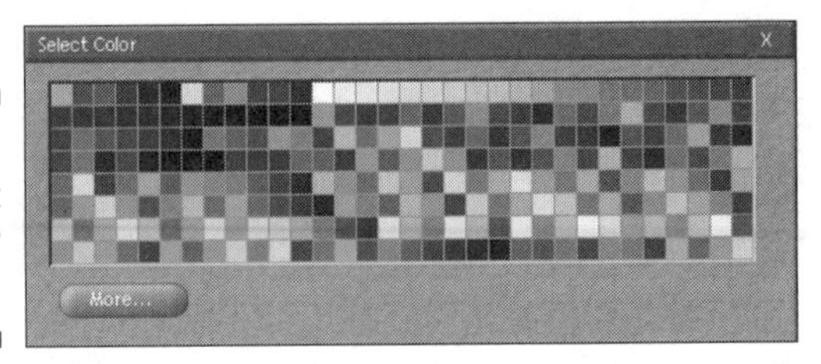

Figure 7-6: The Select Color dialog box.

Flirting with filters

Filters are like Touchup brushes but more efficient. A filter allows you to apply a special effect (for example, brighten or sharpen) to a whole photo all at one time. Table 7-2 summarizes the filters available and the effects they accomplish.

Table 7-2 PhotoSuite 4 Filters

Type of Filter	*Special Effect*
Brightness	Makes underexposed photos appear less dark.
Contrast	Helps correct photos that were shot at too low a shutter speed or with wrong speed of film. Cures blurriness by creating an illusion of greater contrast along all image borders.
Fix Colors	Allows you to adjust the hue, saturation, and value of the colors in the photo. These concepts are discussed in depth in Chapter 10.
Scratch Removal	This feature allows you to use a slider to blur the entire photo slightly to obscure small scratches on its surface.
Soften	This feature allows you to use a slider to blur the entire photo slightly.
Invert	Allows you to create a negative from your photo.
Color Adjustment	Allows you to change the shades and tones that make up the color composition of your photo. These concepts are discussed in depth in Chapter 10.
Gamma Adjustment	This filter is designed especially for use with scanned photos. It's designed to enhance details by working on the mid-range color values while leaving the dark shadows and bright areas alone. Try it on your photos and see whether it has the effect of enhancing detail for that particular photo.

To apply one of the PhotoSuite 4 filters to your photo:

1. **Click the Prepare button on the Navigation bar.**

   The Prepare screen and Activity panel appear.

2. **Click Touchup.**

   Another Activity panel appears.

3. **Click Touchup Filters.**

   The Activity panel shown in Figure 7-7 appears.

4. **Select the filter that you want to use from the drop-down menu.**

   The options in the Activity Panel change to allow you to make the necessary adjustments to apply the filter. For example, in Figure 7-7, the Activity panel contains a slider to allow you to make adjustments to the brightness and contrast.

5. **Make the necessary adjustments to the filter settings, and click Apply to save the changes you've made using the filter.**

6. **Click Return to exit the Touchup Filters Activity panel.**

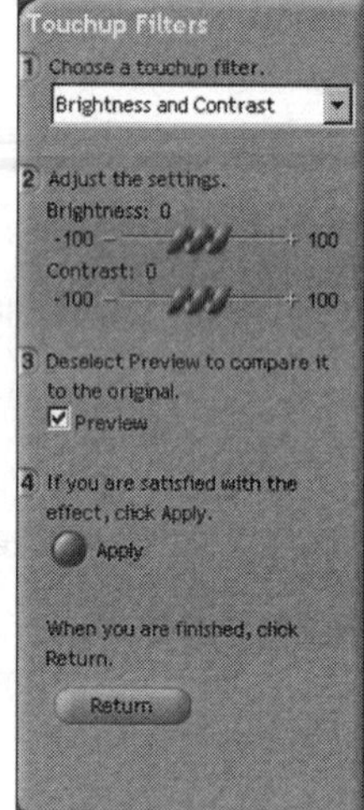

Figure 7-7: The Touchup Filters Activity panel.

Comparing shots before and after touch-up

Figure 7-8 shows an ugly duckling photo waiting to be turned into a swan. Mother and daughter are in perfect focus, and I've applied the automatic Enhance feature. But the left side is still really dark and shadowy. I tried the brighten and contrast tools, but they make my primary subjects look washed-out. Figure 7-9 shows how you can use the Lighten brush tool to selectively brighten the background and foliage otherwise lost in boring shadows.

Figure 7-10 shows an example of a party shot with potential. It certainly captures a mood, doesn't it? My subjects are well centered and cooperative, but they're blurry — partly because the kids won't stay still and partly because the camera is working so hard to adjust for the dramatic differences in light caused by the fire. Figure 7-11 shows the same photo after I've used the Sharpen filter, the Brighten filter, and the Gamma Adjustment to bring the boys out of the shadows.

Figure 7-8: This photo still has underexposed areas after I've applied the auto Enhance feature.

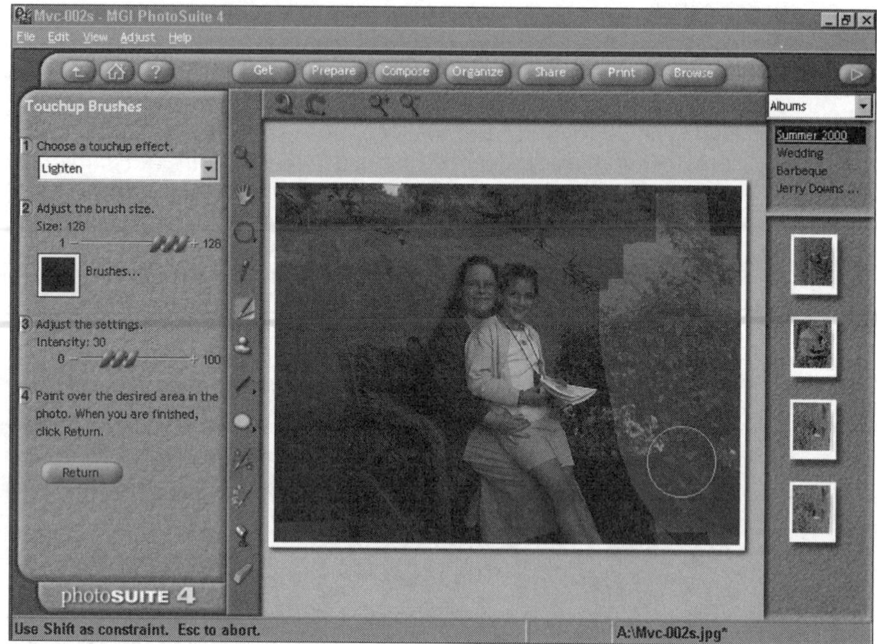

Figure 7-9: The brush tools allow you to selectively lighten areas of the photo.

Figure 7-10: These guys can't stand still, and my camera is adjusting to the firelight.

Figure 7-11: The gamma, brightness, and sharpen filters save the shot.

Send in the Clones

Pixels are the DNA of digital images. Cloning is the process of patching up flaws by harvesting the pixels. You can copy a sampling of them from the adjacent area of the photo, and use the sample to brush over the offending detail that you want to eliminate.

Cloning around

You may remember the example from Chapter 2 in which I show you an example of a model having a truly bad hair day (Figures 2-8 and 2-9 in that chapter). Cloning saved her coiffure by allowing me to copy pixels from the background to cover the clump of hair that was standing straight up.

But it seems that the model's younger sister, shown in Figure 7-12, now has a different beauty problem — she can't get her lipstick on straight. She does have a nice smile, though (and she works cheap). PhotoSuite 4 rescues the shot by allowing you to use surrounding pixels from the model's face to edit out the liberal lipstick. The cloned result appears in Figure 7-13.

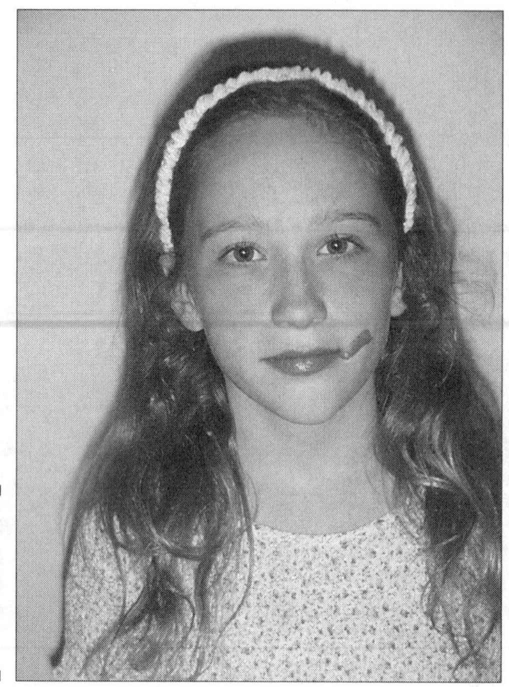

Figure 7-12: Yikes! This girl needs makeup lessons.

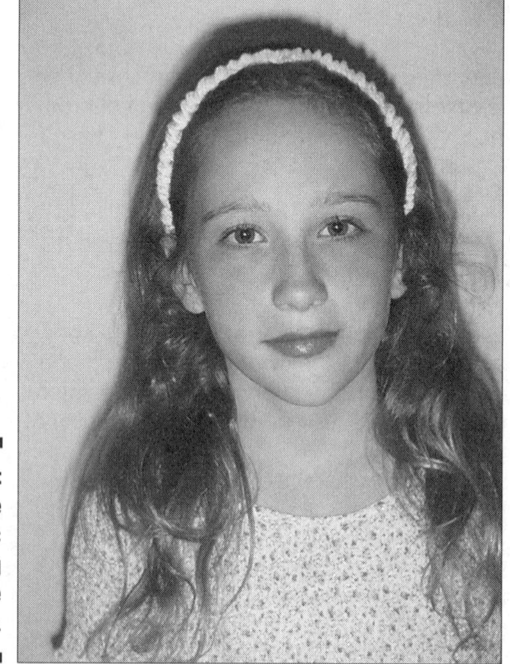

Figure 7-13: A little cosmetic cloning saves the shot.

Harvesting pixels: The DNA of graphics

Cloning is easy but takes a little practice. You may need to use your Undo button and repeat the process a few times to get a final result that bears no telltale traces of editing.

Follow these steps to clone away your photo flaws:

1. **Click the Prepare button on the Navigation bar.**

   The Prepare Screen and Activity panel appear.

2. **Click the Touchup button on the Activity panel.**

   Another Activity panel appears.

3. **Click the Clone button.**

   The Clone Activity panel appears, as shown in Figure 7-14.

   You can also access the Clone screen by clicking the Clone icon on the vertical toolbar on the Prepare screen.

4. **Use the Zoom button located at the top of your screen in the Command bar or on the toolbar to zoom in on the area you want to edit until you can see the individual pixels.**

   I've done away with the excess lipstick from Figure 7-12 (see Figure 7-14.)

5. **Click the Brush Selection tool.**

   An Activity panel with several brush tools of varying sizes and shapes appears.

6. **Select the tool you want to use and click OK.**

7. **Use the slider to adjust the Opacity, which is the color intensity (refer back to Figure 7-14).**

   This is the part that takes some trial and error. You may need to start over several times, adjusting the opacity to just the right level.

8. **Position the Brush tool over some pixels that you want to use to repair the damaged areas. This area is called the *source area.***

9. **Click the pixels over the source area and then over the area you want to repair (called the *destination area*).**

   With each click of your mouse, the source pixels are copied over the adjacent area of destination pixels. This takes practice!

10. **Click Enter when you're finished.**

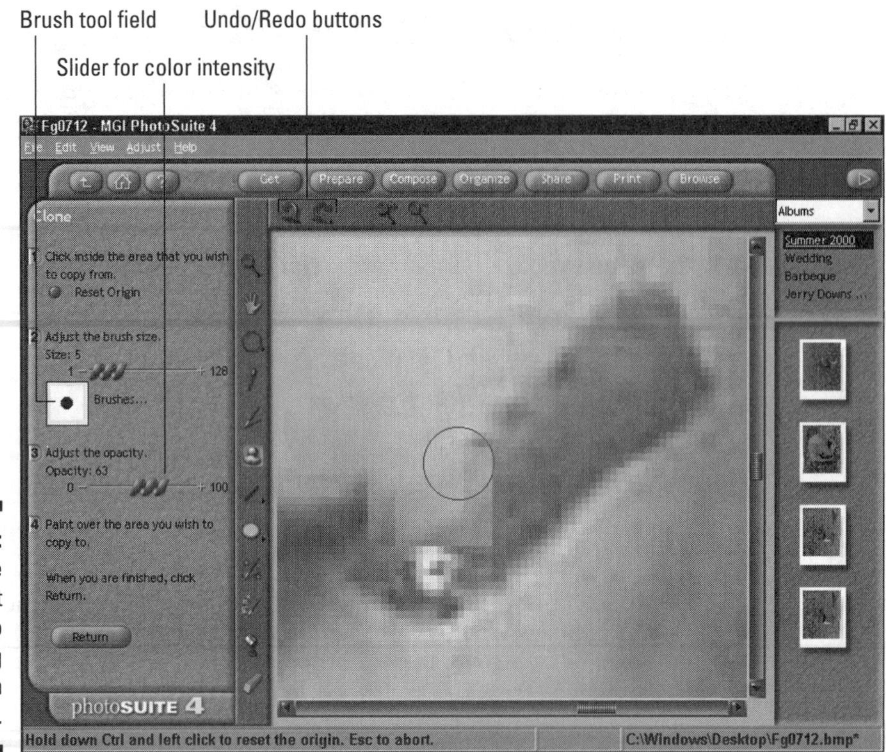

Figure 7-14: Capture the pixels that you want to copy using your brush tool.

Cloning is very much a process of trial and error, so it's a good idea to reacquaint yourself with the Undo button located below your Navigation bar. Each time you click Undo, the previous action is undone. This is a quick way to repeat and adjust the pixel-picking-process until you get a perfect pixel match.

Cloning confidently

Cloning can give you dramatic results and save many a botched photo. It's definitely a skill that every amateur photographer should strive to master. But it's far from intuitive. Here are a few cloning pointers to keep in mind:

- **Test a swatch:** Successful cloning takes place through trial and error; it always takes several stabs to choose just the right source pixels and to adjust the opacity for a well-blended effect.

- **Clone close:** Clone the smallest area necessary to achieve your results. The smaller the area you clone, the more difficult it is to detect that you've edited the shot and the better the quality of your finished result.
- **Use the appropriate brush size:** A smaller brush takes longer to complete the process but ultimately gives you more control.

Getting Rid of Red Eye

Do your relatives turn into alien monsters with glowing red eyes when you photograph them? They're not possessed — just victims of your flash.

Red eye (that *is* the actual technical term for it) is caused when the light from the flash penetrates your eyeballs and reflects off the back of them. It's most likely to occur with blue-eyed people in dimly lit or dark environments. In dim light, your pupils dilate and expose more of the red retina at the back of your eyeball for the camera to capture. (Ewww!)

The red-torical question

Before PhotoSuite 4, you had only the following methods for dealing with red eye:

- **Red-eye reduction flash systems:** These are cameras with flash systems that emit a pre-flash before the actual flash. The pre-flash causes the subjects' eyes to un-dilate. The problem with this method is that you get squinty-eyed subjects or ones who stop smiling or blink after the initial burst of flash because they think the picture's already been taken.
- **Pens and markers:** You can use a blue highlighter to dab over the glowing red hollows, but maybe you want to capture the actual eye color of your beloved. Photography shops sell special pens that allow you to neutralize the red without affecting the subject's eye color. But all that dabbing gets really tedious — especially if you need multiple copies of the shot.

Ridding red eye the PhotoSuite 4 way

PhotoSuite 4 offers you an easy alternative to blinding flashes and smudgy highlighters, as dramatically illustrated in Color Plate 2-1. To get the red out of a subject's eyes:

1. **Click the Prepare button on the Navigation bar.**

   The Prepare screen and Activity panel appear.

2. **Click the Touchup button on the Activity panel.**

   Another Activity panel appears.

3. **Click the Remove Red Eye button.**

   The Remove Red Eye Activity Panel appears on the left side of the screen, as shown in Figure 7-15.

4. **Use the Zoom tools in the Activity panel to zoom in on the subject's red eyes.**

   Keep zooming until you can actually see the color gradations in the picture and distinguish the red pixels from the surrounding ones.

5. **Adjust the brush size using the slider.**

   The smaller the brush size, the more control you can exercise while working and the longer it takes you to complete retouching the entire eye area. If you want to change the brush shape, you can click the Preview button to view and select a different brush shape.

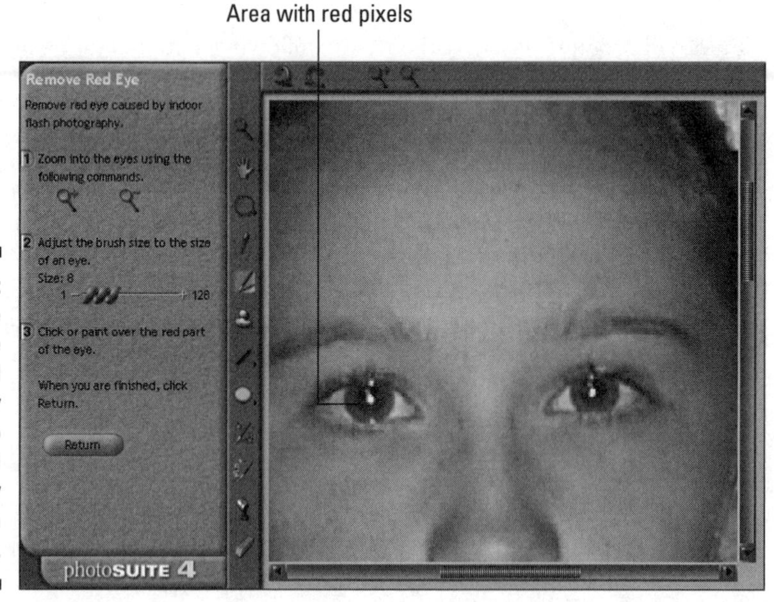

Figure 7-15: Use the tools in the Remove Red Eye Activity panel to zoom in and brush away the alien glow.

6. **Brush over the entire red area that you want to have color-corrected.**

   The brush automatically removes the red hue from the area painted. This is important, because most other programs simply paint black over the eye, making the person look like a robot. By simply removing the red hue, natural highlights that may appear in the eye are retained.

7. **Click Return when you're finished.**

Chapter 8

First Aid for Damaged Photos

In This Chapter

- Clearing up blemishes
- Wiping out wrinkles
- Buffing away the scratches

Sometime a cherished photo becomes the victim of its environment after it's printed or developed. For example, I spilled a big blob of coffee on one of my favorite photos while writing this book and crushed another picture in my desk drawer. I'd be distraught, but fortunately, PhotoSuite 4 helps correct all sorts of abuse and damage to photos.

Applying First Aid

With PhotoSuite 4, you have the ability to rescue your beloved photos from the ravages of time and accidents. The following sections show you how to heal some of the most common injuries — blemishes, wrinkles, and scratches — that your photos can suffer.

Clearing up blemishes

A *blemish* is a mark or damaged area on a photo that you want to eliminate. It can be anything from the blur of your thumb over the camera lens to a drop of coffee or falling leaf that wasn't supposed to fall then and there.

To remove blemishes from a photo:

1. **Click the Prepare button on the Navigation bar.**

   The Prepare screen and Activity panel appear.

2. **Click the Touchup button.**

   Another Activity panel appears.

3. **Click the Remove Blemishes button on the Activity panel.**

   The Remove Blemishes Activity panel appears on the left side of your screen, as shown in Figure 8-1.

4. **Use the Zoom tools to zoom in on the blemished area, as shown in Figure 8-2. Keep zooming until you can actually see the pixels that distinguish the coloration of the blemished area from the surrounding area.**

   Pixels are the individual dots of color that, when viewed together, make up an image. You can learn more about them in Chapter 3, "Photo-Science: Fun with Chemicals and Computer Chips."

5. **Adjust the brush size using the slider (see Figure 8-2).**

   The smaller the brush size, the more control you can exercise while working, but the longer it takes you to complete retouching the damaged area.

6. **Brush over the blemished area.**

   As you brush over the blemish, pixels from the surrounding area are copied to cover the damaged area.

7. **Click Return when you're finished.**

   Your photo is now unblemished.

Figure 8-1: The king of the jungle is stalked by a coffee stain.

Figure 8-2: Zoom in on the blemish and click it using the Remove Blemishes brush tool.

Applying the PhotoSuite 4 anti-wrinkle cream

Wrinkled photos are frustrating. They just don't scan right, and when you try to iron them, the chemicals melt off and stick to the ironing board. Steaming them is even worse.

If you have a treasured photo warped by wrinkles, try these steps to turn back the hands of time:

1. **Click the Prepare button on the Navigation bar.**

   The Prepare screen and Activity panel appear.

2. **Click the Touchup button.**

   Another Activity panel appears.

3. **Click the Remove Wrinkles button on the Activity panel.**

   The Remove Wrinkles Activity panel appears on the left side of your screen, as shown in Figure 8-3.

4. **Using the Zoom tools, zoom in on the wrinkly area, as shown in Figure 8-4.**

5. **Adjust the brush size using the slider (see Figure 8-4).**

   The smaller the brush size, the more control you can exercise while working, but plan to spend longer retouching the wrinkle.

6. **Brush over the wrinkled area.**

As you brush over the area, pixels from the surrounding area are copied to obscure the color variations in the wrinkled area.

7. **Click Enter when you're finished.**

Figure 8-3: The Remove Wrinkles Activity panel appears on the left side of your screen.

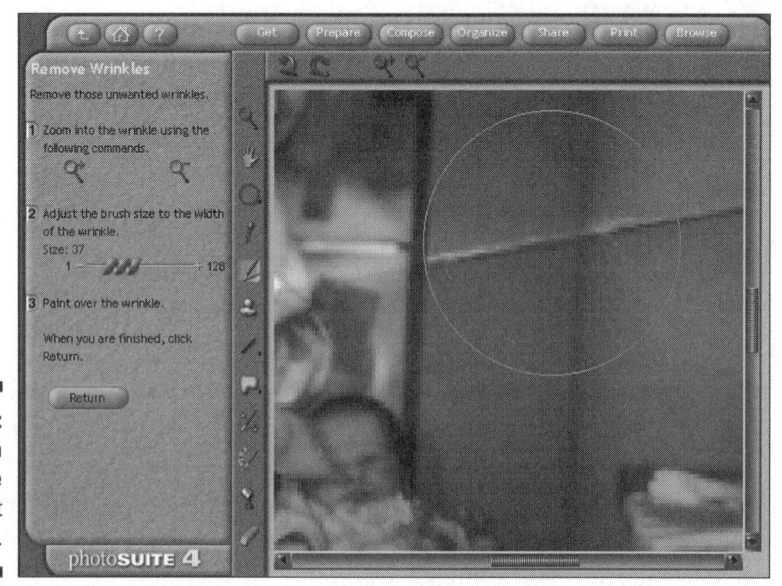

Figure 8-4: Zoom in on that wrinkle and paint over it.

Buffing out scratches

Scratched photos are the most time consuming to fix, but they can be repaired with near-flawless results. The reason they take some effort is that you actually have to use the editing tool to carefully trace the line of the scratch.

To obliterate all evidence of a scratch from the face of your photo:

1. **Click the Prepare button on the Navigation bar.**

   The Prepare screen and Activity panel appear.

2. **Click the Touchup button.**

   Another Activity panel appears.

3. **Click the Remove Scratches button on the Activity panel.**

   The Remove Scratches Activity panel appears on the left side of your screen, as shown in Figure 8-5.

4. **Using the Zoom tools, zoom in on the scratch.**

5. **Adjust the brush size using the slider (see Figure 8-6).**

   This aptly named tool allows you to draw a line over the scratch.

6. **Trace over the scratch using the Remove Scratches Brush tool.**

   As you trace the scratch with the Brush tool, pixels from the surrounding areas are copied, or averaged, to erase the scratch, as shown in Figure 8-6.

7. **Click Return when you're finished.**

   All evidence of the scratch is gone.

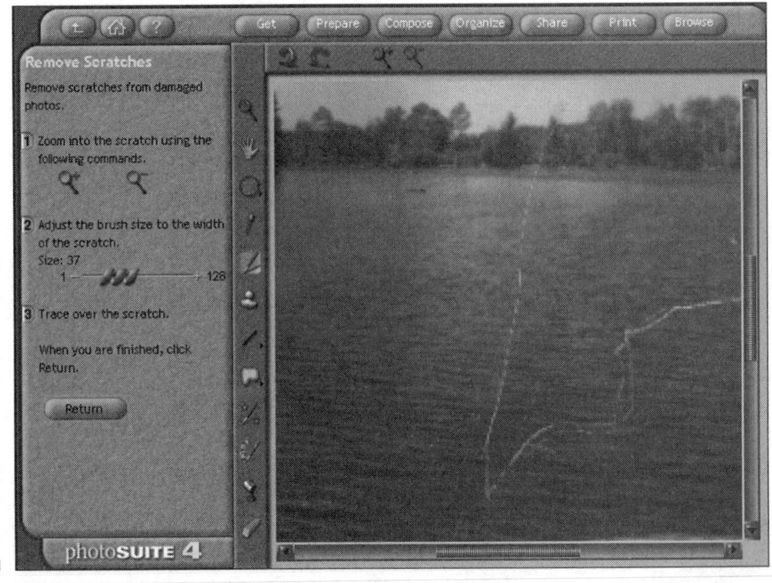

Figure 8-5: The Remove Scratches Activity panel appears on the left side of your screen.

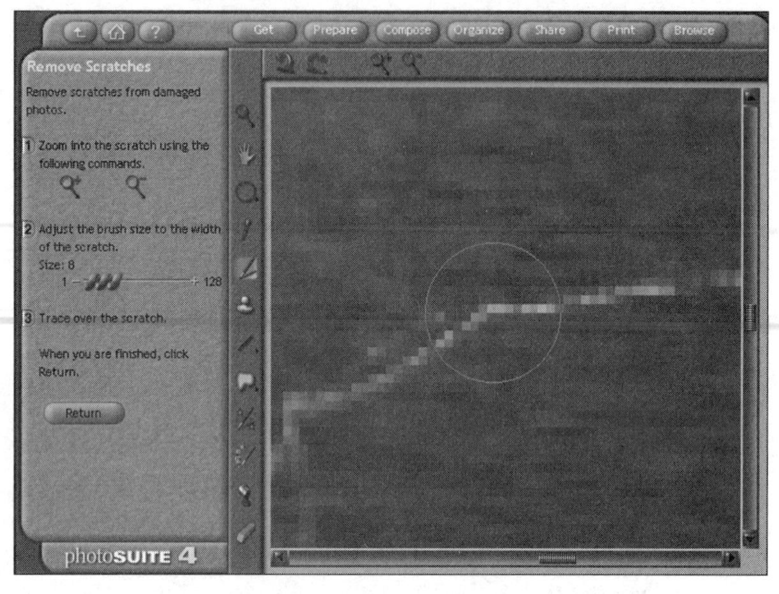

Figure 8-6: Use the Remove Scratches Brush tool to erase the scratch after you've zoomed in on it.

Chapter 9

Performing Photo-Surgery

In This Chapter

- Cutting and suturing photos back together
- Waving the Magic Wand to transform and transplant objects
- Using the amazing Edge Finder for fast cuts
- Switching heads and bodies

Photo-surgery is the latest rage. Like liposuction, it can make posteriors appear smaller and let you transplant who-knows-what onto a body that's less generously endowed. You can use it to improve the scenery — as well as the people in your photos. You can create eerie surrealistic effects and obliterate objects that have no business being in your perfect picture.

Your Instruments and the Operating Room

When you're performing photo-surgery — cutting, pasting, and grafting images — you'll be working in two PhotoSuite 4 screens:

- The Prepare screen, shown in Figure 9-1, gives you access to the cutting tools and features. (I tell you how to access and use them in the next section.)
- The Compose screen, shown in Figure 9-2, allows you to combine photos and parts of photos into what we PhotoSuite 4 aficionados call a *collage*. The collage is your canvas. You can start with a picture that you import and add other images to it, or begin with a totally blank screen, as shown in Figure 9-2.

When working in these two screens, you can transfer images that you've cut from the Prepare screen to the Compose screen using the Clipboard feature.

You can also use the Cutout tools and Clipboard feature covered in this chapter to insert graphics, including a photo, into a Microsoft Word or other text document. For example, you can cut and paste your picture onto your résumé.

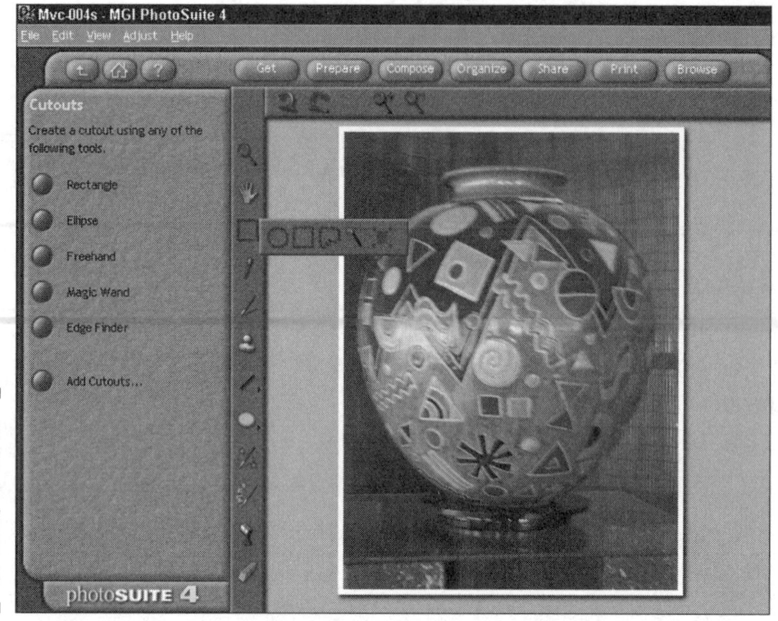

Figure 9-1: The cutting tools Activity panel and toolbar.

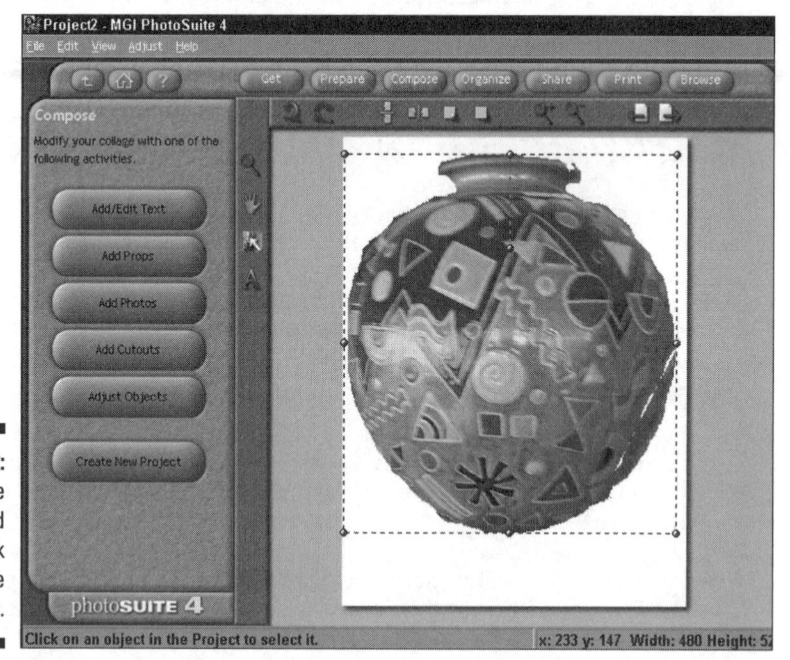

Figure 9-2: An image imported to a blank Collage screen.

Scalpel, Please! The Cutting Tools

You can make people and objects magically appear in your photo, even if they were nowhere near the vicinity at the time of the picture. This section tells you how to lift an image from an existing photo as smoothly and stealthily as a jewel thief to create a Cutout. The next section gives you the options for saving and positioning it.

Finding the cutting tools

PhotoSuite 4 offers you four different photo-surgery instruments:

- **Tools for cutting out elliptical and rectangular selection tools:** These tools allow you to cut out symmetrical, regularly shaped areas in any size and from any part of the photo that you specify.
- **Freehand tool:** This is the equivalent of a digital razor knife. You trace around the edges of the object that you want to cut.
- **Edge Finder:** This feature works by allowing you to click-click-click at multiple points (called *nodes*) all around your object. PhotoSuite 4 finds the edge of your object, which lies between each point. Many users find this to be a faster, more precise alternative to the Freehand tool, depending on the object you're cutting. The use of the Edge Finder tool is illustrated in Color Plate 9-1.
- **Magic Wand tool:** This tool selects areas based on uniform color. You should exercise caution with this one, however, because it selects similarly colored areas throughout the whole photo. It's great if you're selecting a purple object and there's only one purple object in the photo — but if there are multiple purple objects, it may select those, too.

To access the cut tools:

1. **Click the Prepare button on the Navigation bar.**

   The Prepare screen and Activity panel appear.

2. **Click the Cutouts button on the Activity panel.**

   The Cutouts Activity panel appears on the left side of the screen (refer back to Figure 9-1). It contains options for cutting a specific shape or tracing the borders of an object.

As a shortcut, you can click the Selection Tools icon on the vertical toolbar to access the cutting tools (refer back to Figure 9–1).

Cutting out rectangular- and elliptical-shaped areas

PhotoSuite 4 lets you cut out a nice, regularly shaped rectangular or elliptical area in any size you want. You can paste the area you've cut out onto another photo or even into a text document in another program.

Use the Rectangle selection tool to cut out areas with a square shape and the Elliptical Selection tool for areas with a circular shape.

To cut out an area having a regular shape (square, circular, rectangular or elliptical):

1. **Click the button for the shape you want in the Cutouts Activity panel (refer back to Figure 9-1).**

   If you're using the toolbar, click the Selection Tools icon to access the pop-up menu and then click the shape you want.

   A Cutouts Activity panel appears. The Rectangle Selection Activity panel is shown in Figure 9-3.

2. **Click the white arrow to begin working in the Normal selection mode.**

   The sidebar called "Just a little nip and tuck," which appears later in this chapter, explains more about the different selection modes.

3. **Click and hold your mouse over the corner of the area you want to cut.**

   If you're cutting an elliptical or circular area, you need to use your imagination to figure out what would be a corner if an ellipse had corners. In contrast, if you're working with a rectangle or square, you have four corners.

4. **Drag your mouse to the diagonally opposite corner to define the area you're cutting.**

   Again, you need to extrapolate here if you're working with the elliptical or circular object.

5. **Release the mouse button to complete your selection.**

   A white boundary line should appear around the area you've selected (see Figure 9-3).

6. **If you want to erase the selection and start over again, select Reset and Start Over.**

   You can then repeat Steps 4 and 5 to select a new area.

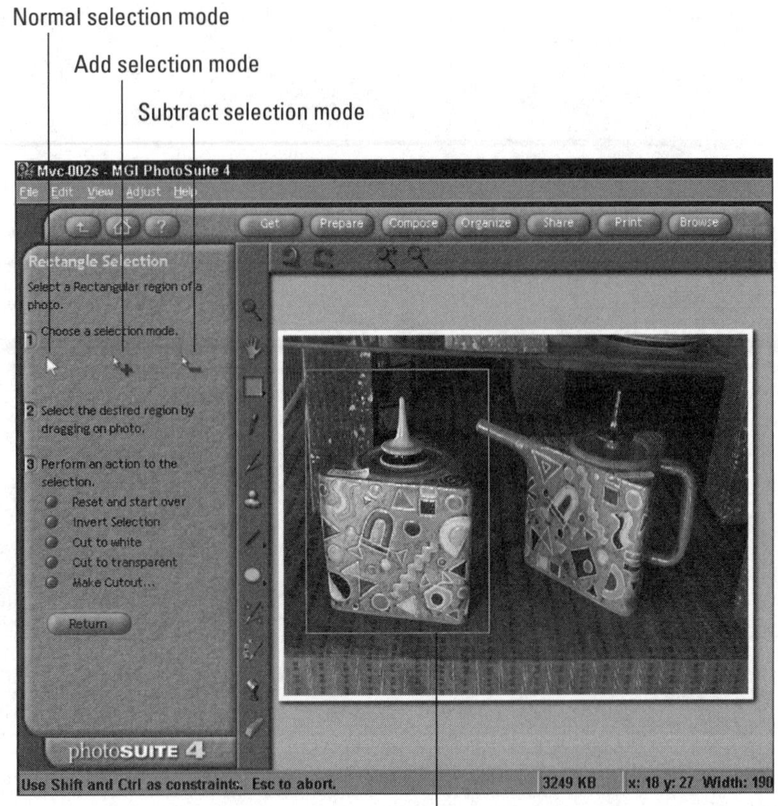

Figure 9-3: The Rectangle Selection Activity panel.

7. **If you want to add or subtract from the selection area, click the Add or Subtract selection mode arrows (shown in Figure 9-3) and repeat Steps 4 and 5.**

   The white boundary line is redrawn to conform to the area you've added or subtracted. (The sidebar "Just a nip and tuck" tells you more about the selection modes.)

8. **Choose one of the following actions to finish making your Cutout:**

   • **Reset and Start Over:** Click this option if you want to define a new selection area.

   • **Invert a Selection:** Selects everything in the photo *outside* the white boundary lines, as shown in Figure 9-4.

   • **Cut to White:** Cuts the selected area to the Clipboard and fills the area with white, as shown in Color Plate 9-2.

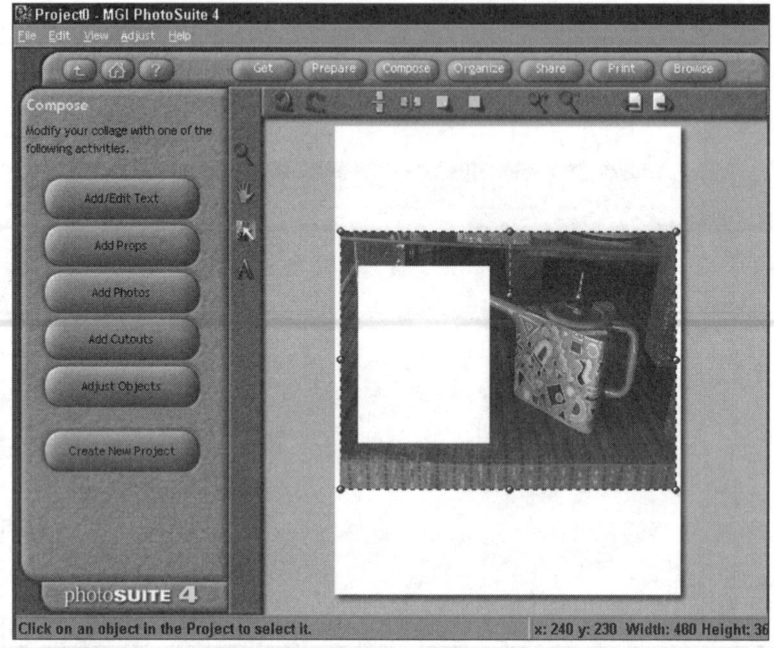

Figure 9-4: This is what the Invert a Selection option does with a cutout.

- **Cut to Transparent:** Cuts the selected area to the Clipboard, leaving the remaining area transparent (see Color Plate 9-2). This feature allows the areas and other photos to show through from behind.

  If you want to preserve a transparency, you need to save it in .TIF, .PNG, or .GIF format (see Chapter 19, "Ten Funky File Formats"). If you save in any other file format, the transparency feature is lost.

- **Make a Cutout:** If you select this option, the Cutout Activity panel appears. I cover these options for pasting and saving your cutouts later in the chapter, in the section "Stick it Here! What to Do with Your Cutout." Color Plate 9-3 shows you an example of how you can save and move your Cutouts.

After you've made a cutout, you can paste it, transplant it to another photo, or save it to the Library or a file. Later in this chapter, I cover how to use the options on the Cutout Activity panel.

Cutting Out Irregularly Shaped Objects

What if the person whose image you'd like to move from one photo to another doesn't have a perfectly rectangular or elliptical head? In fact, most people's heads are pretty irregularly shaped. That's why PhotoSuite 4 offers the nifty Freehand, Magic Wand, and Edge Finder tools, each of which is the equivalent of a razor knife.

Giving the surgeon a free hand

The Freehand tool allows you to trace around the borders of an object to select it. You can add to and subtract from the portions that you select initially, using the selection modes described in the "Just a little nip and tuck" sidebar.

To use the Freehand tool, follow these steps:

1. **Click the Freehand button in the Cutouts Activity panel (refer back to Figure 9-1).**

   The Freehand Selection Activity panel appears, shown in Figure 9-5.

2. **Click the white arrow in the upper left corner of the Activity panel to begin working in the Normal selection mode.**

   You can use the Zoom tool to enlarge the object you want to cut.

3. **Click and hold your left mouse button while you *very slowly* trace around the edges of the object that you want to select, until you end up at your starting point.**

   This is tricky! If you find that you've shaved off a part of the cutout you want to include, or have included part of the background, don't worry. You can clean it up in Step 6.

4. **Double-click when you've traced around the preliminary area that you want to include and are back at your starting point.**

   A white boundary should appear around the area you've selected.

5. **If you want to erase the selection and start over, click once outside the selected area.**

   You can then repeat Steps 3 and 4 to select a new area.

6. **If you want to add or subtract from the selection area, click the selection mode arrows (see Figure 9-5) and, starting from any area on the boundary, trace around the area you want or add or subtract to the cutout; double click when you're finished.**

   The cutout has new boundaries, reflecting what you've added or subtracted.

7. **To finish making your cutout, choose one of the actions listed in Step 8 from the previous section, "Cutting out rectangular and elliptical shaped areas."**

8. **After you've made a cutout, you can paste it, transplant it to another photo, or save it to the Library or a file.**

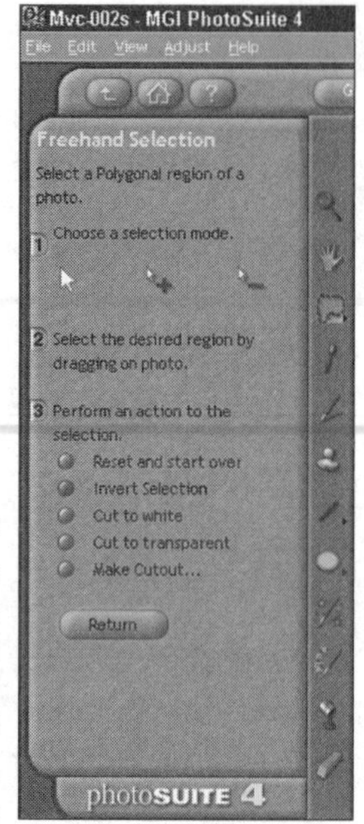

Figure 9-5: The Freehand Selection Activity panel.

Waving the Magic Wand

You can wave the Magic Wand over an object to select it. This feature liberates you from the need to painstakingly trace the boundaries of an object that's fairly uniform in color. Instead, you can "wave" your magic wand by clicking or scribbling over an area within the object. PhotoSuite 4 searches for the color you've scribbled over and encloses it in a boundary.

For example, you can isolate a cloud in a landscape and select it just by clicking it or scribbling with the Magic Wand over its surface. The Magic Wand selects the entire cloud and encloses it within white boundary lines. You can then adjust the boundary lines by using the selection mode tools discussed in the sidebar "Just a little nip and tuck."

Because the Magic Wand selection tool is looking for areas of a similar color, you may end up selecting unintended objects of the same color. For example, if you wave the Magic Wand over a cloud, you may end up selecting a white delivery truck that's also in the picture. If this happens, you can use your Undo button (located beneath the Navigation bar) and start over, after lowering the color tolerance. The Tolerance slide bar, shown in Figure 9-6, determines the range and variance of color that you capture with the Magic Wand.

1. **Click the Magic Wand button in the Cutouts Activity panel (refer back to Figure 9-1).**

   The Magic Wand Selection Activity panel appears (see Figure 9-6).

2. **Click the white arrow to begin working in the Normal selection mode.**

3. **Click your left mouse button and scribble over a portion of the area you want to select.**

4. **Release your mouse button.**

   A white boundary line appears around the entire area on which you've scribbled, provided that the area is fairly uniform in color. The boundary line may be imperfect or irregular, but you can clean it up when you get to Step 7.

5. **If a white boundary line appears in a bunch of areas of the photo and not just around the object that you intended to select, lower the tolerance by moving the Tolerance slider, shown in Figure 9-6, to the left.**

   If you lower the tolerance, PhotoSuite 4 looks for colors closer to the shade you've scribbled over using the Magic Wand. If you increase the tolerance, PhotoSuite 4 selects objects within a greater color range.

6. **If you want to erase the selection and start over, click once outside the selected area.**

   You can then repeat Steps 3 and 4 to select a new area.

7. **If you want to add or subtract from the selection area, click the selection mode arrows.**

   Starting from any area on the boundary, trace around the area you want to add or subtract to the cutout; double click when you're finished.

   The cutout has new boundaries, reflecting what you've added or subtracted.

8. **To finish making your cutout, choose one of the actions listed in Step 8 from the earlier section, "Cutting out rectangular and elliptical shaped areas."**

9. **After you've made a cutout, you can past it, transplant it to another photo or save it to the Library or a file.**

Although Figure 9-6 doesn't show the color, I've selected the purple-tinted area on a glass sculpture. I can correct the boundary lines using the selection mode tools. If I set the color tolerance higher, I also capture the other violet-toned areas in the photo.

Figure 9-6: The Magic Wand Selection Activity panel.

Using the Edge Finder

The Edge Finder is similar to the Freehand tool — only faster, for certain projects. It allows you to more quickly select the boundaries of an object by clicking along it at various points rather than meticulously tracing it. Color Plate 9-1 shows an example of this tool in use.

Here's how to use the Edge Finder tool:

1. **Click the Edge Finder button in the Cutouts Activity panel (refer back to Figure 9-1).**

   The Edge Finder selection Activity panel appears, shown in Figure 9-7.

2. **Click the white arrow to begin working in the Normal selection mode.**

   The sidebar "Just a little nip and tuck" explains more about the different selection modes.

3. **Click along the edge of the area in the photo you want to select.**

   A small rectangle appears at each point you select (see Color Plate 9-1).

4. **Position the rectangle so that it encloses a portion of the area's edge and click again.**

   The portion of the edge that's been captured appears in a contrasting color.

5. **Continue positioning the rectangle and capturing more of the area's edge.**

6. **To close the area, double click at the last selection point or click the Finish Tracing button on the Activity panel (see Figure 9-7).**

7. **If you want to erase the selection and start over, click once outside the selected area.**

   You can then repeat Steps 5 and 6 to select a new area.

8. **If you want to add or subtract from the selection area, click the selection mode arrows (refer back to Figure 9-3) and, starting from any area on the boundary, trace around the area that you want to add or subtract to the cutout; double click when you're finished.**

   The cutout has new boundaries, reflecting what you've added or subtracted.

9. **To finish making your cutout, choose one of the actions listed in Step 8 from the earlier section, "Cutting out rectangular and elliptical shaped areas."**

   After you've made a cutout, you can paste it, transplant it to another photo, or save it to the Library or a file. Drop down to the section of this chapter called "Stick it Here! What to Do with Your Cutout," to find out how to use the options on the Cutout Activity panel.

Just a little nip and tuck

When you're selecting areas for cutting , you can work in three different selection modes. The selection modes are represented by the arrows you see in the Activity panel for each cutting tool (refer back to Figures 9-4 through 9-7.) The selection mode tools allow you to define the initial boundary area and then add to or subtract from it.

There are three different selection modes:

- **Normal:** Defines the boundaries of an area you're selecting when you start the cutting process.

- **Addition Mode:** Adds some more to the portion of the photo you've selected to cut out.

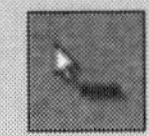

- **Subtraction Mode:** Subtracts a portion from the area you've selected.

Figure 9-7: The Edge Finder allows you to select an object by clicking along the boundaries at various points within the rectangle.

Stick It Here! What to Do with Your Cutout

After you've carefully cut and cropped the image you want to use as a cutout, it's time to transport it. The Cutout Activity panel, shown in Figure 9-8, offers you the following options for transplanting your cutouts and blending them smoothly into the scenery of their destination:

- **Cut to Clipboard:** Removes the image from the original photo and places it on the Clipboard.
- **Copy to Clipboard:** Copies the image from the original photo to the Clipboard.

Using these options can be confusing because you don't get an Activity panel or any text message telling you that the cutout has been successfully transferred to your Clipboard — and there's no way to view the contents of your Clipboard. But as with any Windows Clipboard option, there is indeed a Clipboard storing your image out there.

- **Paste down:** Pastes the image to another area of the *same* photo.
- **Send to Library:** Allows you to temporarily save the photo to the Library so that you can access it at any time during the current session.
- **Save to file:** Saves the cutout to a file on your computer so that you can use it at any time in the future. The default format for the file is .PNG. (Chapter 19, "Ten Funky File Formats," tells you about this and other formats.)
- **Edge Fading:** Blends an object into its background.
- **Opacity:** Allows you to control the extent to which an image is opaque or transparent (see Figure 9-8). Color Plate 9-3 shows an example of an interesting, ghostly image that you can create with your cutouts by adjusting this control.

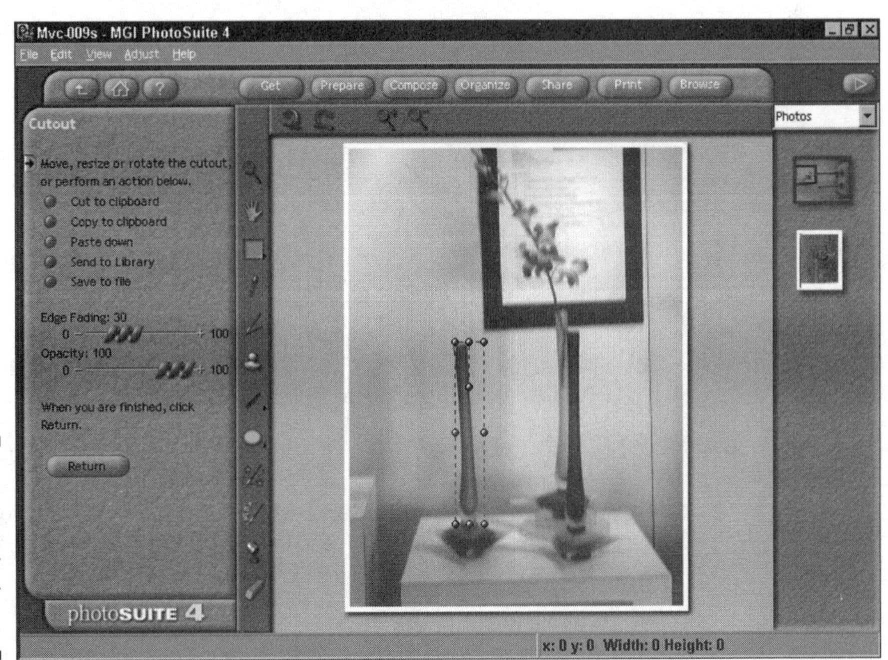

Figure 9-8: Use this screen to paste or save your cutout.

If you drag the cutout to another area of the photo, click the Paste button when you have it correctly positioned; doing so will anchor it.

Ta-Da! Composing a Collage

After you have a cutout on the Clipboard, where do you put it? One versatile choice that gives you virtually unlimited creative options is the collage screen. You can place your cutout on either a blank canvas or on another photo that you select as your background for a collage. You can add as many additional cutouts and photos to your collage as your artistic sensibilities dictate.

Picking a canvas for your collage

To begin creating a photo collage:

1. **Create a cutout and transfer it to the Clipboard using any of the cutting tools described in this chapter in the "Scalpel, Please! The Cutting Tools" and "Cutting Out Irregularly Shaped Objects" sections.**

2. **Click the Compose button on the Navigation bar.**

   The Compose screen and Activity panel appear.

3. **Click the Collage button.**

   If you've been editing a photo, it appears on the screen as the Current Photo.

4. **Indicate whether you want to begin your collage with Blank Canvas, Current Photo, or Other Photo; then Click Next.**

   If you select Blank Canvas, the New Project dialog box, shown in Figure 9-9, appears.

5. **If you're working with a blank canvas, indicate whether you want to display the collage in Portrait or Landscape view as well as the dimensions of your collage and the resolution of the photo; then click OK.**

   The Compose screen reappears.

   Portrait view means that the picture is displayed vertically, with the length as the longest dimension. Landscape means that the width is your project's longest dimension.

6. **You can choose among the following options: Add Props, Add Other Photos, Add Text, or Adjust the Position of the Objects you import.**

   In the next sections of this chapter, I tell you how to add props, text, and other photos and then adjust the position of everything in your screen.

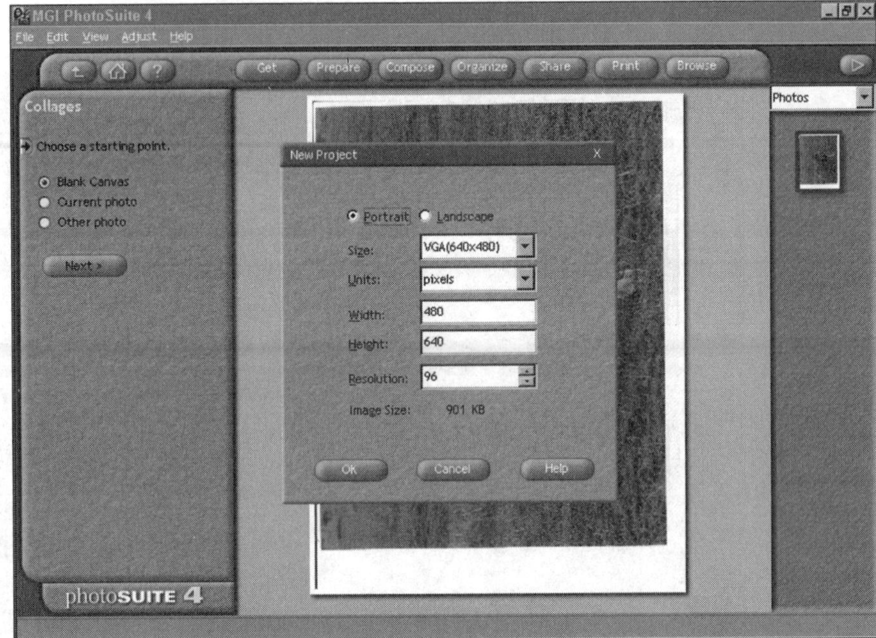

Figure 9-9: You can set the dimensions and resolution of your blank canvas.

Adding and editing text

A picture may be worth a thousand words, but a few words add a lot to a picture. PhotoSuite 4 allows you to add text, such as a caption, to a photo by following these steps:

1. **From the Collage screen (see Figure 9-2), click the Add/Edit text button.**

   The Add or Edit Text Activity panel appears.

2. **Click anywhere on the collage to add text.**

   When you click, a blue bounding box appears (see Figure 9-10).

3. **Enter your text in the Edit Text box.**

4. **Select a font style from the drop-down menu.**

   PhotoSuite 4 offers you several dozen fonts, colors, and styles from which to choose.

5. **Resize and position the text by clicking the handles (the blue spheres) and dragging them.**

   After you've positioned the text you've initially added, you can repeat Steps 2 through 4 as needed.

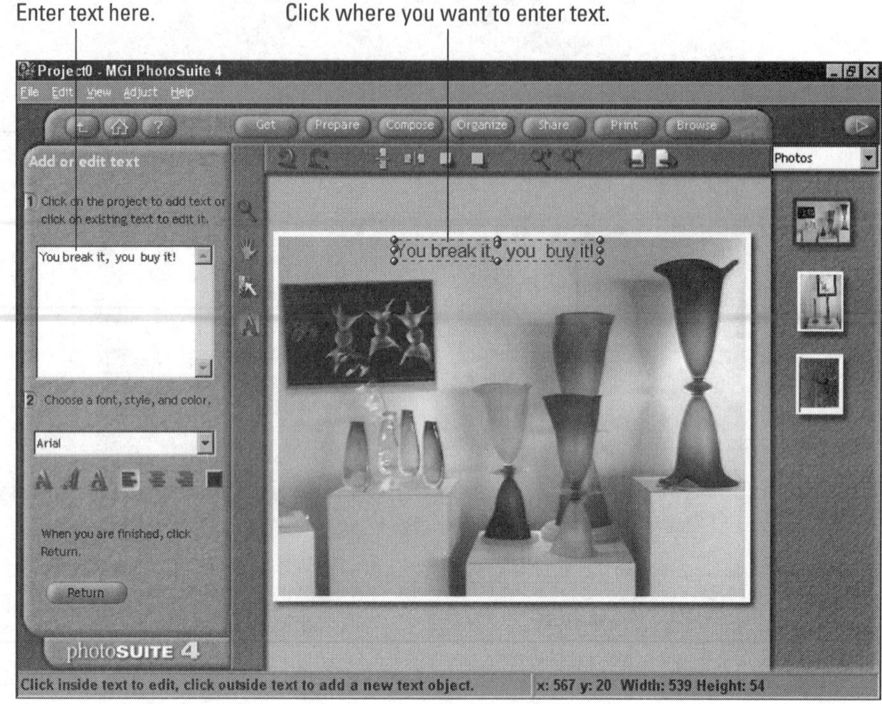

Figure 9-10: Add text to your collage using this Activity panel.

6. **Click Return when you're finished adding, positioning, and resizing the text.**

   The Compose screen appears on your desktop, with the added text.

Adding more photos and saved cutouts

One is a lonely number when it comes to digital images — or at least it's not as much fun as multiple images. So combining photos is something every amateur photographer should know how to do.

Adding more photos

You add entire photos to an existing collage or stick in a cutout you've previously created and saved.

To get two or more photos on your screen simultaneously:

1. **From the Collage screen, click the Add Photos button.**

   The Add Photos Activity panel appears, as shown in Figure 9-11.

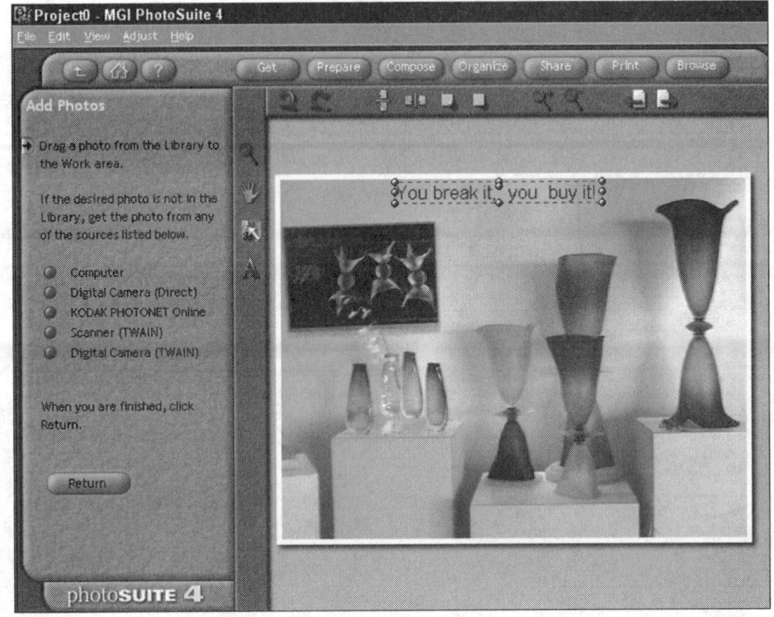

Figure 9-11: The Add Photos Activity panel.

2. **Click a button on the Activity panel that indicates the source of the photo.**

   For more information on how to locate and open an image file, see Chapter 5.

Adding a saved cutout

To add a cutout that you've previously created or saved to your project, follow these steps:

1. **From the Cutouts Activity panel (refer back to Figure 9-1), click the Add Cutouts button.**

   The Add Cutouts Activity panel, shown in Figure 9-12, appears.

2. **Do one of the following:**
   - Drag a previously saved cutout from the Library.
   - Click Computer and browse the Browse dialog box that appears for the file in which the cutout is saved.
   - Click Paste from Clipboard if the photo was previously saved from the Clipboard.
3. **You can now move, rotate, or edit your cutout.**
4. **Click Return if you're finished, or use the Undo and Redo buttons (see Figure 9-12) to repeat the process.**

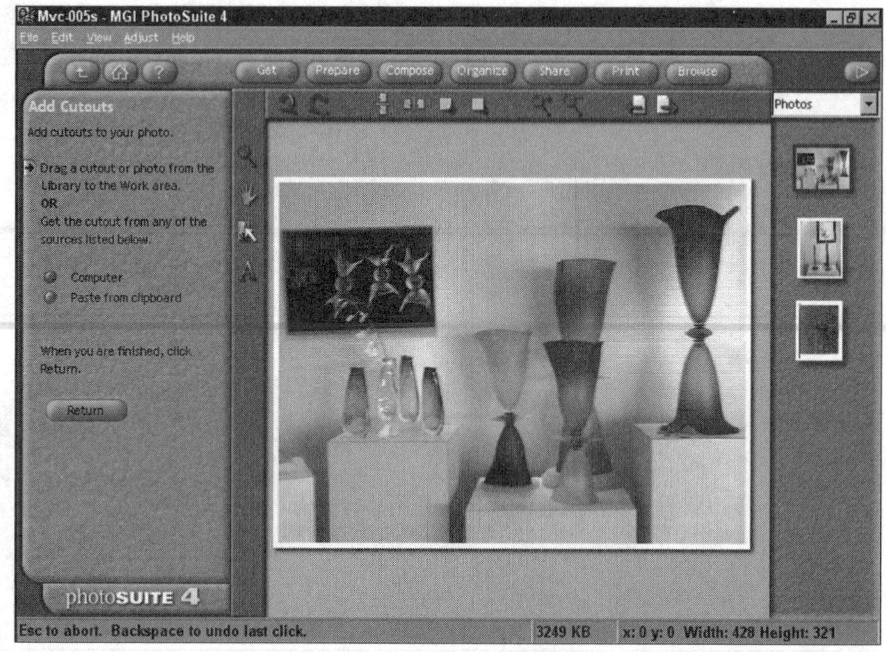

Figure 9-12: Add cutouts to your photo using this Activity panel.

Adjusting objects on the screen

Importing images into your collage is only the beginning of your artistic efforts. You still need to arrange them and add the details that bring a sense of order and realism to what you've created.

To access options for adjusting and positioning objects on your collage:

1. **Click the Adjust Objects button on the Compose screen.**

   The Adjust Objects Activity panel, shown in Figure 9-13, appears.

2. **Select from among the following options to position and adjust the objects in your collage.**

   - **Edit:** This option allows you to edit text or a photo.
   - **Rotate and Flip:** You can turn objects upside-down or sideways by rotating them 90 or 180 degrees or at any other angle.
   - **Change Order:** When you're importing objects into a collage, they're stacked on top of each other, just as if you were cutting and pasting them by hand. This tool allows you to change the order in which they're stacked, as shown in Figures 9-14 and 9-15.

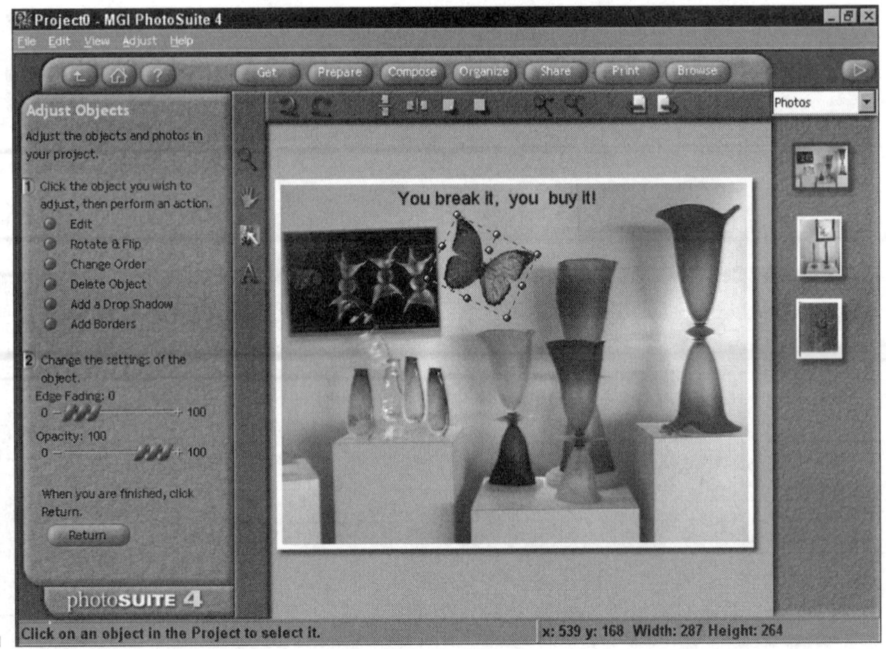

Figure 9-13: The Adjust Objects Activity panel.

Figure 9-14: Photos in a collage are stacked in layers.

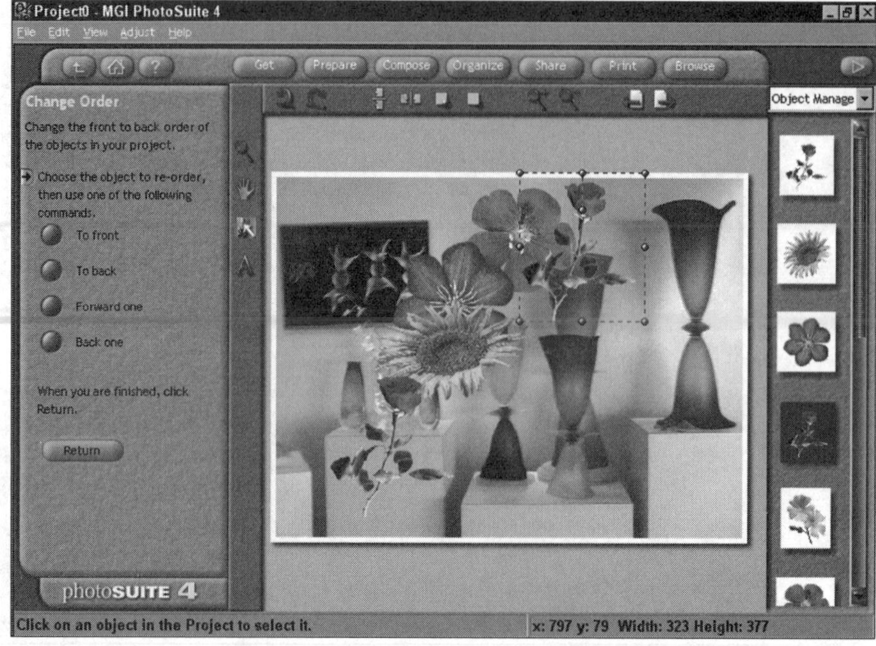

Figure 9-15: The Adjust Objects options let you change the stacking order of your photos, frame them, and do other tweaking.

- **Delete Object:** You can click an object to delete it. (A bounding box appears around the object you've selected.)

  If you accidentally delete an object, use the Undo button.

- **Add a Drop Shadow:** If you add an object to a photo, it should cast a shadow like the other objects in the photo, right? The next section of this chapter, "Adding and dropping a shadow," tells you how to work with this option.
- **Add Borders:** This option allows you to add frames and borders to your collage.
- **Edge Fading:** This is a blending tool that enables you to smooth the edges of an imported object until they blend naturally into the rest of your photo.
- **Opacity:** You not only can import images but also can turn them into transparent, ghostly apparitions. This slider lets you make the images you import more or less opaque.

Adding and dropping a shadow

A dead giveaway that an image has been imported into an original scene is that it casts either no shadow or some sort of unnatural shadow. PhotoSuite 4 allows you to add and drop shadows in a way that will make your altered photos appear authentic to even the most diligent sleuth.

To add or drop a shadow into a project:

1. **From the Compose screen, click the Adjust Objects button on the Activity panel and then click the Add a drop shadow button.**

   The Activity panel shown in Figure 9-16 appears.

2. **Select an object in your project.**

   The selected object is enclosed within a bounding box.

3. **On the Activity panel, select a shadow direction by looking at the shadows that appear around the yellow boxes.**

   Each box has a shadow aimed in a different direction.

4. **Adjust the distance between the shadow and the object using the Movement slider.**

   Moving the slider to the right makes the shadow appear larger.

5. **Adjust the intensity of the shadow using the Opacity slider.**

   Moving the slider to the right makes the shadow appear more intense, as though it's being cast on a bright, sunny day.

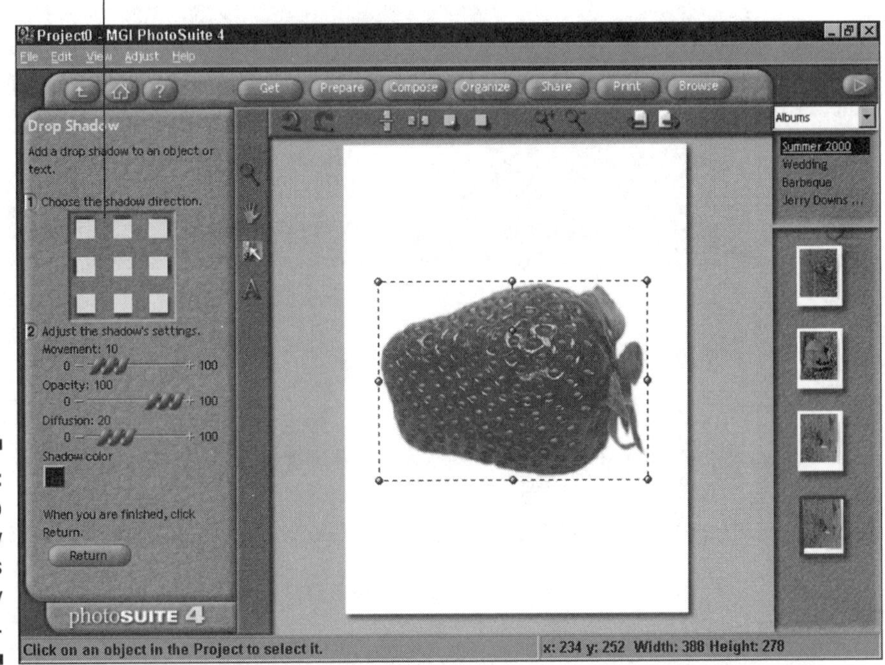

Figure 9-16: Add a drop shadow using this Activity panel.

6. **Adjust the diffusion, or blurriness, of the shadow using the Diffusion slider.**

   As you move the Diffusion slider to the right, the edges of the shadow appear more faded and blurred.

7. **Choose a shadow color by clicking the Shadow Color field; then click Return to exit the Activity panel.**

   The default color in the Shadow Color field is black (see Figure 9-17).

You can get some fascinating aura effects by selecting different colors for your drop shadows and by adjusting the Opacity and Diffusion settings.

Figure 9-17: The drop shadow appears in this photo.

Polishing with props

PhotoSuite 4 comes with clip art that you can import into your picture. You can easily resize and reposition the props until you get just the level of reality or hilarity you're striving for.

To add props to your photos:

1. **From the Compose screen, click the Add Props button on the Activity panel.**

   The Add Props Activity panel appears, as shown in Figure 9-18.

Select props category.

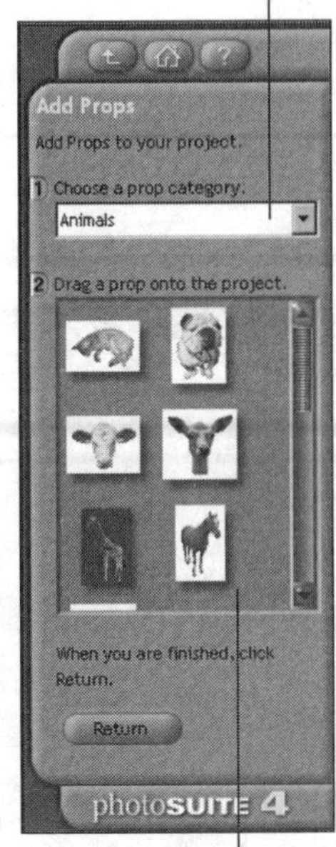

Available props appear here.

Figure 9-18: Add props using this screen.

2. **From the drop-down menu, select the type of props you want to use.**

   You can choose from among the following categories:

   - Animals
   - Body Switch
   - Flowers and Food
   - Hair
   - Hats
   - Music
   - Objects
   - Special Occasions
   - Sports
   - Tools
   - Word Balloons

A Word about Word Balloons

Word balloons, like the one that appears in Figure 9-19, can be a little tricky to add. Doing so comprises a process that involves the use of the Add/Edit Text tools as well as the Props feature.

Here's how to get that dialog going:

1. **From the Compose screen, click the Add Props button on the Activity panel.**

   The Add Props Activity panel appears.

2. **Select Word Balloons from the drop-down menu.**

   A number of different types of Word Balloons appear on your screen.

3. **Drag and drop the Word Balloon you want to use onto the screen and then click Return.**

4. **Click the Add/Edit Text button on the Activity panel.**

   The Add or Edit Text Activity panel appears (see Figure 9-19).

5. **Add or edit text in the Activity panel, following the steps detailed previously in this chapter in the section "Adding and editing text."**

Figure 9-19: Word balloons give a voice to your props.

How to Do That Old Body-Switch Trick

I bet you've been waiting to get to this — or maybe you just skipped right to it. What image-editing feature could be cooler?

When it comes to switching heads on bodies, you have several choices:

- You can take a photo, and switch around the heads and bodies using the cutting tools and Compose screen discussed throughout this chapter.
- You can use the cartoon bodies provided with PhotoSuite 4 on which to place the heads of your friends and family, after you've digitally decapitated them.

Switching heads onto familiar bodies

In Figures 9-20 and 9-21, I do a father-son head trip. You can't tell the men from the boys, can you?

If you're cutting a head (or other object) from a smaller subject and pasting it in the head of the larger subject, you can blend in the extra background around the new head using the clone tools I tell you about in Chapter 7.

Figure 9-20: Dad and son with heads attached.

Figure 9-21: Now they're really the spitting image!

Putting heads on PhotoSuite 4 body props

In Figure 9-22, I've made the guys into superheroes using the PhotoSuite 4 props to access a bevy of bodies and other importable images:

1. **Click Compose on the Navigation bar.**

   The Compose screen appears.

2. **Indicate whether you want to import a photo or begin working on a blank white canvas.**

   The New Project Activity panel appears.

3. **Enter the photo dimensions and layout you want and then click Next.**

   The Compose screen and Activity panel reappear.

4. **Click the Add props button.**

   The Add Props Activity panel appears.

5. **Select Body Switch from the drop-down menu.**

6. **Select the cartoon body you want to use in your picture by double-clicking it or by dragging and dropping it onto your PhotoSuite 4 project.**

   The body appears on your desktop, surrounding by a bounding box.

Figure 9-22: Ready to save the world!

7. Click and drag the handles around the body prop to resize and position it in your picture.
8. Click Return to exit the Add Props Activity panel and return to the Compose screen for more editing fun.

COLOR PLATE 2-1: The Touchup feature allows you to fix your photo by removing blemishes, scratches, wrinkles, and the chronic red-eye problem caused by flash photography.

COLOR PLATE 2-2: Create a PhotoTapestry using a database of small thumbnail images like the ones shown here.

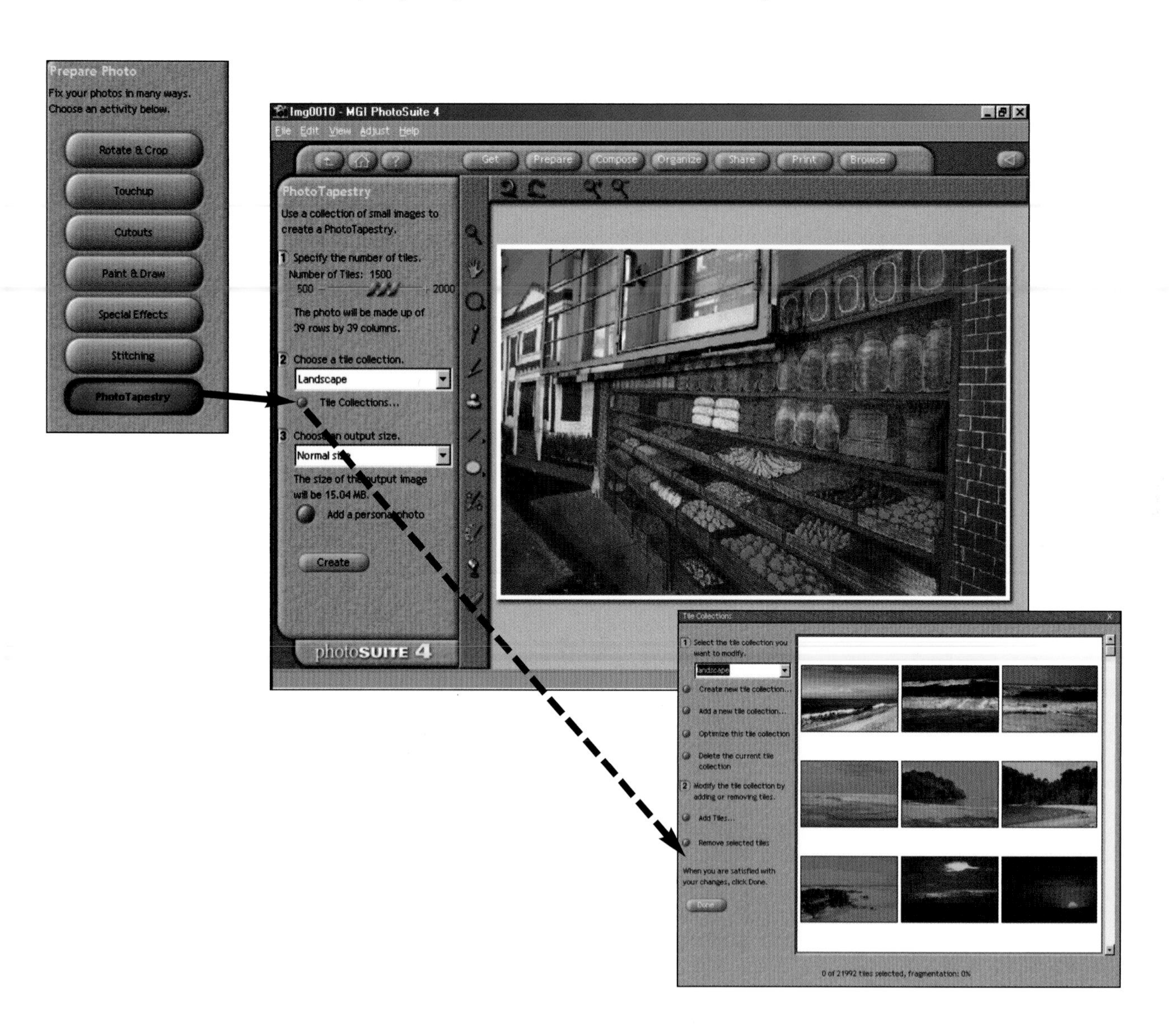

COLOR PLATE 2-3: You can import your own images into the PhotoTapestry.

COLOR PLATE 2–4: You can stitch photos together to capture the excitement of expansive panoramas.

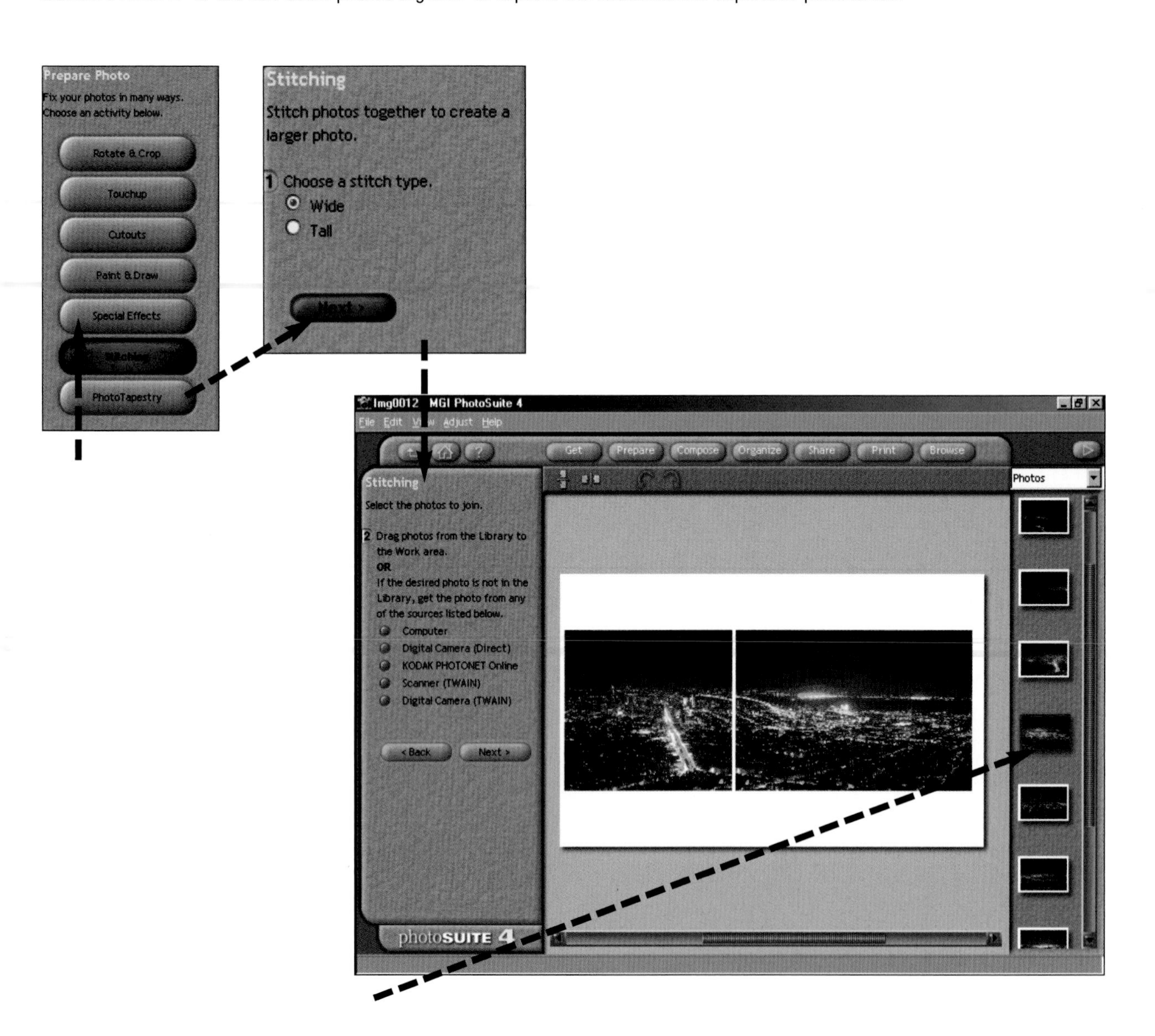

COLOR PLATE 2-5: PhotoSuite 4 comes with extensive preset and interactive warp features.

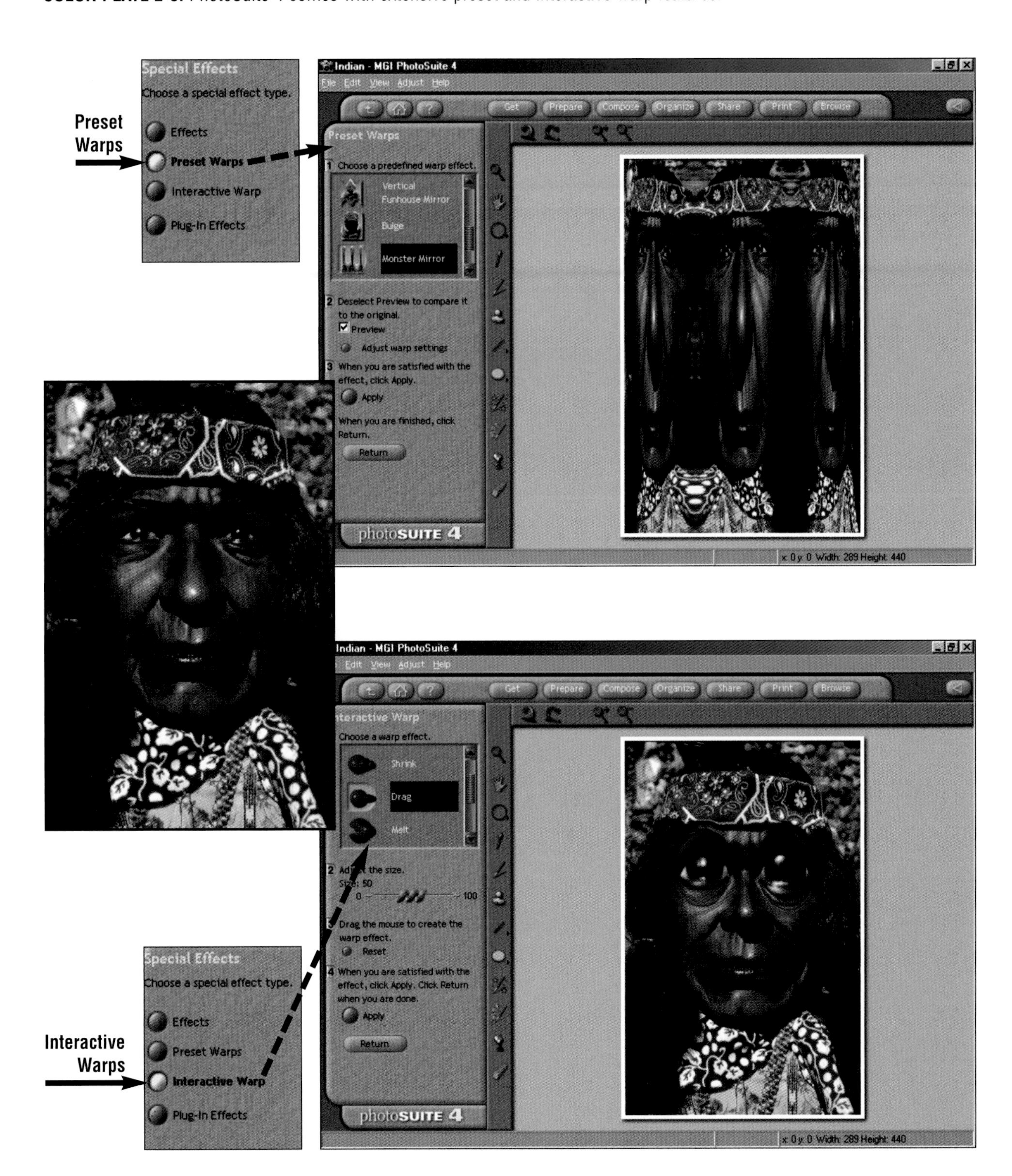

COLOR PLATE 9-1: The Edge Finder tool makes it easy to make stunning cutouts of images with detailed, irregular edges. An outline forms between selection nodes that appear at the outer edge of your object each time you click your mouse.

COLOR PLATE 9-2: PhotoSuite 4 allows you to cut out a white or transparent area and to save objects that you've cut out to transport to other photos.

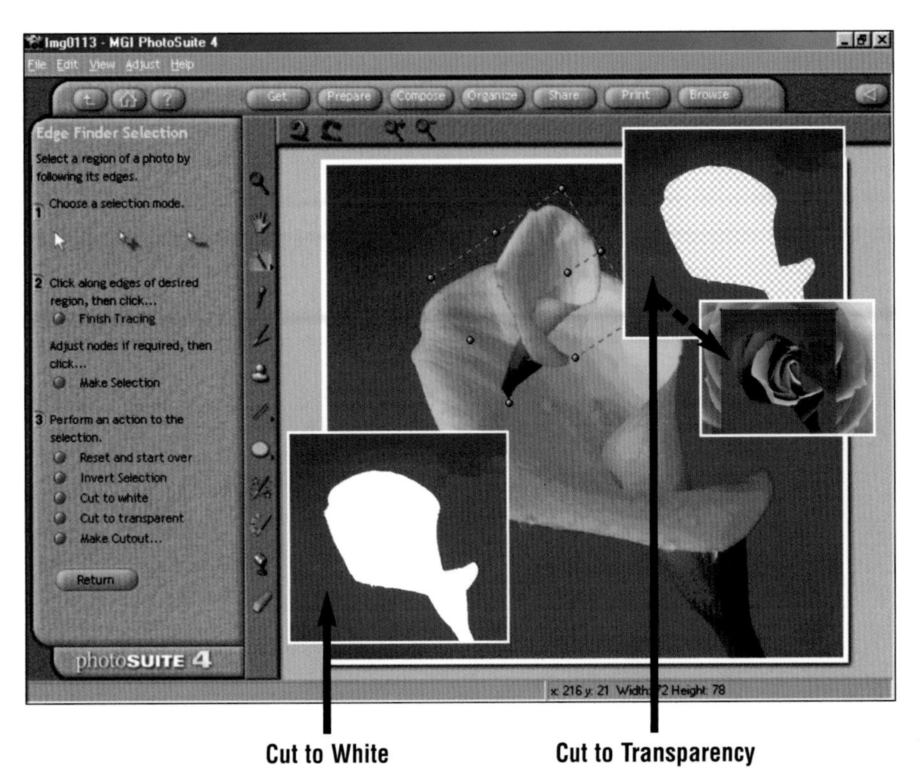

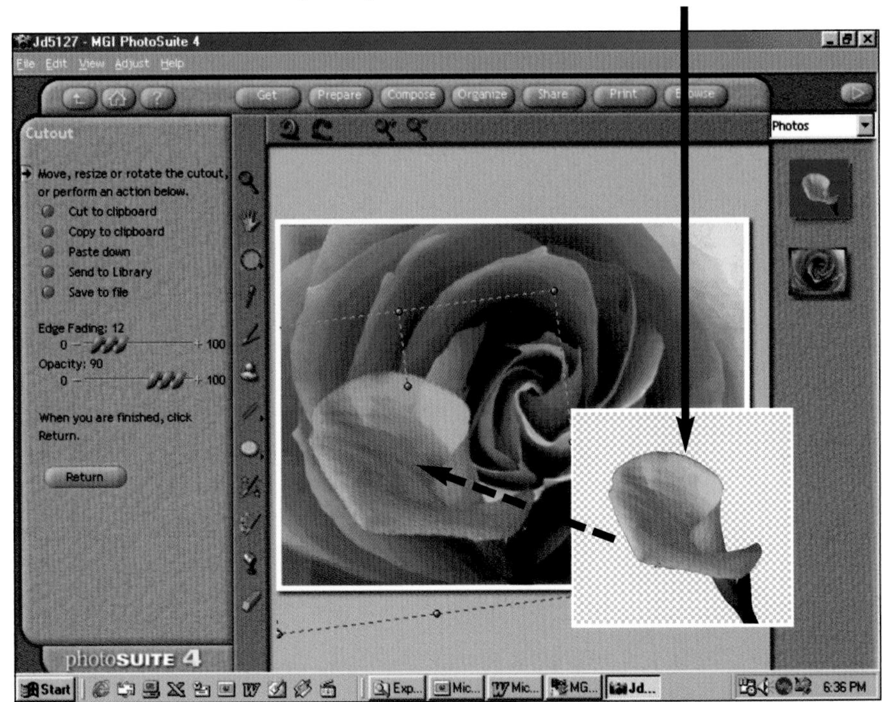

COLOR PLATE 9-3: You can create dramatic and haunting works of art by using the Cut to Transparent tool and experimenting with the tinting and colorizing features.

COLOR PLATE 10-1: In this example, the girl's face was colorized to black and white using a brush tool, and the colors of the flower are enhanced using simple painting and colorizing techniques discussed in Chapter 10.

COLOR PLATE 10-2: Photos can be artistically enhanced by selectively colorizing.

COLOR PLATE 10-3: PhotoSuite provides a sophisticated array of painting, drawing, and tinting tools.

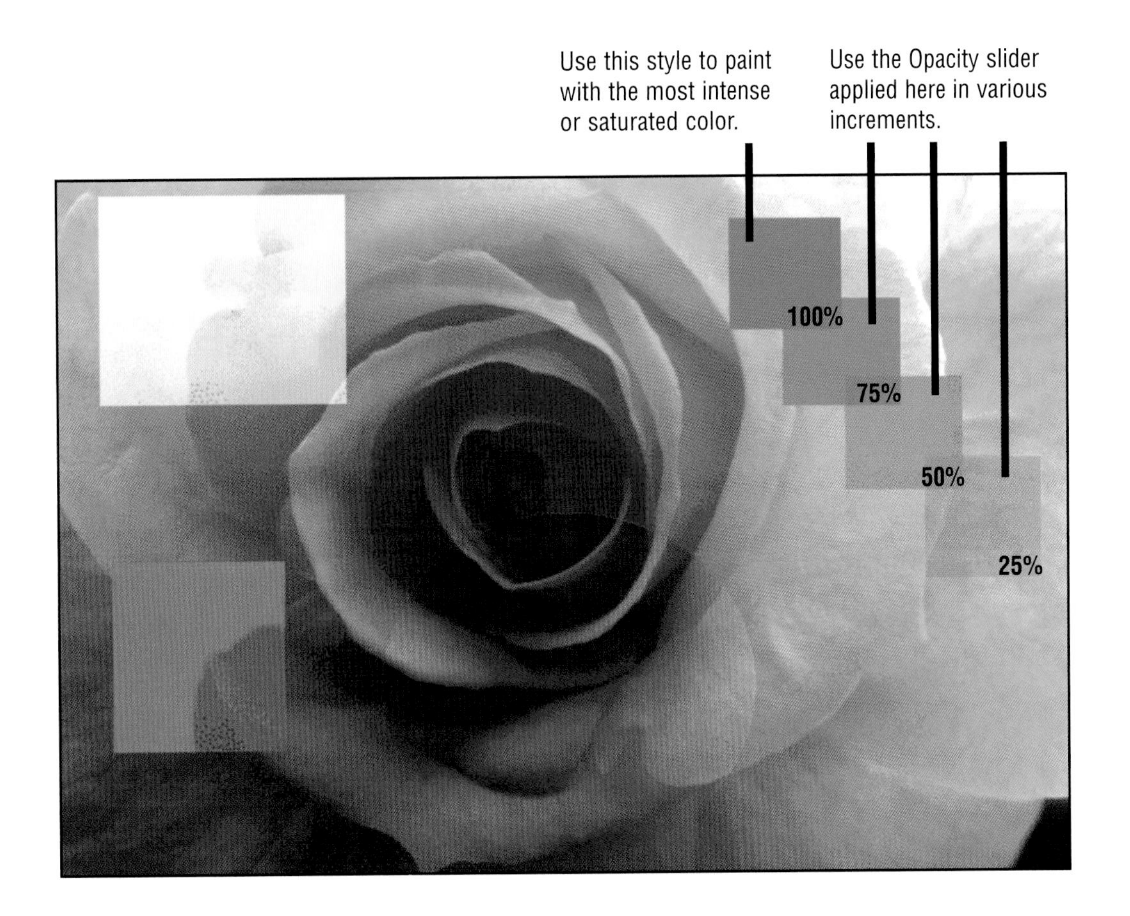

COLOR PLATE 11-1: Chapter 11 tells you how to create callouts or use the Photo Sprayer tool to stamp a pattern of objects on your photo, like the flowers here.

COLOR PLATE 11-2: Use the Flood Fill tool to fill areas with color and create interesting filled and unfilled shapes.

COLOR PLATE 12-1: You can vary your effects using the Sepia Filter, Antique Filter, and Moonlight Filter.

Sepia Filter

Antique Filter

Moonlight Filter

COLOR PLATE 12-2: PhotoSuite allows you to add interesting Scenic or Abstract backgrounds for your photos.

Scenic background

Abstract background

Share...Create Web Items — Web Page

COLOR PLATE 13-1: PhotoSuite allows you to create media-rich Web Pages from easy-to-use templates.

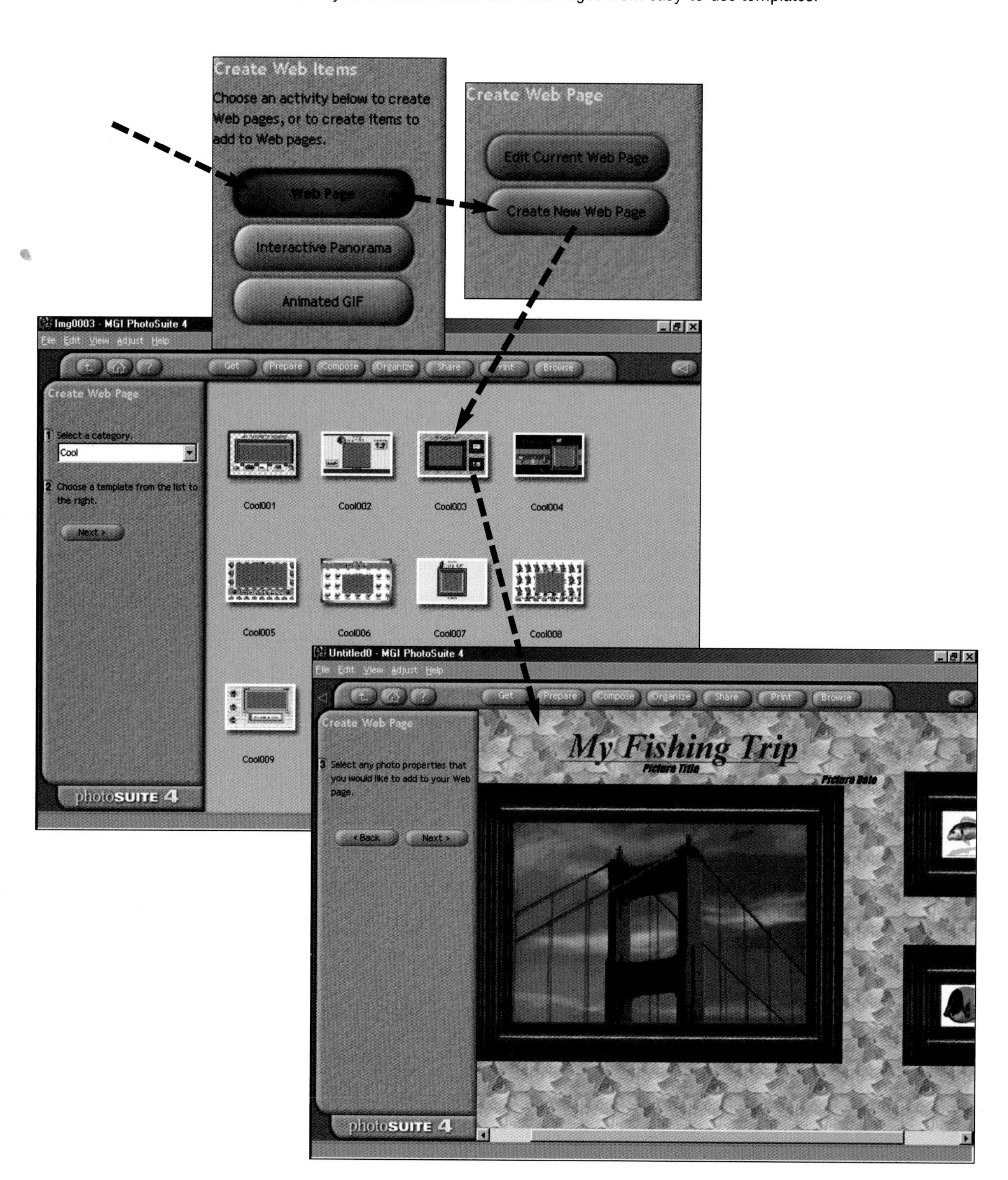

Part III
Step into the Drawing Room

In this part . . .

The world is full of color, and you don't want your camera to miss a single pixel of it! Of course, it helps to know what a pixel is. This part gives you some basic color theory and tells you how to apply it — literally and figuratively.

Chapter 10

In Color Living

In This Chapter

- Color concepts for the new millennium
- Resolving color conflicts with your equipment
- Hue-who?
- Getting saturated
- Andy Warhol lives!

Today's kindergartners are using sophisticated software at an age when most of us were learning not to eat the finger paint. Instead of experimenting to find that red and blue make purple, they may be learning that taking away magenta and green makes cyan on their dye sublimation printers.

And what kid wants a 64-color box of crayons when she has a monitor that can produce 16 million different colors?

Colors Posing as Primary

Just as you know that the earth is round, you probably accept that it's also made up of primary colors. And you can even identify those primary colors — red, green, and blue. Yes, green! Or is it cyan, magenta, yellow, and black?

What? You disagree that green is a primary color? And what, exactly, is cyan? Well, in the world of on-screen images (as opposed to Tempera paints) it is green — not yellow — that's a primary color. (Hence the term RGB, standing for red, green, and blue.) And in the universe of most — but not all — printers, cyan, magenta, yellow and black are the primary colors from which all other printed shades are descended.

Revisiting kindergarten: What's a primary color?

In kindergarten, I learned that the *primary* colors are the basic colors that generate all other colors. This is still accurate.

Miss Kasseri, my blue-haired kindergarten teacher, also taught me that by mixing red, blue, and yellow, I could create every other color in the universe, given enough finger paint and time. But this last bit of information has gone the way of the Tooth Fairy.

Miss Kasseri's rendition of color theory was complete back when first graders did their art projects with Tempera paints. But today's precocious Web babies paint with computers and peripherals. These days, Miss Kasseri would probably have expanded her spiel to include theory about different *primary color groups*.

Kindergarten 2001: Primary colors come in groups

Contrary to what you may have learned in a kindergarten of the previous millennium, there is not one group of primary colors, but three. They are as follows:

- **Traditional:** This is the group we were taught about as kids. It consists of red, yellow, and blue. This group is great for mixing Tempera paints but you won't be doing much with it in PhotoSuite 4.
- **Subtractive (CMYK):** This is the color group that applies to printers and most ink-based devices. It consists of magenta, yellow, cyan, and black. It goes by the acronym CMYK. The *K* stands for black — they use K because whoever devised this theory figured that *B* would be confused with blue. In theory, you shouldn't even need the K, because magenta, yellow, and cyan should combine to create black — but this doesn't quite work with most printers. They have to add the black ink.
- **Additive (RGB):** This is the primary color group used by monitors, scanners, and television sets. It includes red, green, and blue, hence the acronym of RGB. Oddly, if you combine red, green, and blue light on a wall or a computer monitor, you get white.

Figure 10-1 shows a color wheel diagram for each of the three primary color groups. (And by the way, cyan is a sort of sky-blue color.)

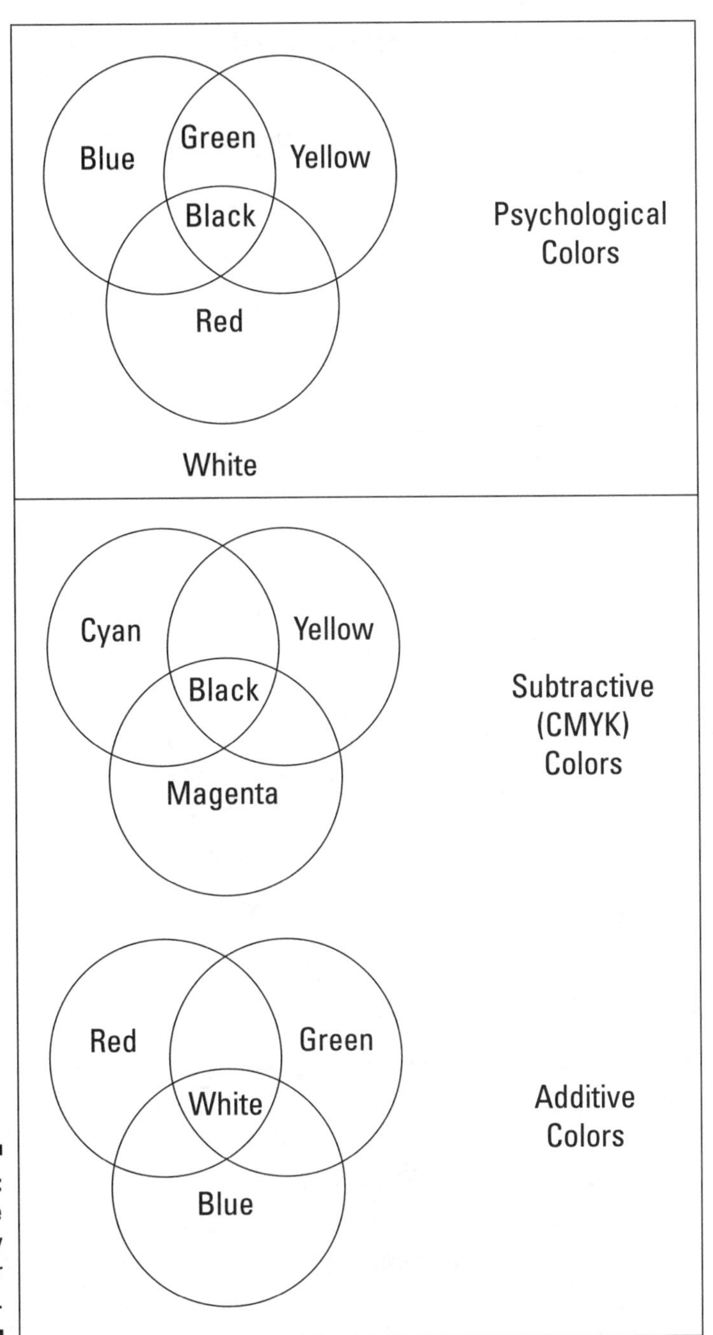

Figure 10-1: The three primary color groups.

Combating color-confused equipment

The color confusion begins when your monitor displays a vibrant on-screen image that you can't, try as you might, replicate with your printer. The printed image is muted and well, blah, in comparison. What are you doing wrong?

The answer is, of course, nothing. It is simply impossible for your CMYK-based printer color scheme to replicate the more vivid RGB color scheme used by your monitor. The two pieces of equipment are working off different palettes.

Figure 10-2 shows a chart for helping you coordinate what you see on your monitor with the results you get on your printer. The diagram shows how the RGB and CMYK primary color schemes are related. The colors opposite the dotted lines are spectral opposites.

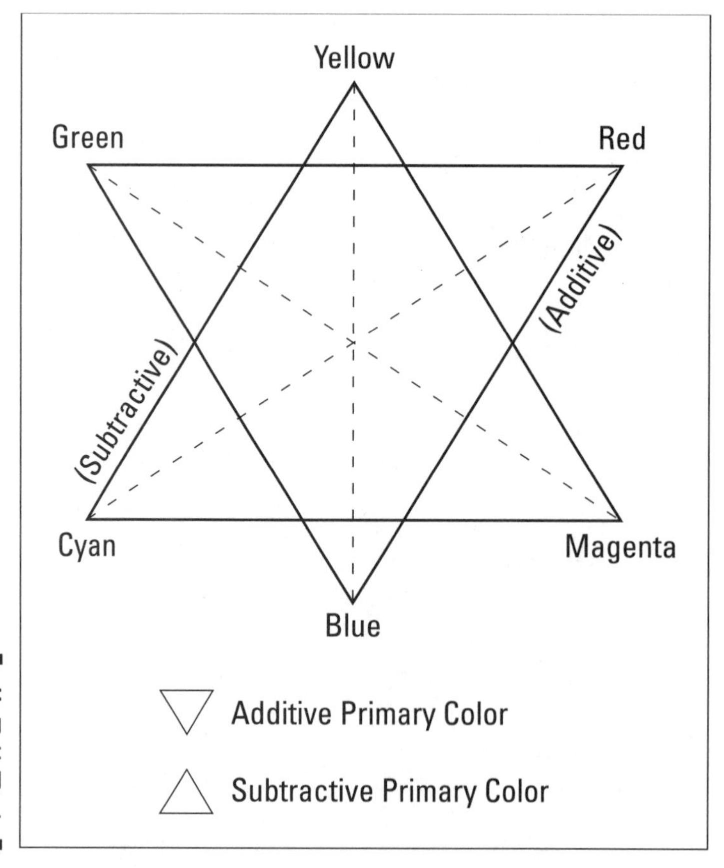

Figure 10-2: Making adjustments: the spectral opposites.

If, for example, your printed copy is coming out a bit too magenta, you want to move your image along the color spectrum and put some more green in the image. This is, of course, because green is the opposite of magenta.

Stop singin' the blues: The color adjustment filter

PhotoSuite 4 allows you to compensate for the differences in the RGB and CMYK schemes using the Color Adjustment filter shown in Figure 10-3. The feature also allows you to compensate for other color quirks, such as funky indoor lighting or the tendency that digital cameras have to be skewed a bit toward the blue end of the spectrum.

To access the Color Adjustment filter:

1. **Click the Prepare button on the Navigation bar.**

   The Prepare screen and Activity panel appear.

2. **Click the Touchup button.**

   Another Activity panel appears.

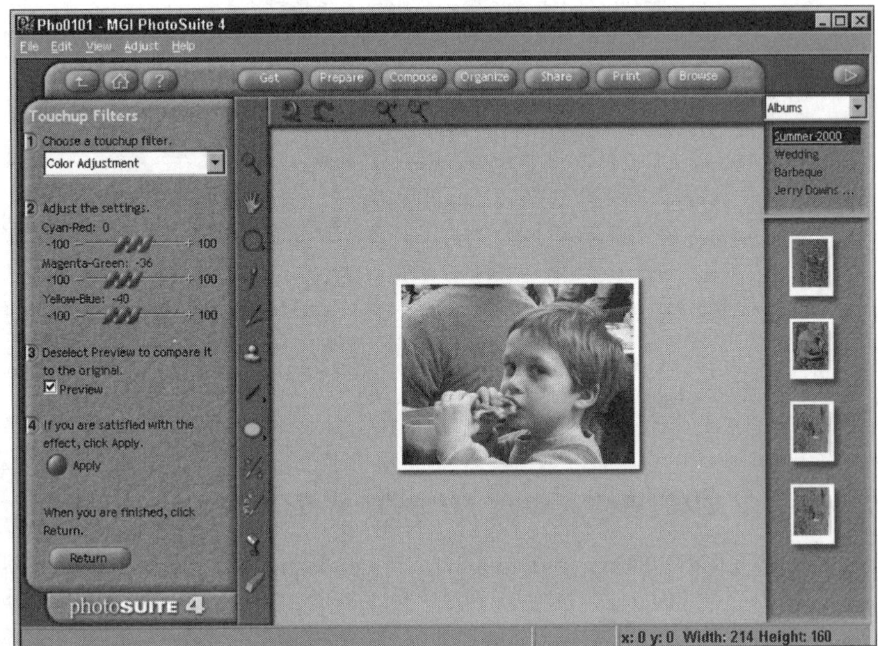

Figure 10-3: The Touchup Filters Activity panel.

3. **Click the Touchup Filters button.**

   The Touchup Filters Activity panel appears.

4. **Select Color Adjustment from the drop-down menu.**

   The Activity panel shown in Figure 10-3 appears, displaying sliders for the following color continuums:

   - Cyan-red
   - Magenta- Green
   - Yellow-Blue

Now, if you decide that your photo is a bit too green, it's not quite as simple as merely adjusting the green slider. You have to adjust the *other* colors, too. For example, if you decrease the green, you need to increase the red and blue in your photo by half as much to keep all the colors in your photo in balance.

Table 10-1 summarizes the adjustments you need to make to keep your RGB colors in balance.

Table 10-1 RGB Color Adjustment Table

Problem	*What to do*
Too blue? (Common with digital cameras)	Decrease the blue; then increase both the red and green by half the amount you decreased the blue.
Too red? (Happens a lot with artificial light)	Decrease the green; then increase both the red and blue by half the amount you decreased the green.
Grossly over-green?	Decrease the red; then increase both the green and blue by half the amount you increased the red.

If digital photography is your hobby, you develop a discerning eye for which hue is overpowering and needs to be toned down. But while you're developing that eye, you need to go through a lot of trial and error with the sliders in the Color Adjustment Activity panel.

Viewing RGB images on-screen

Quick! What do your computer screen, camera, and scanner all have in common? The answer: They're all using the RGB primary color group to process images.

Your camera, scanner, and monitor mimic the human eye and brain. Your eyes capture red, green, and blue light spectrums and record the *brightness value* of each in separate portions of your brain. Your brain then mixes the data from the different channels to create a full-color-spectrum image.

Digital devices work the same way. Cameras, scanners, and computer monitors use RGB color channels to record the intensity of the three spectrums and transform them into images.

PhotoSuite 4 allows you to view each channel independently, and adjust it, using the Color Adjustment filter I tell you about earlier in this chapter, in "Stop singin' the blues: The color adjustment filter."

Printing the CMYK way

Most domestic printers and professional printing presses apply dotted layers of cyan, magenta, yellow, and black. If your printed copies are off-color, you can tweak them using the Color Filter Activity panel.

You can introduce more or less cyan, magenta, and yellow by moving the slider in the Color Adjustment Activity panel to the right (see Figure 10-3). Cyan, magenta, and yellow have negative values, so you need to decrease the number above the slider to increase their values. (For example, –28 is a higher cyan rating than a +5 rating.)

A Tribute to Andy Warhol: Colorizing and Tinting

Colorizing and tinting your photos are perhaps some of the most dramatic and artistic things you can do with PhotoSuite 4. Just ask any Andy Warhol fan.

Remember Andy Warhol? That avante-garde 1960s artist? Andy was an icon of the pop movement and considered by many to be a genius. Andy used to take black and white shots of famous people such as Marilyn Monroe, Mick Jagger, and Mao Tse Tung and colorize them to make a statement. For example, he'd emphasize Marilyn's lipstick and eye shadow.(Color Plate 10-1 shows an artistically colorized photo using several of the colorizing and tinting effects discussed in this chapter.)

Much of Andy's work is ensconced in the Andy Warhol museum in Pennsylvania. You can view some great examples of his colorizing genius at `http://www.clpgh.org/warhol/`.

Turning a photo to black and white

Black-and-white photos provide an excellent canvas for creative colorizing techniques. Some subjects (such as old movie stars blowing smoke rings) look better in black and white. Black and white can capture a mood and a sense of history. It's also cheap to reproduce.

To transform a color photo into a black-and-white rendition of the same subject:

1. **Click the Prepare button on the Navigation bar, after you've imported the photo into PhotoSuite 4 using the Get screen (as explained in Chapter 5).**

   The Prepare screen and Activity panel appear.

2. **Click the Touchup button and then Touchup Brushes.**

   The Touchup Brushes Activity panel appears, as shown in Figure 10-4.

3. **Select Colorize from the drop down menu (see Figure 10-4).**

   The Colorize options appear in the Touchup Brushes Activity panel.

4. **Click the Brush selection tool.**

   The Brushes Activity panel appears with a variety of Brush tool sizes and shapes.

5. **Select the largest Brush tool available, shown in Figure 10-5. by clicking it and then clicking OK to exit the Brushes Activity panel.**

   The Brushes Activity panel closes.

6. **Move the brush size slider (shown in Figure 10-4) all the way to the right.**

   Doing so makes the brush size as large as possible.

7. **Click the Paint Color swatch (also shown in Figure 10-4).**

   The Select Color Activity panel appears, as shown in Figure 10-6. This Activity panel contains 265 different hues.

8. **Select either a black or white color in the Select Color Activity panel by clicking it once.**

   The Select Color Activity panel closes.

9. **Holding your mouse button down, "paint" over the entire area of the photo to turn it from color to black and white.**

10. **Click Return to exit the Touchup brushes Activity panel when you're finished.**

Figure 10-4: The Touchup Brushes Activity panel with the Colorize options.

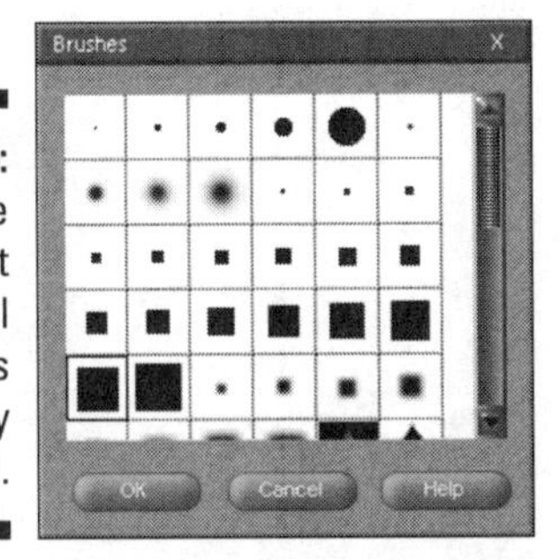

Figure 10-5: Select the largest brush tool using this Activity panel.

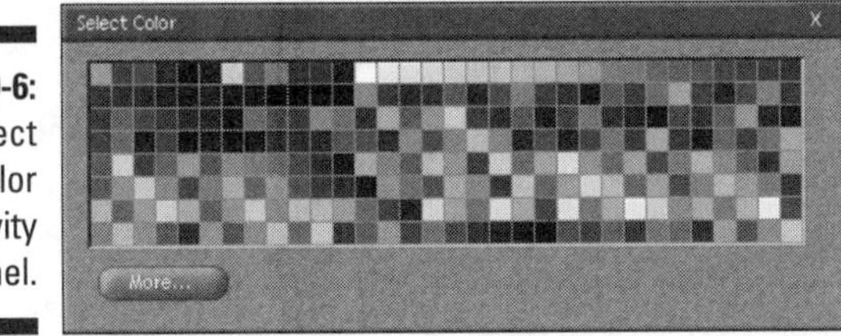

Figure 10-6: The Select Color Activity panel.

Adding and removing color in sections

Art is a matter of what you add to an existing image — your perspective, interpretation, and stylistic effects. You can achieve some of your most highly stylized pictures by selectively removing and adding back color to a photo.

Painting portions of a photo black and white

Selectively turning portions of your photo to black and white makes an interesting statement. Here are three ways you can control which parts of your photo are reduced to black and white:

- Paint parts of a color photo, using the Touchup Brushes tools.
- Click the Flood Fill icon on the vertical toolbar and click one area of the photo at a time to transform it to black and white (see Figure 10-7).
- Color the entire photo black and white and then use the Erase tool to selectively return the color to portions of the photo. I tell you more about how to use the handy Erase tool in Chapter 11, "Drawing Tools That Amaze and Delight."

Inverting the color

The Invert effect makes a photo appear as though it were a negative. It replaces the pixels in the photo with the contrasting opposite colors in the color chart (refer back to Figure 10-1). For example, black pixels are replaced with white and red pixels are replaces with green. Figures 10-8 and 10-9 show this effect applied to a black-and-white photo. If only Andy Warhol could see this!

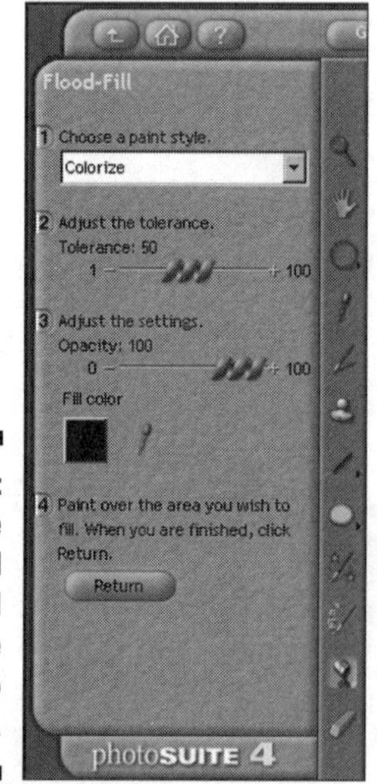

Figure 10-7: Use the Flood-Fill tool to add or remove color to sections.

Figure 10-8: This is a standard photo.

Figure 10-9: Here's the same photo with the Invert tool applied.

You can access the Invert tool in either the Touchup Filters or Touchup Brushes Activity panel.

Creatively colorizing

Selectively colorizing portions of a photo render it an interpretive work of art. Color Plate 10-2 exemplifies how a photo can be artistically enhanced by selectively colorizing portions of it.

To selectively colorize a portion of a photo, follow these steps:

1. **Click the Prepare button on the Navigation bar.**

   The Prepare screen and Activity panel appear.

2. **Click the Touchup button.**

3. **Click the Touchup Brushes button on the Activity panel.**

   The Touchup Brushes Activity panel appears.

4. **Select Colorize (or Tint) from the drop-down menu.**

   The Colorize (or Tint) options appear in the Touchup Brushes Activity panel.

5. **Click the Paint Color field to display the Select Color Activity panel.**

   The Select Color Activity panel appears.

6. **Select a color in the Select Color Activity panel by clicking it.**

   The color you've selected is displayed in the Paint Color swatch.

7. **Test a "swatch" of color on the area of the photo you want to colorize.**

   Is it too light or too dark?

8. **Click the Undo button to remove the color you added as a test in Step 6.**

   The Undo button is located just below the Navigation bar (it looks like a backward arrow).

9. **Adjust the Opacity using the slider in the Activity panel and repeat Steps 5 and 6 until you achieve the color you want.**

   Opacity is the extent to which the color you apply is transparent and allows the existing hue to show through it.

   Color Plate 10-3 shows how to control saturation using the Opacity slider.

10. **Select a Brush type by clicking the Brush selection tool.**

    The Brushes Activity panel appears.

11. **Select a Brush tool shape from the Brushes Activity panel and click OK.**

    The brush shape you select reflects how color is painted on the area.

12. **Adjust the Brush size using the slider in the Activity panel.**

13. **Paint over the area in the photo you want to colorize; repeat Steps 7 through 12 to apply additional colors to other areas of the photo.**

    Use your Undo button as needed to adjust your results. Consider saving the image to files with different names so that you can go back to something you tried previously.

14. **Click Return when you're finished colorizing your photo.**

You can't use the Undo button after you click Return. It's a good idea to save "drafts" along the way.

Singin' the blues with tints

Sometimes colorizing a photo is overkill. What you really want is the subtle effect of *tint.*

Tints are transparent applications of colors — sort of like colored cellophane. Tints are great for setting the mood and tone of a photo. Blue tints can give your photo a cool, melancholy mood. Reddish tints project warmth and can add an antique feel to your subject matter.

How tints work

The tint paint style allows you to paint with less saturation of color than the Colorize tool. Tint applies color subtly, as though you were looking through a tinted lens. This can help retain detail in a photo. Also, tints have no effect on grayscale, so they don't effect black and white images. (For more information about this, see Chapter 3.)

You can use the Opacity slider to control the degree of color saturation. Color Plate 10-3 shows how to control saturation using the Opacity slider.

Trying it with a tint

To apply a tint to portions of your photo:

1. **Click the Prepare button on the Navigation bar, after you've imported the photo into PhotoSuite 4 using the Get screen (as explained in Chapter 5).**

   The Prepare screen and Activity panel appear.

2. **Click the Touchup button and then Touchup Brushes.**

   The Touchup Brushes Activity panel appears.

3. **From the drop-down menu, select Tint.**
4. **Click the Brush selection tool.**

   The Brushes Activity panel appears with a variety of Brush tool sizes and shapes.
5. **Select the largest Brush tool available by clicking it; then click OK to exit the Brushes Activity panel.**
6. **Move the brush size slider all the way to the right.**

   This makes the brush size as large as possible.
7. **Click the Paint Color field.**

   The Select Color Activity panel appears.
8. **Select the color that you want to use as a tint by clicking it once.**

   The Select Color Activity panel closes.
9. **Holding your mouse button down, "paint" over the entire area of the photo to apply the tint to the area you want.**
10. **Click Return to exit the Touchup brushes Activity panel when you're finished.**

Pleased to Meet Hue

Hue is the property that gives the color its name, for example blue or red. By manipulating the hue you can, for example, turn flower petals from pink to blue.

In PhotoSuite 4, you use the Fix Colors Activity panel to alter the hue of the entire photo. Alternatively, you can use the Touchup Brushes to alter the sections to which you apply color.

All of hue: Altering a whole photo

To access the Fix Colors Activity panel:

1. **After importing a photo into PhotoSuite 4 using the Get screen, click the Prepare button on the Navigation bar.**

   The Prepare screen and Activity panel appear.
2. **Click the Touchup button.**

   An Activity panel appears.

3. **Click the Touchup Filters button.**

   The Touchup Filters Activity panel appears.

4. **Select Fix Colors from the drop-down menu, as shown in Figure 10-10.**

   The Fix Colors options appear in the Touchup Filters Activity panel.

5. **Use the Hue slider at the top of the Activity panel to experiment with the Hue settings.**

   Moving the hue slider to the right introduces more green, with the hues becoming blue and magenta as you move the slider across. The effect is as if you were starting at the green point of the diagram in Figure 10-2 (shown previously) and moving clockwise around the circle back to green.

6. **When you're satisfied with the hue as it appears on-screen, click Apply.**

7. **Click Return to exit the Touchup Filters Activity panel.**

Figure 10-10: Adjust the hue using this Activity panel.

The hues that you view on-screen may appear differently on a printed version of the same photo. The section of this chapter called "Combating color-confused equipment" explains why.

Adjusting the hue of an entire photo with the Touchup Filter can give you some unintended results. For example, as you adjust the slider to achieve a certain effect for one part of the photo — such as pink to blue petals — you need to be aware of the effect this is having on the rest of the photo. You may be getting pink-to-green faces as well.

Pieces of hue

If you want to paint portions of a photo, you can adjust the hue to get just the right shade. For example, you may want to paint the face of an ordinary citizen Martian green. But suppose that ordinary leaf green or an avocado green is not complementary to your subject's hair and eye color.

This is a job for the hue adjustment feature in the Touchup Brushes Activity panel. You can access this feature and find the perfect green hue for your Martian by doing the following:

1. **Click the Prepare button on the Navigation bar.**

   The Prepare screen and Activity panel appear.

2. **Click the Touchup button.**

   An Activity panel appears.

3. **Click the Touchup Brushes button.**

   The Touchup Brushes Activity panel appears.

4. **Select Colorize from the drop-down menu.**

   The Colorize options appear in the Touchup Brushes Activity panel.

5. **Click the Paint Color field.**

   The Select Color Activity panel appears.

6. **Click the More... button at the bottom of the Select Color Activity panel.**

   The Activity panel shown in Figure 10-11 appears.

7. **Adjust the hue either by increasing or decreasing the numeric value in the Hue field or by moving the arrows up or down the Spectrum bar on the left side of the Activity panel.**

   The Select Color Activity panel displays both the original shade and the color as it appears after any adjustments are made using the Activity panel options.

8. **Click OK when the New field displays a color you want.**

9. **Click the Brush selection tool.**

   The Brushes Activity panel appears.

10. **Select a Brush tool and click OK to exit the Brushes Activity panel.**

    The smaller the Brush tool, the greater the control you can exercise when colorizing details.

11. **Paint over the area in the photo you want to colorize.**

12. **Click Return to exit the Touchup Tools Activity panel.**

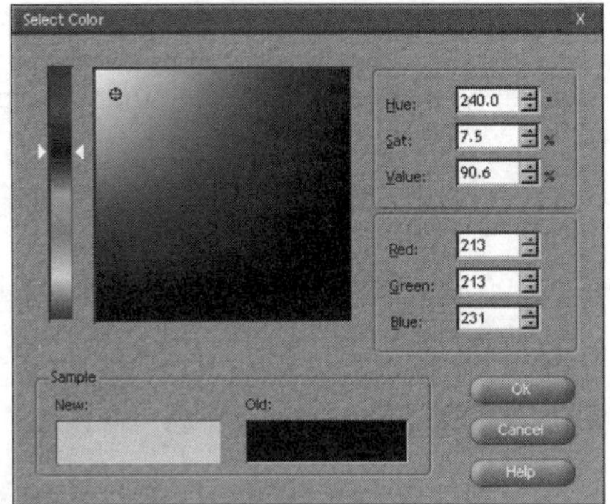

Figure 10-11: When using the Brush tools, adjust the hue using this Activity panel.

Can't Get No Saturation

Saturation is the miracle image-laundering product that makes whites whiter and brights brighter. It's the concentration of each color in your picture. Saturation doesn't change the color itself; it just intensifies it.

Although increasing saturation can pep up a dull image, it's not something you can do with impunity. You can lose image detail if you go for too much saturation. This is because many printers can reproduce the level of saturation that you see on your screen, and the printed shot appears blurry with the color boundaries running together.

Slathering saturation on the whole photo

To adjust the saturation level of an entire photo:

1. **Click the Prepare button on the Navigation bar.**

   The Prepare screen and Activity panel appear.

2. **Click the Touchup button.**

   Another Activity panel appears.

3. **Click the Touchup Filters button.**

   The Touchup Filters Activity panel appears.

4. **Select Fix Colors from the drop-down menu.**

   The Fix Colors options appear, with sliders to adjust hue, saturation, and color value.

5. **Use the Saturation slider to increase and decrease the level of saturation in the entire photo.**

   Colors will appear more vibrant on-screen as you move the Saturation slider to the right. However, you need to make sure that your printer can accommodate the increased saturation levels.

6. **Click Apply when you're satisfied with the level of saturation; adjust other settings in the Activity panel as necessary.**

7. **Click Return to exit the Touchup Filters Activity panel.**

Upping saturation for part of a photo

To adjust the saturation level of a color for which you're using the Touchup Brushes to paint portions of a photo:

1. **Click the Prepare button on the Navigation bar.**

   The Prepare screen and Activity panel appear.

2. **Click the Touchup button.**

   An Activity panel appears.

3. **Click the Touchup Brushes button.**

   The Touchup Brushes Activity panel appears.

4. **Select Colorize (or Tint) from the drop-down menu.**

   The Colorize (or Tint) options appear in the Touchup Brushes Activity panel.

   In the next section, I tell you more about the results you get by selecting Tint rather than Colorize.

5. **Click the Paint Color field.**

   The Select Color Activity panel appears.

6. **Click the More... button at the bottom of the Select Color Activity panel.**

   Another Activity panel appears.

7. **Adjust the saturation level by increasing or decreasing the numeric value in the Saturation field or by moving the arrows up or down the Spectrum bar on the left hand side of the Activity panel.**

   The Select Color Activity panel displays both the original shade and the color as it appears after any adjustments are made using the Activity panel options.

8. **Click OK when the New field displays the color at the saturation level you want.**

9. **Select an appropriate brush tool and paint the areas of the photo you want to colorize.**

10. **Click Return to exit the Touchup Tools Activity panel.**

Too Light? Too Dark? Shopping for Color Value

Value refers to how light or dark a color is. The higher the color value, the darker it appears, and vice versa. For example, lowering the value of a red hue may make it appear pink.

Value for a whole photo

Reducing the value of an entire photo can give it a dreamy, watercolor appearance. It can also make your photo look washed out, if you overdo it. Adjusting value upward and downward can be a good way to control the quality of a printed copy.

You can experiment with the Value settings for a photo by accessing the Fix Colors Activity panel the way as described earlier in this chapter in the section "Pleased to Meet Hue." This time, however, move the Value Slider up and down, to increase value rather than hue.

Lighten it up

You can manipulate the value of a color you're painting with, in case you think it's a shade too light or too dark. Follow these steps:

1. **When working with a Touchup Brush effect (such as Colorize or Tint), click the Paint Color swatch that appears in the Activity panel.**

   The Select Color Activity panel appears.

2. **Click the More... button at the bottom of the Select Color Activity panel.**

   Another Activity panel appears.

3. **Adjust the saturation level by increasing or decreasing the numeric value in the Value field.**

   The Select Color Activity panel displays both the original shade and the color as it appears after the value is increased or decreased from any adjustments made using the Activity panel options.

4. **Click OK when the New field displays the value you want.**

5. **Select an appropriate brush tool and paint the areas of the photo you want to colorize.**

6. **Click Return to exit the Touchup brushes Activity panel.**

Chapter 11

Drawing Tools That Amaze and Delight

In This Chapter

- Adding the signature and uniqueness to your photos
- Getting fantastic Flood-Fill results
- Picking your paint color and paint on effects
- Drawing shapes and filling them up

Sometimes a perfectly cropped, centered, and illuminated photo is somehow lacking. It's missing some undefined magical element. Maybe the subject is, well — boring. Or maybe everything is just *too* perfect.

This chapter contains a few more tools you can use to add interest and artistry to a photo.

Signatures and Other Unique Brush-On Feats

Props and special effects are lots of fun, but there are times when you may want to draw or mark or brand a photo in a way that's unique. Here are a few ways to make *your* mark:

- **Signatures and handwritten messages:** You may want to include a handwritten message — in your own writing — along with your signature. I've added the artist's signature to the photo in Color Plate 11-1.
- **Callouts:** You may notice that some of the figures have lines drawn to point to certain program features, and the lines are accompanied by some explanatory text. These are *callouts*. You can draw a line using the drawing tools and then add text to a photo in PhotoSuite 4, as described in Chapter 12, "A Walk on the Wild Side: Special Effects." Color Plate 11-1 shows a callout I created.

- **Photo Sprayer:** This tool lets you paint with colorful objects — analogous to using a rubber stamp. In Color Plate 11-1, I've used the flower object.
- **Drawing something that isn't in the prop menu:** The PhotoSuite 4 props are pretty extensive but they don't include every conceivable object you might want in a photo. Depending on your level of talent and motivation, you may just want to draw and include your own cartoon-like prop, as I've done by adding the moustache to the baby shown in Figure 11-1.

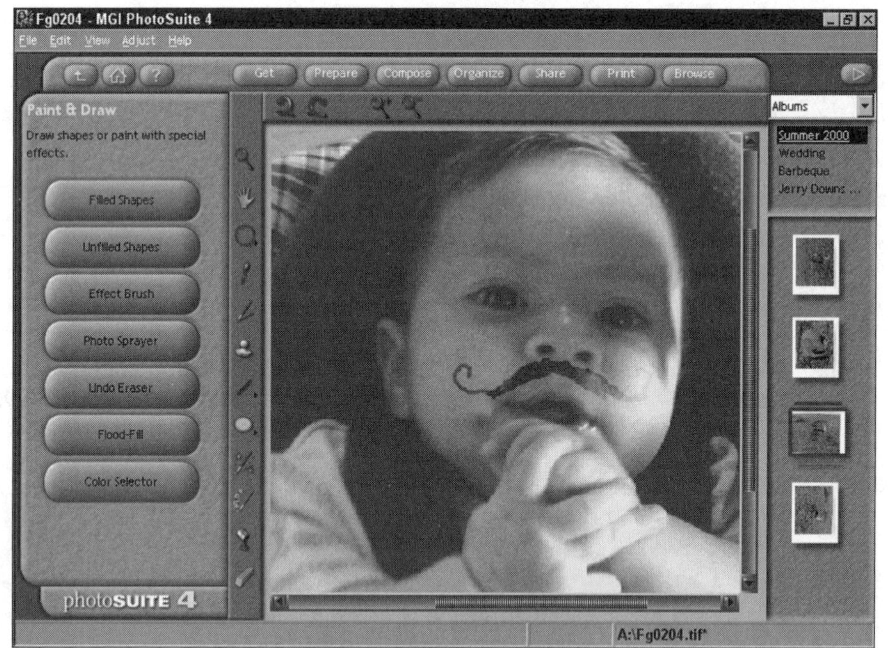

Figure 11-1: Draw your own touches.

Here's how to use to use the basic drawing tools to add signatures, autographs, and other unique touches:

1. **Click the Prepare button on the Navigation bar.**

   The Prepare screen and Activity panel appear.

2. **Click the Paint & Draw button.**

   The Paint & Draw Activity panel appears.

3. **Select Effect Brush from the Activity panel.**

   The Effect Brush Activity panel, shown in Figure 11-2, appears.

   This option allows you to select a Brush tool type and paint color directly on your photo (for example, to add a signature).

4. **Click the Brush selection tool.**

   The Brushes Activity panel appears.

5. **Select a brush type and then click OK to close the Brushes Activity panel.**

6. **Use the Adjust brush size slider to adjust the size of the brush.**

   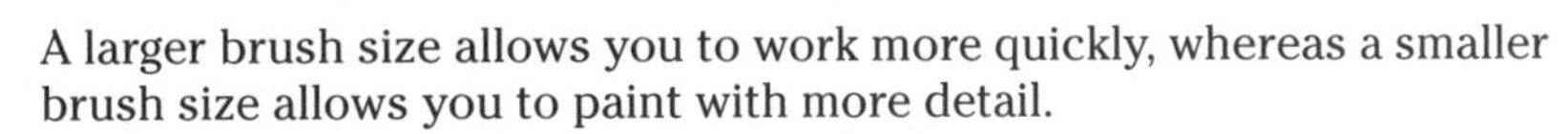

   A larger brush size allows you to work more quickly, whereas a smaller brush size allows you to paint with more detail.

7. **Click the Paint Color swatch if you want to change the color that's displayed (see Figure 11-2).**

   The Select Color Activity panel appears.

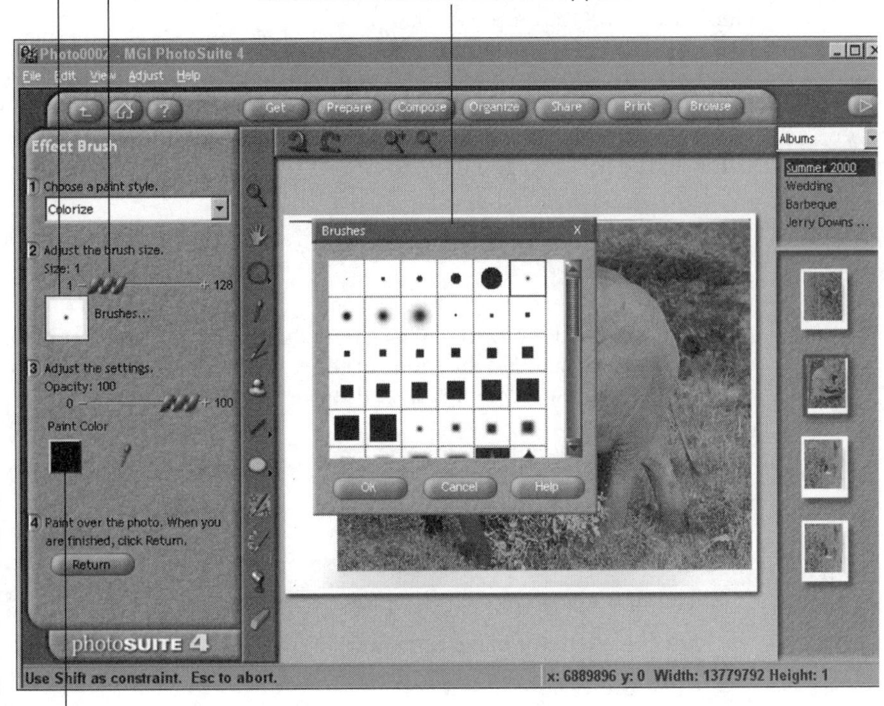

Figure 11-2: More stylistic enhancements.

8. **Select a color and click OK to exit the Select Color Activity panel.**

   The new color you've selected appears in the Paint Color swatch.

9. **Left-click and drag your mouse, using it as a paintbrush to write or draw on the photo.**

   You can use the Undo button or change paint colors as needed.

10. **Click Return when you've finished painting over the photo.**

You can paint with Special Effects, applying them to the desired area of your photo using the steps outlined above. Chapter 12 tells you more about the effects available to you and how to paint with them.

Fathoming the Flood-Fill Tool

Flood-Fill is a rejuvenating tool. Use it to fill an area that's uniform in color with areas of a new color. For example, in Color Plate 11-2, I've changed my elephant friend to the proverbial pink.

What may look like an area that's uniform in color may not really be uniform. For example, a sky that looks blue to you may actually be made up of a lot of varying shades of blue. If so, the Flood-Fill tool won't fill the sky with the new color on the first try. You have to repeat the process several times.

Fill 'er up!

Filling an area with color (or with a Special Effect) is a quick process. You don't have to painstakingly paint, prepare, or trace the way you do when you're fixing flaws, cropping, or cutting.

To fill an area with color using the Flood-Fill tool:

1. **Click the Prepare button on the Navigation bar.**

   The Prepare screen and Activity panel appear.

2. **The Paint & Draw Activity panel appears.**

   Another Activity panel appears.

3. **Click the Flood-Fill button.**

   The Flood-Fill Activity panel appears, as shown in Figure 11-3.

   You can click the Flood-Fill button on the vertical toolbar (shown in Figure 11-3) to display the Flood-Fill Activity panel.

Figure 11-3: Fill areas with color using this Activity panel.

4. **Choose a paint style from the drop-down menu.**

   Table 11-1 lists all the available paint styles.

5. **Adjust the tolerance level using the Tolerance slider in the Activity panel.**

   Tolerance is the amount of variance in the pixels that will be tolerated, or included, in the area subject to the Flood-Fill. For example, a high tolerance might allow you to use a Flood-Fill for a wide variation of trees and foliage in an area. A low tolerance would capture a more restricted range of green hues within the Flood-Fill area.

6. **Click the Fill color swatch to select a different color to draw or paint with.**

   Clicking the Fill swatch causes the Select Color Activity panel to appear.

   You can then select a color and then click OK to exit the Activity panel. The new color appears in the Fill swatch.

7. **Set the level of transparency of the color using the Opacity slider.**

   The higher the Opacity setting, the less transparent the color appears.

8. **Click once in the area of the photo you want to fill.**

   All the pixels of the same color, or within the range of tolerance, are filled with the Fill color. (See Color Plate 11-2.)

Table 11-1 Paint Styles

Style	*What It Does*
Normal	Paints with the most intense or saturated color, at the maximum level of opacity. This level of opacity obscures detail in the photo. (See Color Plate 10-2.)
Tint	Paints with less saturation than the Normal paint style, and retains the detail in the photo. (See Color Plate 10-2.)
Colorize	Paints with more color saturation than the tint setting but less than the Normal setting. (See Color Plate 10-2.)
Lighten	Lightens areas of the photo; good for downplaying or minimizing shadows.
Darken	Darkens areas of a photo.
Transparency	Makes the areas you paint transparent. This is effective if you have another photo behind the one you're painting (see Chapter 9 for more information about collages).
Invert	Substitutes pixels in a photo for other pixels that are opposite in color. Dark pixels are made light; light pixels are made dark.
Remove Red Eye	Darkens red pixels in a photo to get rid of that demon monster effect caused by your flash.
Remove Blemishes	Removes blemishes in a photo by averaging the pixel colors in the immediate area of the photo to obscure the blemish.
Soften	Softens and obscures the detail in a photo. (May help if your subject is ugly.)
Sharpen	Sharpens detail in a photo by increasing color contrast around the edges of objects.
Crystallize, Mosaic, and Randomize	Applies a hexagonal, square, or random patterns, respectively, to the surface of the photo.

Style	What It Does
Emboss	Creates a three-dimensional effect by selectively enhancing the edges in the photo.
Splatter	Reduces the resolution of a photo by replacing pixels with the average pixel color.
Fog, Glass, Snow, Wind, Smoked Glass	Gives the impression you're looking at the photo through one of these effects.
Painting	Simulates the appearance of an oil painting or watercolor.
Posterize	Reduces the number of colors in the photo to facilitate reproducing or enlarging it.

Flood-Fill factoids

The Flood-Fill tool gives you quick and dramatic results. Here are a few often-overlooked techniques to make the process even easier:

- **To increase the level of saturation of the Flood Fill color gradually:** Click your mouse repeatedly over the area you've selected to fill. With each click of your mouse, the color becomes more intense.
- **To fill a larger area of multiple colors:** Scribble over the area you want to fill with your mouse. All the pixels in the area you drag over are filled, regardless of their color.
- **To color only one area of a similar color:** What if there are multiple areas in your photo with colors that look pretty close, and you don't want to change the color of all the similarly colored areas? Try lowering the tolerance. But if that doesn't work, you can use the techniques described earlier in this chapter in the section "Signatures and Other Unique Brush-On Feats."
- **If you don't get the desired result the first time:** Flood-Fill can be a bit unpredictable. The tool fills an area within the tolerance range of whatever pixels you happened to click. But because so many different-colored pixels can be present within an area of the photo, you can never be sure exactly what you're capturing in your tolerance range. If you get a weird result on your first attempt with the Flood-Fill tool, use the Undo button. Then move your mouse over a bit and try again.

Drawing Shapes for Show

Shapes are handy little additions that come in handy for things such as labeling objects in your photo or adding an artistic effect or pattern. You can use PhotoSuite 4's shape-drawing tools to create:

- An ellipse
- Standard rectangles
- Rounded rectangles
- A Word Balloon shape called a polygon
- Freehand shapes

You can create both *filled* and *unfilled* shapes. Filled shapes are solid, or filled with a color you've selected. Unfilled shapes are simple outlines.

Creating filled shapes

Filled shapes are solid areas of color. A solid area of color, as opposed to an outline, provides greater visibility and impact. You can create filled shapes with or without borders. The border adds yet more impact and attracts additional attention to the shape. PhotoSuite 4 lets you select one color for the border of the shape and a second color to fill the shape. In Color Plate 11-2, I've adorned my elephant friend with shapes that have a green outline and pink fill color.

To add a filled shape to your photo, follow these steps:

1. **Click the Prepare button on the Navigation bar.**

   The Prepare screen and Activity panel appear.

2. **Click the Paint & Draw button.**

   Another Activity panel appears.

3. **Select Filled Shapes.**

   The Filled Shapes Activity panel, shown in Figure 11-4, appears.

Figure 11-4: Select shapes with or without outlines using this Activity panel.

4. **Select one of the shapes listed in the Activity panel.**

   You can select shapes with or without an outline. Shapes with an outline have a border around them. PhotoSuite 4 allows you to select a border that is a different color from the inside area of the shape. (I've used shapes with an outline in Color Plate 11-2.)

   After you select a shape, the Activity panel shown in Figure 11-5 appears.

5. **Select Normal, Colorize, Tint, or another paint style from the drop down menu.**

   The available paint styles are summarized in Table 11-1.

   Normal, Colorize, and Tint allow you to paint with a color you've selected with varying levels of saturation, as described in Table 11-1. You can also paint on other special effects, which are covered in Chapter 12.

6. **Click the Brushes selection tool to open the Brushes Activity panel, select a brush type by clicking it, and then select OK to exit the Brushes Activity panel.**

   The Brush tool Activity panel is identical to the one used with the Flood-Fill feature (refer back to Figure 11-2).

7. **Adjust the size (width) of your border using the Outline slider.**

   Moving the slider to the right makes the border wider. This means that you see more of the border color and less of the fill color.

8. **Select both a Border color and a Fill color by clicking each swatch to open the Select Color Activity panel.**

   The Select Color Activity panel appears, offering you more than 264 colors from which to choose (see Figure 11-5).

Figure 11-5: Fill areas with color using this Activity panel.

9. **After you've selected a color, click OK to close the Select Color Activity panel.**

10. **Adjust the Opacity setting using the slider.**

    Lowering the opacity level by moving the slider to the left makes the shape more transparent.

11. **For shapes other than the freehand shape, click and hold the mouse button at one corner point of the shape your want to draw; then drag it to the diagonally opposite point. (If you're creating a freehand shape, simply draw the shape.)**

    As you're dragging your mouse, the outline of a shape appears on your screen.

12. **When the outline of the shape has the dimensions you want, release the mouse button to anchor it (or, if you're drawing a freehand shape, double-click your mouse at the point where your close your shape, which is your original starting point).**

If you hold your left mouse button to draw the shape, the border is drawn in the active paint color and the shape is filled with the active Fill color. If you hold your right mouse button to draw the shape, the border is drawn in the active Fill color and the shape is filled with the active Paint color.

Creating unfilled shapes

Unfilled shapes are outlines of shapes. You can use them to enclose objects within a photo, or to create patterns.

Follow these steps to add unfilled shapes to your photo:

1. **Click the Prepare button on the Navigation bar.**

   The Prepare screen and Activity panel appear.

2. **Click the Paint & Draw button.**

   Another Activity panel appears.

3. **Select Unfilled Shapes.**

   An Unfilled Shapes Activity panel appears, from which you may select to draw one of the following shapes:

   - Line
   - Rectangle
   - Rounded Rectangle
   - Ellipse
   - Freehand Shape

4. **Select one of the shapes listed in the Activity panel.**

   The Unfilled shapes Activity panel appears.

5. **Select Normal, Colorize, Tint, or another paint style from the drop-down menu.**

   The available paint styles are summarized in Table 11-1.

   Normal, Colorize, and Tint allow you to paint with a color you've selected with varying levels of saturation, as described in Table 11-1. You can also paint on other special effects, which are covered in Chapter 12.

6. **Click the Brushes swatch to open the Brushes Activity panel; select a brush type by clicking it; then select OK to exit the Brushes Activity panel.**

   The Brushes Activity panel is identical to the one used for the Flood-Fill and Filled Shapes features (refer back to Figure 11-2).

7. **Adjust the outline size for the shape using the slider in the Activity panel.**

   Moving the slider to the right makes the border wider.

8. **Select a Border color by clicking the Border color swatch to open the Select Color Activity panel.**

   The Select Color Activity panel appears. This box is identical to the one you use for selecting colors for filled shapes (refer back to Figure 11-5).

9. **After you've selected a color, the Color Activity panel automatically closes.**

10. **Adjust the Opacity setting using the slider.**

    Lowering the opacity level by moving the slider to the left makes the shape more transparent.

11. **For shapes other than the Freehand Shape or line, click and hold the mouse button at one corner point of the shape your want to draw and drag it to the diagonally opposite point. (If you're creating a Freehand Shape or line, simply draw it with your mouse.)**

    As you're dragging your mouse, the outline of a shape appears on your screen.

12. **When the outline of the shape has the dimensions you want, release the mouse button to anchor it (or, if you're drawing a Freehand Shape, double-click your mouse at the point where you close your shape, which is your original starting point).**

The Line un-Filled Shape is great for creating callouts and pointing to objects within your photo. (See Color Plate 11-1.)

Chapter 12

A Walk on the Wild Side: Special Effects

In This Chapter

- Changing the climate of your photo
- When blurry is better
- Turning photos into impressionistic masterpieces
- Weird warp effects
- The surprises on your CD

This chapter takes you on a wild tour of wacky weather, splatter effects, strange planetary backdrops, and geographical locations. PhotoSuite 4 is a digital amusement park with hundreds of themes, effects, and awe-inspiring features.

You can find all these intriguing add-ons in two places. The first spot is the Special Effects menu on the Prepare screen. The other place is the Content folder on your PhotoSuite 4 CD-ROM.

Ordering Special Effects Off the Menu

PhotoSuite 4 offers you a smorgasbord of exotic special effects. Sampling them is more fun than eating your way through a dessert tray.

MGI's research shows that the typical user (you) likes to have a mental image of what each different special effect looks like. Then, when the right opportunity arises, you can recall the one you need to express yourself and creatively capture the moment.

Surveying the special effects

PhotoSuite 4 offers you six categories of effects, plus the bizarre Warp effects. Warp effects are in a twisted little category of their own and have separate menus and Activity panels. They're discussed in this chapter in the section "For People Who Are Really Warped."

The Special Effects menu is your ticket and map to the following categories of PhotoSuite 4 features, which are illustrated throughout this chapter:

- **Natural:** Makes your photo appear as if it were victim of a natural phenomenon such as fog, glass, snow, wind, or smoked glass.
- **Artistic:** Turns a photo into a work of art by duplicating it for a mirage effect, making it appear as a three-dimensional embossed image, or reducing colors to create the effect of a poster, cartoon, or painting. You can also add the more impressionistic effects called Splatter, Swirl, Ripple, and Spherize, which pretty much do what their names indicate.
- **Geometric:** These effects provide you with the ability to give your photo the appearance of a Mosaic or Tile image. You can also use the Randomize feature to apply a random pattern to the pixels in the photo.
- **Enhancements:** Applies various blur effects to your photo.
- **Lens:** Makes your photo look as though you're viewing it through a colored lens, similar to the effects you'd expect to see if you attached colored filters through a camera lens.
- **Painterly:** This category of effects makes your photo appear textured by canvas, rain, frosted glass, brick, weave, or even a grass effect, which makes the image appear as though it's a field of grass.
- **Warps:** Use this feature to stretch, shrink, and distort portions of your photo beyond recognition.

Accessing and adjusting special effects

Professional photographers used to spend countless darkroom hours achieving the same effects *you* get with a click of your the mouse (and the PhotoSuite 4 program).

To access the Special Effects menu, follow these steps:

1. **Import a photo into PhotoSuite 4 using the Get screen, as explained in Chapter 5.**

   You must open an image file in PhotoSuite 4 to access the full range of special effects.

2. **Click the Prepare button on the Navigation bar.**

   The Prepare screen and Activity panel appear.

3. **Click the Special Effects button.**

   The first Special Effects Activity panel appears, as shown in Figure 12-1. You can select Effects, Preset Warps, Interactive Warp, or Plug-In Effects.

4. **To access Special Effects other than Warp, click Effects.**

   The Activity panel shown in Figure 12-2 appears. (I tell you about the Warp effects later in this chapter.)

5. **Select one of the Special Effects categories from the drop-down menu.**

6. **Click the Adjust Effect Settings button.**

   Another Activity panel appears, as shown in Figure 12-3. This Activity panel allows you to adjust the intensity of the special effect. (The Adjust Effects Activity panel shown in Figure 12-3 is for the Wind effect.)

7. **Adjust the slider for the Special Effect and click Return when you're satisfied with your adjustments.**

   The Special Effect Activity panel reappears.

8. **Click Apply to apply the special effect to your photo; then click Return to exit the Special Effect Activity panel.**

Figure 12-1: The first Special Effects Activity panel.

Figure 12-2: This Activity panel allows you to access special effects other than Warp.

Figure 12-3: Adjust the intensity of a special effect using an Activity panel such as this one.

Sampling some special effects

PhotoSuite 4 lumps Special Effects — other than Warp effects — into six quirky categories. My vulture-like friend, Zoë, is about to experience them all. Zoë appears *un*-effected and in her naturally beautiful state in Figure 12-4.

If the special effect you choose doesn't give you the desired effect on the first try, remember that you can adjust its intensity by clicking the Adjust Effect Settings button in the Special Effects Activity panel, after choosing a special effect from the drop-down menu (refer back to Figure 12-2).

Figure 12-4: An un-effected picture of Zoë.

Smart Blur

In Figure 12-5, I've applied a special effect to Zoë that's actually an old photographer's trick. The Smart Blur effect blurs only the background of a photo, to make the subject appear sharper. How does the feature know what to blur? Well, that's *why* they call it Smart blur, of course!

To apply the Smart Blur effect:

1. **Select Enhancement from the first drop-down menu in the Special Effects Activity panel.**

   The previous section tells you how to access the Special Effects Activity panel.

2. **Select Smart Blur from the second drop-down menu in the Special Effects Activity panel.**

   The background appears slightly blurred, making the subject of your photo (in this case, Zoë) appear sharper and more prominent, as you can see in Figure 12-5.

Select the Gaussian Blur feature, rather than Smart Blur, if you want to blur the whole photo. Blurring the whole enchilada works great if your primary subject needs features that you want to obscure — such as wrinkles or a bad paint job on a car you're trying to sell after an accident.

3. **Click the Adjust Effect Settings button.**

   An activity panel with a slider appears so that you can adjust the intensity of the blur effect.

4. **After you've adjusted the intensity of the blur effect to your satisfaction, click Return.**

   The Special Effect Activity panel reappears.

5. **Click Apply to apply the blur effect to your photo; then click Return to exit the Special Effect Activity panel.**

Figure 12-5: Here's Zoë with the Smart Blur effect applied.

Through all kinds of weather

If you select Natural from the first drop-down menu in the Special Effects Activity panel, you can bring on the following adverse weather conditions:

- **Fog:** This one makes your image kind of gray and blurry, like London or Seattle.
- **Wind:** Whoosh! Check out Zoë's wind-ruffled feathers (Figure 12-6) brought on by selecting the Wind feature.
- **Snow:** This one's great for Christmas cards, or for a family photo to your landlord reminding him to do something about the heat. Brrr! Zoë looks cold in Figure 12-7, doesn't she?

Figure 12-6: Whoosh! Here's Zoë ruffled by the Wind special effect.

Figure 12-7: Brrrrr! Zoë gets the Snow special effect.

It's a mirage

The Mirage effect duplicates a copy of your primary photo subject (in this case, Zoë) and displays it just below the original as if it were a reflection (see Figure 12-8).

To get this mirage effect in your photos, follow these steps:

1. **From the Special Effects Activity panel, select Artistic from the drop-down menu.**
2. **Select Mirage from the second drop-down menu and click the Adjust Effect settings button.**

   The Mirage Activity panel appears.
3. **Adjust the height of the duplicate (reflection) image using the Height slider.**

   Sliding it to the right makes the reflection appear bigger.
4. **Select a Blend option (Strong, Medium, or Weak) to blend the image into the background.**

   This slider controls the intensity of the reflective image.

5. **Click Apply when you're satisfied with the Mirage effect on your screen; click Return to exit the Mirage Activity panel.**

If you want to view the original image before you applied the Mirage effect, de-select the Preview check box.

Figure 12-8: Reflections of Zoë with the Mirage effect.

Making photos look like paintings, drawings, and sculptures

When is a photo not a photo? Or at least unrecognizable as a photo? The answer is when you use the Artistic Effects from the drop-down menu in the Special Effects Activity panel.

The Posterize, Paint, Cartoonize, and Embossing options are all accessed from the Artistic Effects via the artistic drop-down menu in the second Special Effects Activity panel. Here's how these features create art from reality:

- **Posterize:** Reduces the number of colors in an image so that it looks better when it's enlarged and is more economical to reproduce. You can click the Adjust effect settings button to increase or decrease the number of colors that appear in the poster.
- **Cartoonize:** Turns your picture into a cartoon, as shown in Figure 12-9, with only a few colors. Use the Adjust effect settings button to choose from among three different colorization levels.
- **Embossing:** Makes your subject look as though its been chiseled in stone. You can click the Adjust Effect Settings button to get to a slider that makes the sculptured effect appear in more or less relief.

Figure 12-9: A Zoë cartoon.

Some even weirder artistic effects

Are you looking for something more impressionistic than realistic? Try these effects by accessing them via the Special Effects drop-down menu.

- **Crystallize:** This applies a pattern in the form of a series of hexagons to your image, then randomly jumbles the hexagons within certain color areas to give you the feeling of viewing your subject through a multifaceted piece of crystal.
- **Splatter:** You get the splatter effect because PhotoSuite 4 replaces each pixel in your photo with pixels of the average color within an area. This makes everything look all runny and splattery. You can use the Pattern Size option accessed by clicking the Adjust Effect Settings button to make the splatter pattern larger or smaller. You can also use the Intensity slider to blend the edges of the pattern more or less to vary the splatter effect.

Adjust the settings and intensity of the special effects using the options and Activity panel discussed in the section of this chapter called "Accessing and adjusting special effects."

Geometric gyrations and effects

The Swirl, Ripple, and Spherize special effects are in a surrealistic league of their own. You can access them by selecting the Artistic option in the Special Effects Activity panel. Here's a brief tour:

- **Swirl:** This one makes your image look as though it's being viewed from the eye of a tornado. Click the Adjust Effect Settings button to access a scroll bar that lets you control the direction of the swirl and the intensity of the effect. Figures 12-10 and 12-11 show Zoë swirled at two different intensity levels.

You can also use the Adjust Effect Settings button to control the direction of the swirl.

Figure 12-10: Zoë gets the Swirl effect.

Figure 12-11: A more intense Swirl effect turns Zoë to butter.

- **Ripple:** This is a funhouse mirror effect. Its result is similar to the Warp features I tell you about later in this chapter, in the section "For People Who Are Really Warped."
- **Spherize:** This effect makes the subject look as though it's either wrapped around a ball or trapped inside a ball. Click the Adjust Effect Settings button and specify the height of the Spherize effect using the slider. More height makes the subject look as though it's wrapped around the outside of the ball. Less height makes it look as though the subject is inside the ball. For example, when you apply the Spherize effect to Zoë with a low height setting as shown in Figure 12-12, it looks as though she's back in the egg, huh?
- You can access more impressionistic effects by selecting Geometric from the drop-down menu on the Special Effects screen (See Figure 12-2). The Geometric features are as follows:

Figure 12-12: The Spherize effect makes Zoë look as though she's back in the egg.

- **Mosaic:** This one makes your photo look like a mosaic by replacing the pixels in the photo with the average pixel color for each square area. You can use the slider under the Adjust effect settings button to adjust the size of the mosaic squares, as shown in Figures 12-13 and 12-14.
- **Tile:** This effect is supposed to make your subject look as though it's made up of tiles, by superimposing a sort of grid pattern over the photo. I think it looks more like a wire mesh fence. You can see for yourself in Figure 12-15.
- **Randomize:** This one's too weird for me! It takes all of the pixels in your image and randomly jumbles them, as shown in Figure 12-16. You can use options under the Adjust effect settings button to vary the effect, and its intensity. Can you find Zoë in there?

Figure 12-13: The Mosaic effect uses the average color of pixels within square areas.

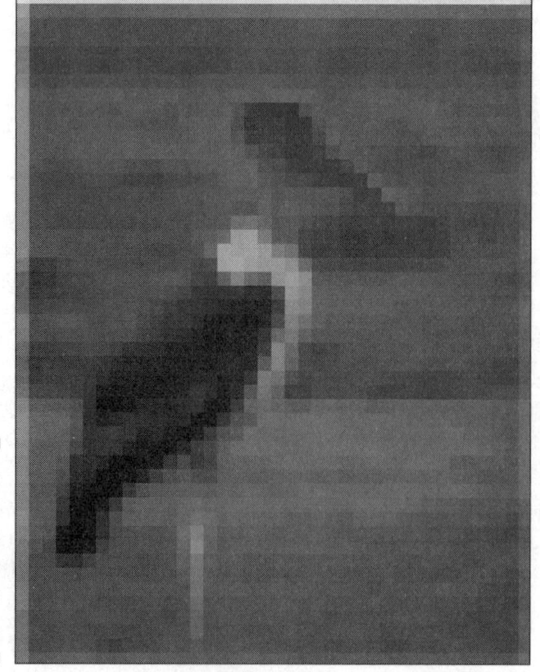

Figure 12-14: You can vary the size of the Mosaic squares.

Figure 12-15: Zoë is a prisoner of the Tile effect.

Figure 12-16: Do you recognize Zoë? This is the Randomize effect.

Look through a lens

These features make you look like a real photographer who has invested lots of money in expensive equipment. The lens effects, true to their name, make your photo look as though they've been shot through some expensive, special lens.

PhotoSuite 4 makes the following lens effects available to you (see Color Plate 12-1, which shows some of these effects):

- **Warm:** This lens gives your photo a warm, reddish-brown cast.
- **Cool:** Use this filter to give your photo cool blue tones.
- **Sepia:** This is a sort of rose-colored lens.
- **Tan:** Everything is given a tobacco-colored tint.
- **Moonlight:** The effect of this filter is an aqua-gray cast.
- **Antique:** This is one of my favorites. The gold tones make your photo appear aged and give it a classic mood.

Giving your photo texture

Of course, you can't actually add texture to your photo. But you can give it the appearance of being reproduced on a textured surface by selecting from among the Painterly options in the Special Effects Activity panel.

Here are the textured effects you can achieve:

- **Frosted glass:** Makes it look as though you're viewing your subject through frosted glass.
- **Canvas:** Gives the photo a simulated canvas texture.
- **Rain:** Makes the photo look as though it were taken in the middle of a rainstorm.
- **Grass:** This effect, illustrated in Figure 12-17, makes it look as though the photo is made up of millions of blades of grass.
- **Weave:** Makes the photo appear to be woven.
- **Brick:** Gives the photo a psuedo-brick texture.

You can find options to adjust the intensity for all the painterly effects by clicking the Adjust Effect Settings button.

Figure 12-17: The Painterly effects, such as Grass, give your photo a textured appearance.

For People Who Are Really Warped

The Warp effect allows you to stretch and manipulate your subject's features as though they were made of silly putty. It's fun and possibly therapeutic.

You can apply the Warp feature two different ways:

- **Preset Warp:** This feature allows you to apply the Warp features using the following predefined settings:
  - Vertical Wave
  - Horizontal Wave
  - Predefined Funhouse
  - Bulge
  - Monster Mirror

There's no logical way to explain the visual impact of the different Preset Warps. Experiment with them all! I've used the Vertical Wave on Zoë in Figure 12-18.

- **Interactive Warp:** This feature lets you choose your own Warp settings and apply them selectively to portions of the photo.

For fun, I've taken the four kids in Figure 12-19 and applied a different warp effect on each of their faces. From left to right, I've used the Vertical Wave, the Horizontal Wave, the Predefined Funhouse Effect, and the Interactive Warp.

Figure 12-18: Zoë does the Vertical Wave (Preset Warp) here.

Figure 12-19: Four out of the five kids here have a different Interactive Warp feature applied to their face.

To access the Warp special effects, follow these steps:

1. **Import a photo into PhotoSuite 4 using the Get screen, as explained in Chapter 5.**

   You must open an image file in PhotoSuite 4 to access and experiment with the Warp effects.

2. **After you import a photo, you are brought to the Prepare Activity panel.**

   The Prepare screen and Activity panel appear.

3. **Click the Special Effects button.**

   The Special Effects Activity panel appears.

4. **Select Preset Warps or Interactive Warps.**

   If you select Preset Warps, the Activity panel shown in Figure 12-20 appears. If you select Interactive Warps, the Activity panel shown in Figure 12-21 appears.

   If you're using the Preset warp, experiment with each of the predefined settings by clicking them. If you're using Interactive Warp to achieve the setting you want, drag your mouse to control the effect.

5. **Click Apply when you're satisfied with the Warp image that you see on your screen; then click Return to leave the Interactive Warp or Preset Warp Activity panel.**

If you're using Interactive Warp, you can choose from among the following Warp effects:

- **Grow:** After selecting this effect, click an area of the photo or drag your mouse across it to enlarge the pixels and make the feature or area of the photo appear larger.
- **Shrink:** After selecting this effect, click an area of the photo or drag your mouse across it to shrink pixels and make the feature or area of the photo appear smaller.
- **Drag:** Click this setting and then drag your mouse over an area of the photo to stretch it as though it were made of rubbery putty.
- **Melt:** The proportions of the image are retained, but shifted.
- **Restore:** Use this to fix mistakes or undo some of the effect applied.

Figure 12-20: The Preset Warps Activity panel.

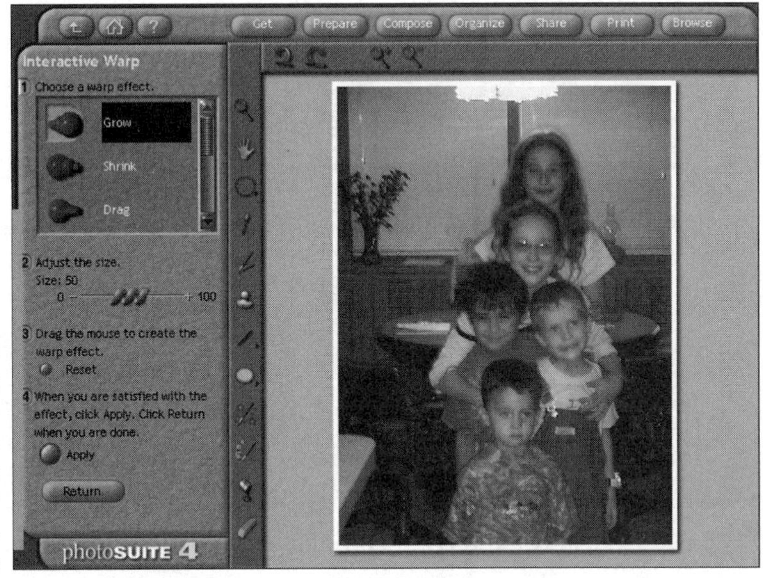

Figure 12-21: The Interactive Warps Activity panel.

The Undo and Redo features are really useful when you're trying to get just the right Warp effect.

The Wonders on Your Content CD

PhotoSuite 4 comes with a surprise CD. Not only do you get the CD with the program and installation files, you get a whole *extra* CD of professionally photographed backdrops, enhancements, props, and other images that you don't need to run the program. The surprise CD — labeled Content Disc — is probably one of the most intriguing freebies ever to be provided by a software manufacturer.

Here's a sampling of just a few of the surprises your Content Disk contains:

- Announcements
- Backgrounds
- Bookmarks
- Certificates

- Wedding album pages and covers
- Postcards
- Signs and stationery

Most of these features are covered in Chapter 15, "Cheap Gifts and Chic Digital Accessories," and in Chapter 16, "PhotoSuite for Fun and Profit." But there's one file on the content disc that isn't covered anywhere else in this book, and it's too good to miss.

To access the different backgrounds on your content CD:

1. **Click the Compose button on the Navigation bar.**

   The Compose screen and Activity panel appear.

2. **Click Fun Stuff.**
3. **Click Backgrounds.**

   Thumbnails of various backgrounds appear on your desktop.

4. **Select one of the categories of backgrounds from the drop-down menu.**

   Thumbnails for all of the backgrounds for that category appear on your desktop (see Color Plate 12-2).

5. **Double-click the thumbnail for the background you want to use.**

   The Compose screen reappears with the scene you've selected displayed at full size in the Workspace.

6. **Complete your project by following the directions for using the features on the Compose screen in Chapter 9.**

   I've used the techniques in Chapter 9 to add a cutout of Zoë to my background, as shown in Figure 12-22.

Figure 12-22: Zoë gets a surrealistic backdrop (Abstract Background Number 5).

Part IV

Being a PhotoSuite 4 Paparazzo

"THAT'S A LOVELY SCANNED IMAGE OF YOUR SISTER'S PORTRAIT. NOW TAKE IT OFF THE BODY OF THAT PIT VIPER BEFORE SHE COMES IN THE ROOM."

In this part . . .

Photography is a social hobby. What good is a photo if no one looks at it? This part tells you how to send your friends photos and to throw a photo party on the Web using the free GatherRound.com site. It also tells you how to use the Stitching feature to stitch multiple photos together to create stunning, interactive panoramas, and how to make dozens of useful items such as calendars and greeting cards.

Chapter 13

Graphics on the Go

In This Chapter

- E-mailing yourself all over the world
- Gathering round the computer screen
- Making your own Web Site in thirty minutes or fewer
- Sending your photos to the lab with PhotoNet Online

Amateur photographers are by nature gregarious folks who want to share what they create. With PhotoSuite 4, you can e-mail photos to friends individually or throw one big picture party for anyone who wants to attend, using the Gather Round feature. You can even create your own Web site in less time than it takes to watch a television sitcom.

E-Mailing Your Images

Will stamps someday become obsolete? PhotoSuite 4 gives you one more reason to abandon them in favor of e-mail forever. Paper photos can be crushed, wrinkled, or snickered at by postal employees. With PhotoSuite 4, you can discreetly send copies to multiple recipients with a click of your mouse.

You can even send your e-mail in the form of a slide show. PhotoSuite 4 sends your recipient the necessary software to view it. (See Chapter 14, "Say 'Cheese!' Family Albums, Slide Shows, and Screen Savers," for more about slide shows.)

Photos are sent via e-mail in files called attachments. (Chapter 19, "Ten Funky File Formats," tells you about the different file formats you can select for your attachments.) JPEG is a very popular format for Internet use because it doesn't take up a lot of space, so it's pretty quick. But this format has the drawback of data loss due to its compression scheme. You can opt to send your photos in another format, as explained in Step 3 in the following steps.

Here's how to send your photos into the great e-mail beyond:

1. **Click the Share button on the Navigation bar.**

   The Save & Share Activity panel appears.

2. **Click the Send E-Mail button on the Activity panel.**

   The Send E-Mail Activity panel appears, as shown in Figure 13-1.

3. **Select one of the following options for sending your photo attachments:**

   - **Send it as it is:** Sends the file in its current format.
   - **Send as Slide Show with Player:** Sends the file as a slide show, along with the necessary software for the recipient to play it.
   - **Send As JPEG:** Sends your file in JPEG form.
   - **Send as JPEG with an approximate size of:** You can specify an approximate JPEG file size with more or less aggressive compression.

4. **Click Send to send your message, or Save for e-mailing later.**

   The first time you send a message, a wizard appears to set up your e-mail application/service to use the PhotoSuite 4 e-mail feature. Follow the prompts that appear with this wizard to confirm that you want to use the default application, or to specify another application for sending e-mail.

   You can subsequently change to another application by clicking the Change e-mail method button.

   An e-mail message box appears. The filenames of the photos you're sending appear on the attachment line (see Figure 13-1).

5. **Enter the e-mail address for the recipient.**

   Before sending an attachment, make sure that you know the attachment size limits of the system that's receiving your file. If it's too large an attachment for that particular system, the message and attachment may be undeliverable. It will bounce back to you with a message saying so. Handle this problem by sending multiple messages with fewer attached files.

6. **Use the default message or enter your own message.**

   A default message appears, telling the recipient that he or she received a PhotoSuite 4 image. You can add to this message or delete it in favor of your own clever quips.

7. **Click Send and then click Return to exit the Send E-mail Activity panel.**

   Zoom! Your message and photos are off.

PhotoSuite 4 also enables you to use a Web based e-mail service such as MSN Hotmail. To use this feature:

1. **Click the Change E-Mail Method button.**

   A drop-down list appears, listing several e-mail methods and applications.

2. **Select an e-mail method from the drop-down list.**

3. **Click the Create New Web-Based Method button to set the Web-based e-mail as your new default e-mail and enter a Web address and name for the Web-based service.**

   The Web-based service is now set as your default e-mail application for e-mailing images from PhotoSuite 4.

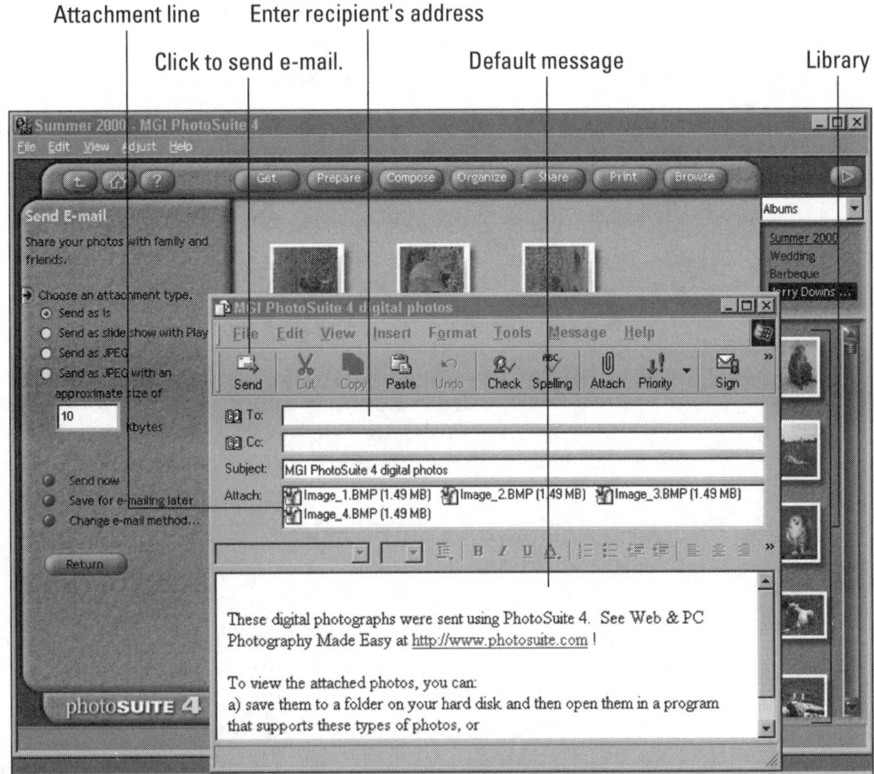

Figure 13-1: You can e-mail photos directly from the PhotoSuite 4 program.

Gather Round! Posting Pictures to the Web

The GatherRound feature lets you put password-protected photo albums on the Web using the GatherRound.com Web site. This is a free service to you, and it allows your friends and family to view your pictures 24 hours a day.

Here's how to take advantage of the GatherRound feature:

1. **Click the Share button Navigation bar.**

   The Save & Share Activity panel appears.

2. **Click the Share Your Pictures at GatherRound.com button on the Activity panel.**

   The GatherRound Activity panel Appears.

3. **If you're a first time user, click the Create Account button. Then click the GatherRound hypertext link and then the Signup button. (If you're not a first-time user, proceed to Step 4).**

   You're automatically logged onto the GatherRound Web site, where you're prompted to enter your name, e-mail address, and an account password that's between four and eight characters.

4. **Type in your e-mail address and password.**

   If you're a new user, you must also agree to accept the Terms of Use. If you're already a GatherRound member, just type your e-mail address and password in appropriate fields on the GatherRound Activity panel; then click the Login button. After you do so, the Upload Activity panel appears.

5. **Select an album from the drop-down list in the Library, or click the Create New Album button.**

   Drag and drop the photos you want to Upload (post) onto your Workspace. If you're creating a new album, an activity panel appears that prompts you to retrieve photos from other sources, such as your computer, camera, or scanner. Chapter 5, "Where Do Little Images Come From?," tells you more about how to retrieve and import files.

6. **Click the Upload button and enter a password for your album when prompted.**

   The password for each album must be different than the password you selected in Step 3 to limit access to your GatherRound site.

   All the photos currently displayed in your Workspace are transferred to the GatherRound Web site. The album appears on your desktop for viewing, as shown in Figure 13-2.

7. **Invite your friends and relatives to the GatherRound.com Web site by clicking the hypertext link that reads "Invite Family and Friends to Visit Your Album."**

   Enter e-mail addresses for the invitation as prompted. Your guests don't need to use a password to access your album the first time but they will for subsequent visits. You can add the password to the generic invitation message (or modify the message in any other way that you like).

Click here to mail invitations to friends and family.

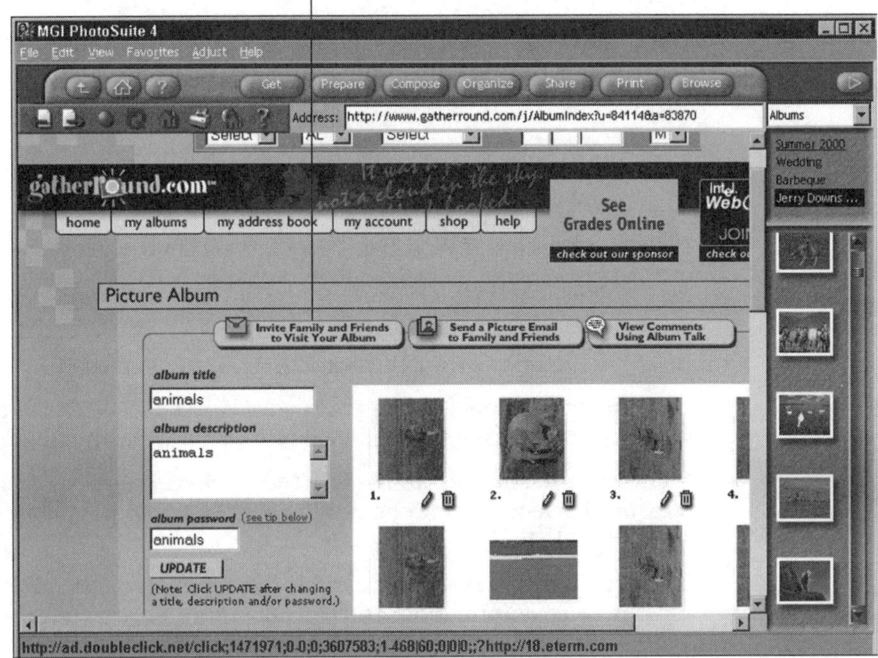

Figure 13-2: Posting photos on the GatherRound Web site.

Creating Your Own Little Web Site

Sometimes you just need a Web space to call your own. PhotoSuite 4 helps you satisfy this creative longing by providing templates and wizards that allow you to create a sophisticated Web page, as shown in Color Plate 13-1 — complete with sound and animation — in thirty minutes or less. (Sorry, there's no guarantee — that's only for soggy pizzas.)

Creating a Web page in 12 easy steps

Okay — start the timer! You're about to create your very own Web page in twelve easy steps, as follows:

1. **Open a photo, project album, or slide show in your PhotoSuite 4 Workspace and click the Share button on the Navigation bar.**

   The Save & Share Activity panel appears.

   (If you need a review of how to open a file or project, Chapter 5 tells you how.)

2. **Click the Create Web Items button on the Activity panel, and on the next Activity panel, click the Web Page button.**

   The Web Page Activity panel appears.

3. **Click the Create New Web Page button.**

   The Create Web page Activity panel appears.

4. **Select a category of Web Page templates from the drop-down menu.**

   All the available templates within that category are displayed within the Workspace.

5. **Select the template that you want to use and click Next.**

   The Web page template appears in your Workspace with the photo, album, or project you opened in Step 1 displayed within it.

6. **Select the check boxes to include the photo properties on the Web site, or deselect them if you don't want the photo properties to appear, and click Next.**

   The default text is really a prompt for you to include the photo's name, date, or other information. You can substitute your own text on the screen in the position of the default text using the Activity panel shown in Figure 13-3.

Click to make adjustments to any object on-screen.

Animated object

Default text

Figure 13-3: Edit your Web page using this Activity panel.

7. **Click the Add Text button to modify the default text.**

   The Add or Edit Text Activity panel appears.

   Chapter 9, "Performing Photo-Surgery," tells you more about how to use the Add/Edit Text Activity panel.

8. **Add additional photos, images, and links to your Web site by clicking the Photo, Interactive Panorama, Animated GIF, or predesigned Web link buttons.**

   Animated GIF files are covered in the later section "GIF or take." You can retrieve predesigned Web links if you have some on your computer already.

9. **To modify any object on the Web page, click the Select Object button to modify any of its properties; click Return when you're finished.**

   The Web Object Settings Activity panel appears, allowing you to modify the size, order, border, and other properties of the selected object.

10. **Click the Page Background button to modify the color or pattern of the page background; click Return when you're finished.**
11. **Click the Page Sound button and browse for a sound file on your system to play continuously or upon opening your Web page; click Return when you're finished.**

    To use this feature, you must have a sound file on your system.
12. **Click the Edit links button to modify the colors of any links that appear on your Web page; click Return when you're finished.**

    Congratulations! Your Web page is complete. Now proceed to the next section to post it to the Internet.

Posting a page to the Web

After you've finished editing and adding stuff to your Web page, follow these steps to get it on the Web.

1. **From the Create Web page Activity panel, click Next and then click the button labeled Post It to Web Page.**

   The Post Web Page Activity panel appears.
2. **Select your Web Service Profile from the drop-down list if you already have a profile, or click the Profiles button and then New (in the Activity panel that appears) to create a new profile.**

   Your Internet service provider must provide you with a profile (which includes settings and specifications) to post your page on the Web. If a profile doesn't appear in the drop-down list, click the New button to access a series of Activity panels needed to create a profile. You must provide a user or login name and a password and then select your Web service from a drop-down list. If your Web service isn't listed, you must contact the Internet service provider to obtain the Web service's FTP address, Web page directory, and Web address to enter in the text field of the Web Profile Activity panel.

You can also send your Web page as an e-mail by clicking the Send as E-Mail button in the Post Web page Activity panel.

Making your own animated files

Now here's something really exciting! PhotoSuite 4 lets you create and edit animated images using something called .GIF files. You can even import animated files from the Web. A colleague of mine used PhotoSuite 4 to nab an image of a planet with satellites orbiting it, and used the PhotoSuite 4 .GIF editor to colorize the satellites. I plan to take the whole thing one step further and replace the satellites with images of human faces when I knock off work today. This feature is so extraordinarily sophisticated, but no more difficult to use than an editing feature on a word processing program.

GIF or take

A .GIF file is a special file that brings an animation to a Web page. You can create your own animated .GIF file using several photos or frames within a single file. When the file is viewed on a Web browser, it runs sort of like a multiframe cartoon.

The best photos to combine into a .GIF file are the ones that convey motion to begin with. For example, try taking a series of photos of someone opening a gift and expressing surprise and delight. Or capture the essence of a great practical joke. And by all means, don't forget to scour the Web for animated images, which you can simply drag and drop into PhotoSuite 4.

GIF'ing your files some animation

Photos of a moving scene taken in quick succession "GIF" you the best results. You can also drag and drop an existing .GIF image from any page on the Web, just as you would any old boring, still image. (See Chapter 6, "Getting That Slippery Photo Where Your Want It," for a refresher on the old drag-and-drop maneuver.) When you've successfully imported the image into PhotoSuite 4, use the .GIF editor as you would for any other PhotoSuite 4 .GIF image; here's how to create and edit your own animated GIF file:

1. **Click the Share button on the Navigation bar.**

   The Save & Share Activity panel appears.

2. **Click the Create Web Items button on the Activity panel.**

   Another Activity panel appears.

3. **Click the Animated GIF button and then click the Create New Animated GIF button on the following Activity panel.**

   An Activity panel appears with height and width fields representing the dimensions of the .GIF you want to create.

4. **Enter the height and width dimensions you want for the .GIF file and click OK.**

   The Edit Animated GIF Activity panel appears.

5. **Click the Add button to add the photos to your .GIF file.**

   An Activity panel appears for you to browse for the image files you want to use in your .GIF.

   If you add a file that is a different size than the other images, an Activity panel appears which gives you the option of either cropping the photo to reduce the size or rescaling it.

6. **If you want to add transitions (which are effects that occur when you proceed from one frame to the next), Shift+Click on two adjacent photos and then click the Create Transition button.**

   You must select two adjacent photos by Shift+Click-ing them to make the Create Transition button active.

   The Transition effect frames are inserted between the .GIF photos. The Activity panel offers you a drop-down menu of different transition effects such as sliding, wiping, and spiraling.

7. **Use the options in the Edit Animated GIF Activity panel to delete frames from your .GIF, play back your .GIF, save your .GIF file, or Create a Web page with the .GIF.**

8. **Click the Playback button to view your .GIF.**

   An Activity panel appears, which allows you to indicate whether you want to replay the GIF continuously or a specific number of times. You can use the controls on the Command bar to Play and Pause your animation.

9. **Click Return when you're finished to Exit the Edit Animated GIF Activity panel.**

To control the duration of time that an individual .GIF frame is viewed, select the frame and click the Frame Duration button. An Activity panel appears that allows you to control the number of seconds the frame is viewed.

To edit a particular photo within a .GIF:

1. **Select the photo and click the Edit Frame button.**

   The Prepare screen and all the Editing options are launched.

2. **Edit the photo using all the available PhotoSuite 4 editing tools.**

   You have been taken to the editing section of the program.

3. **To return to the Edit Animated GIF Activity panel, click the Share button on the Navigation bar, then click Create Web Items, then click Animated GIF, and finally click Edit Current Animated GIF to get back to the editing panel from which your started.**

Plain-Vanilla Printing

Not a new and exciting topic — but one that bears a mention in any chapter called "Graphics on the Go."

Printing your photos couldn't be simpler with PhotoSuite 4. Just follow these steps:

1. **Open the photo you want to print and click the Print button on the Navigation bar.**

   A preview of the photo appears on your screen the way it will be printed.

   Chapter 5 tells you how to open photos from all sources, if you need a refresher.

2. **Click Print in the Activity Panel.**
3. **If you have more than one printer, select the one you'll be using from the drop-down menu.**
4. **Click the Nudging button if you want to manually adjust the position of the photo for printing.**

   The photo is nudged, or moved, in increments of 1⁄32 of an inch.

5. **Select a print size.**

   You can select specific dimensions or select the Fit to Page option from the drop-down menu.

6. **Select an orientation — Portrait or Landscape.**

   Portrait means that the longest side of the paper is vertical, whereas Landscape means that the long side in horizontal.

7. **If your project has more than one page, indicate whether you want to print one page or multiple pages.**
8. **Click Print.**

Chapter 16 tells you how to print multiple copies of smaller objects, such as business cards, on one page.

The quality of your paper can greatly enhance the quality of your printed image, making it appear sharper and more vivid.

Sending Your Photos to the Kodak Lab

Sometimes the quality of home printing just isn't satisfactory. You need a real photography lab at your disposal.

Those clairvoyant creators of PhotoSuite 4 have foreseen this possibility and have included the capability for you to upload photos to Kodak PhotoNet Online. Kodak PhotoNet Online lets you send your photos to a *real* lab for high-quality reprints, enlargements, and gift items.

To send your photos to the Kodak lab:

1. **Open the photo project or album you want to load.**
2. **Click the Print button on the Navigation bar.**
3. **Click Print to PhotoNet Online to access the Kodak PhotoNet Online Web page and place your order.**

Chapter 14

Say "Cheese!" Family Albums, Slide Shows, and Screen Savers

In This Chapter

- Organizing your photos into albums
- Creating a slide show extravaganza
- Repapering your Windows desktop
- Creating spectacular screen savers

What good is a photo (or anything else) if you can't find it when you want it? Fortunately, PhotoSuite 4 doesn't fail you here. It provides remarkably efficient database systems — called albums — for organizing, retrieving, and displaying photos.

You can create digital albums that never yellow, tear, or mildew. Then you can produce your own slide shows, complete with sound effects, to display the contents of your albums. You can even create wallpaper for your Windows desktop to show off your favorite photo every time you boot up.

Creating Albums

Albums are the databases of PhotoSuite 4. They allow you to systematically organize your photos so that you can access and retrieve them later. PhotoSuite 4 maintains shortcuts to your photos in the form of thumbnails, which are postage stamp replicas of the full-size photos. You can view the thumbnail shortcuts in the album at any time, and simply click them to retrieve the actual photos.

You can also use albums to store and save sound and video files that you take with your digital camera and open into PhotoSuite 4 using the same steps described in this chapter for still photos.

Looking at photos in albums

Whenever you add a photo to an album, the thumbnail is automatically created for it. Thumbnails are stored inside the album, side by side. The thumbnail is a shortcut to the image file, sort of like an icon on your desktop.

When you want to view a photo, double-click its thumbnail. The Prepare screen appears on your desktop, with the image file displayed in the Workspace.

It's important to remember that thumbnails are shortcuts to an image file and not an actual image file. If you remove the actual image file from your computer, you get an error message when you click the thumbnail; the message tells you that PhotoSuite 4 can't access the image file. For example, if you remove the floppy disk on which the file is located, you won't be able to access the photo by clicking its thumbnail.

Viewing the master album

The albums that you create in PhotoSuite 4 are stored within a Master Album. The Master Album isn't a photo album — it doesn't contain any photos. It's actually a list of other albums you create. Each time you create a new album, its name shows up on the Master Album list.

To view a list of albums on your computer using the Master Album list:

1. **Click the Organize button on the Navigation bar.**

   The Organize screen and Activity panel appear, as shown in Figure 14-1.

2. **Click the Albums button on the Activity panel.**

   The Master Album Activity panel, containing a list of albums maintained in the Master Album, appears, as shown in Figure 14-2.

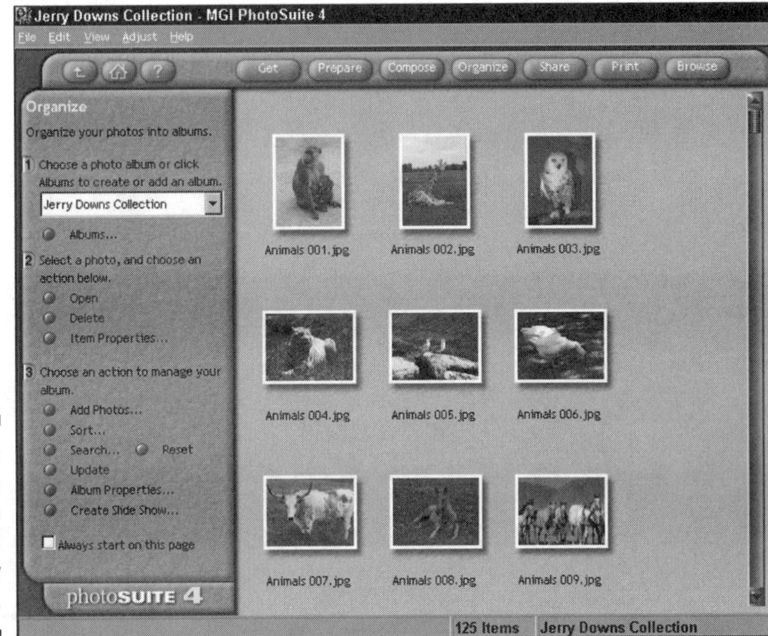

Figure 14-1: The Organize screen and Activity panel.

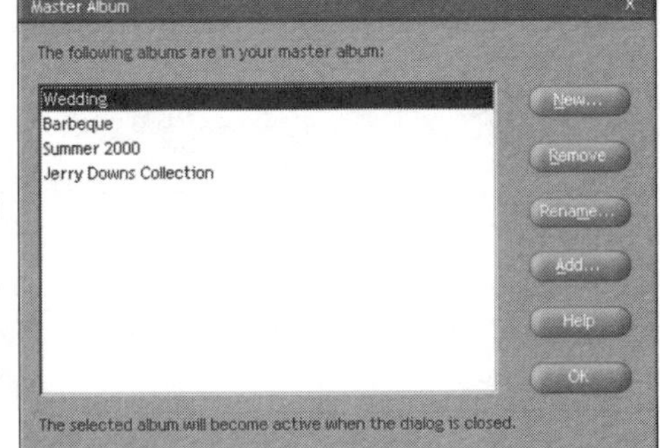

Figure 14-2: The Master Album Activity panel.

Creating and removing albums

You can create as many albums as you need to conveniently organize and store all your photo themes. After an album is created, you can add photos and mulimedia files to it.

To create a new album, follow these steps:

1. **Click the Organize button on the Navigation bar.**

   The Organize screen and Activity panel appear.

2. **Click the Albums button on the Activity panel.**

   The Master Album Activity panel, containing a list of Albums maintained in the Master Album, appears.

3. **In the Master Album Activity panel, click the New button.**

   The New Album Activity panel appears, as shown in Figure 14-3.

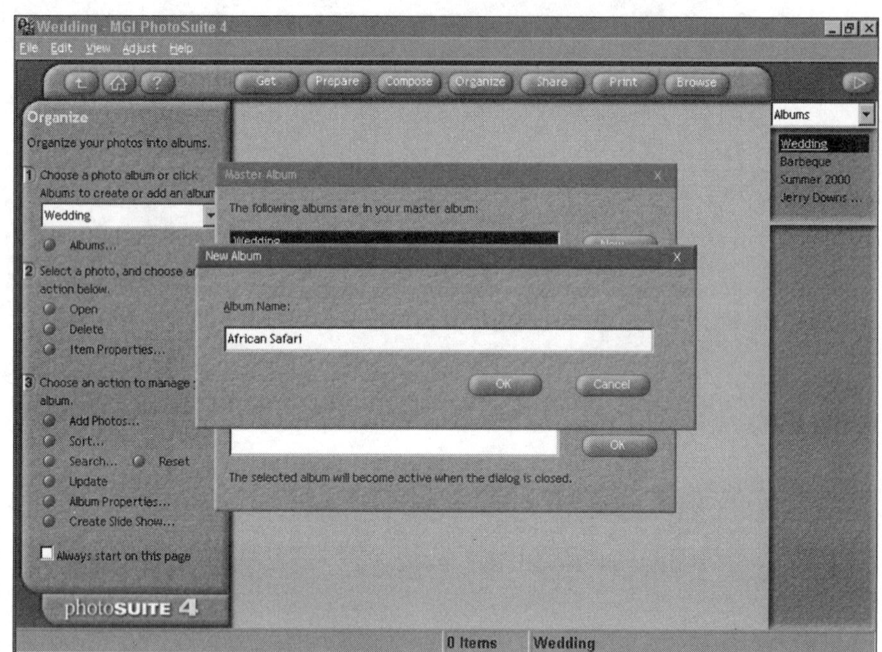

Figure 14-3: Name a new album.

4. **Enter a name for your new album in the New Album Activity panel; then click OK.**

To remove an album from the Master Album list:

1. **Click the Organize button on the Navigation bar.**

   The Organize screen and Activity panel appear.

2. **Click the Albums button on the Activity panel.**

   The Master Album Activity panel, containing a list of Albums maintained in the Master Album, appears.

3. **In the Activity panel, select the name of the album you want to remove and then click the Remove button.**

   If you've made changes to the album, you're prompted to save the changes first.

If you remove an album from a Master list, it's not deleted from your computer. You can add it back at any time, using the steps in the next section for adding an existing album. To completely remove an album from your system, go to C:/My Documents/MGI/PhotoSuite 4/Albums/ and delete the album file.

Adding an existing album to the Master Album list

Maybe you have an album of compromising pictures that you don't want anyone to know about. If so, you can delete this album from the Master Album list, using the steps in the previous section. That way, no one knows it's there because it doesn't appear on the list of available albums. When *you* want to access it, you can add it back to the Master Album list by following these steps:

1. **Click the Organize button on the Navigation bar.**

   The Organize screen and Activity panel appear (refer back to Figure 14-1).

2. **Click the Albums button on the Activity panel.**

   The Master Album Activity panel, containing a list of Albums currently in the Master Album list, appears (refer back to Figure 14-2).

3. **Click the Add button in the Master Album Activity panel.**

   An Activity panel appears, from which you may browse and select a file.

When you're working in the Master List Activity panel, you use the New button for creating an album, whereas you use the Add button for adding an existing album to the Master Album list.

Renaming albums

Renaming an album is no different than renaming any other file. Follow these steps to do it:

1. **Click the Organize button on the Navigation bar.**

   The Organize screen and Activity panel appear.

2. **Click the Albums button on the Activity panel.**

   The Master Album Activity panel, containing a list of albums, appears.

3. **In the Activity panel, select the name of the album you want to rename and then click the Rename button.**

   The Rename Activity panel appears.

4. **Type a new name for the album in the Rename field provided; then click OK.**

   The album now appears in the Master Album list with its spiffy new name.

Adding photos and other graphics files

You can add to your albums indefinitely, the only limitation being the available space on your computer. To add photos and other graphics files to your album, follow these steps:

1. **Click the Organize button on the Navigation bar.**

   The Organize screen and Activity panel appear.

2. **Click the Albums button on the Activity panel.**

   The Master Album Activity panel, containing a list of Albums maintained in the Master Album, appears.

3. **In the Activity panel, select the name of the album to which you want to add a photo, project, sound file, or video file and double-click to open it.**

   The thumbnails from the album you've selected appear on your desktop.

4. **To add the photo(s) you want, do one of the following:**

   - Drag each thumbnail from the Library to the album you've selected.
   - From the Activity panel, click the Add button to view a list of sources you can use to obtain photos.
   - If you need a refresher on how to get photos from any of these sources, flip back to Chapter 5, "Where Do Little Images Come From?"
   - From the File menu, Select Add Photos and browse the Activity panel shown in Figure 14-4. Select a photo and click Open to add it.

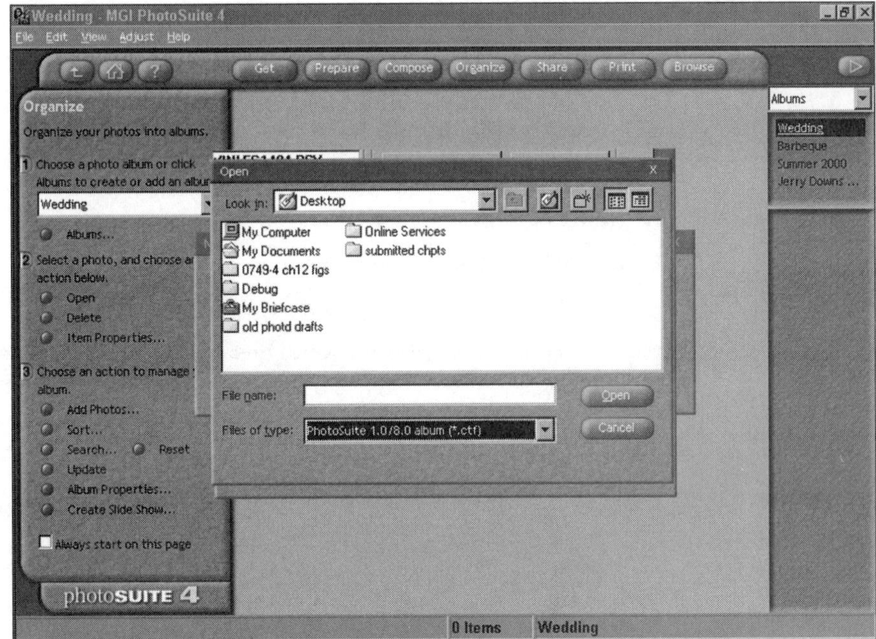

Figure 14-4: You can browse your computer drives to add a photo.

Assigning properties to albums and photos

Properties are characteristics of a file or album that you can modify or, in some cases, assign. These properties affect how the albums are displayed and how photos are sorted and referenced.

Assigning properties to whole albums

Albums have the following two properties associated with them that you can modify:

- **Thumbnail size:** The size of the thumbnails displayed for your album (the smaller the thumbnail, the larger the number of them that can be simultaneously displayed on your desktop).
- **Text mode:** If you select None, your album displays thumbnails only. Selecting Label displays the photo's filename below the thumbnail, and Full Text displays the file's full name and path.

To view and modify the entire album:

1. **Click the Organize button on the Navigation bar.**

   The Organize screen and Activity panel appear.

2. **Click Album Properties on the Activity panel.**

   The Album Properties Activity panel, shown in Figure 14-5, appears.

3. **Click one of the sample thumbnails in the Album Properties Activity panel to set the thumbnail size for the album.**

4. **Select one of the following text modes:**

   - **None:** Displays no text
   - **Label:** Displays the filename only
   - **Full Text:** Displays the photo's full filename and path

5. **Click OK to close the Album Properties Activity panel and save the changes you've made.**

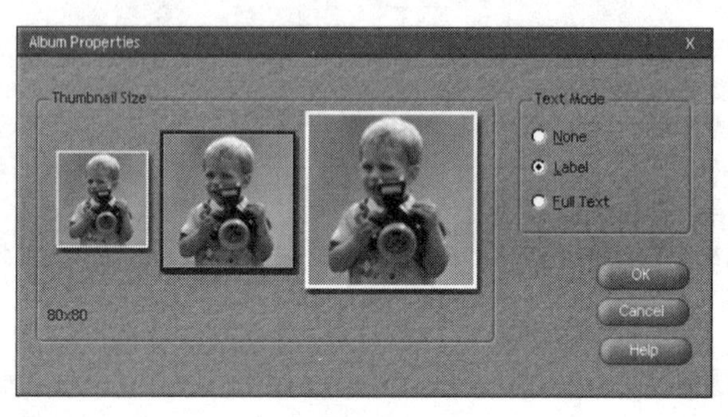

Figure 14-5: Modify album properties using this Activity panel.

Assigning properties to individual photos

You can save a surprising amount of information about a photo using properties settings. The properties information can be used for sorting, retrieving, and accessing the photos, as discussed in the next section, "Sorting your thumbnails."

You can use the Item Properties Activity panel, shown in Figure 14-6, to provide information about each of the following properties of individual photos:

- **Title:** Provide the name of the photo.
- **Author**, **Owner:** Provide the name of the photo's creator or owner.
- **Aperture, Shutter Speed, Lens, Filter, Camera:** Document the type of equipment and settings used to take the photo (see Chapters 3 and 4 for more information about these properties).
- **Comments, Description, Category, Event, Department, Place, People in the Photo:** Include additional information you want to include about the photo.
- **Copyright:** Include information about any copyright protection you've obtained here (see a lawyer about this one).

- **Keywords:** Supply words you want to use in any search to access, retrieve, or sort the file.
- **Rating:** Assign ratings to your photos based on any criteria you can dream up.
- **Sound:** Assign a sound file to a photo by clicking the Browse button and selecting a sound file from the Activity panel.

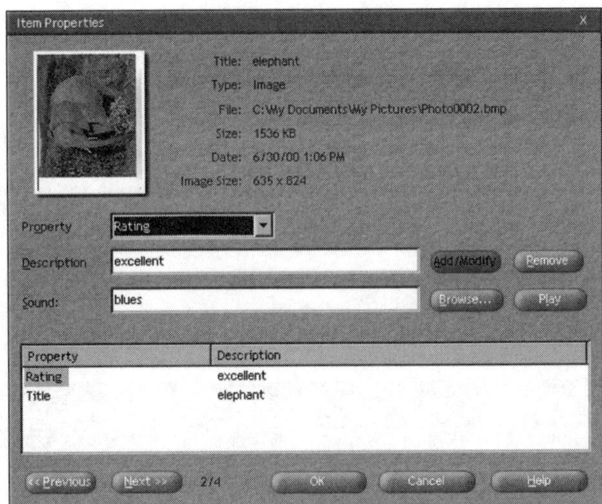

Figure 14-6: The Item Properties Activity panel.

To access the Item Properties Activity panel and assign properties to a photo, follow these steps:

1. **Click the Organize button on the Navigation bar.**

   The Organize screen and Activity panel appear.

2. **Click the Albums button on the Activity panel.**

   The Master Album Activity panel, containing a list of Albums maintained in the Master Album, appears.

3. **In the Activity panel, double-click the album you want open to rename; click the Rename button.**

   The thumbnails for that album appear on your desktop.

4. **Select the thumbnail for the photo you want to open and click the Item Properties button on the Activity panel.**

   The Item Properties Activity panel appears.

5. **In the Property field, select an attribute from the drop-down menu.**

   Some of these attributes are used for the Sort and Search commands discussed in this chapter in "Sorting your thumbnails."

6. **Type a text description for the attribute you've selected in the Description field; then click Add/Modify to enter the text.**

   The descriptive information you've entered is associated with the photo and is summarized in the table at the bottom of the Item Property Activity panel.

7. **If you want to assign a prerecorded sound to the photo, click the Browse button, select a sound file, and open it.**

   The sound file you've opened in the Browse Activity panel will play every time the photo is opened. (You can preview the sound by clicking the Play button.)

8. **Click Previous or Next to go to another photo in the album and assign properties to it.**

9. **Click OK to save the changes you've made and exit the Properties Activity panel.**

You can right-click a thumbnail on your desktop and select Properties from the menu displayed, as shown in Figure 14-7.

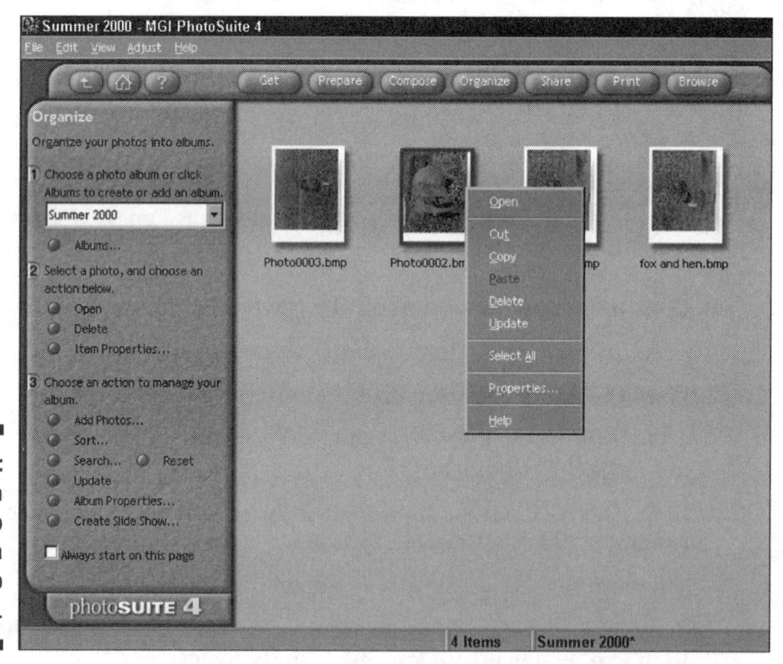

Figure 14-7: Right-click a thumbnail to access a pop-up menu.

Sorting your thumbnails

Albums wouldn't be very effective as databases if you couldn't sort their contents or update them, would they?

You can sort the photos and thumbnails within an album using most of the criteria you assigned to individual photos as properties in the previous section. Here are a few examples of ways you might choose to sort your thumbnails:

- **File Name:** Sorts in ascending or descending order if you've assigned a number to your file, or in alphabetical order if you've used words to name them.
- **File Size:** Sorts in ascending or descending order according to image file size.
- **File Date:** Sorts files chronologically in ascending or descending order.
- **Title:** Sorts in ascending or descending alphabetical order.
- **People in the Photo:** Sorts photos alphabetically by names of the people you've identified as being in the photo.

Here's how to sort the contents of an album:

1. **Click the Organize button on the Navigation bar.**

   The Organize screen and Activity panel appear.
2. **Click the Sort button on the Activity panel.**

   The Sort Activity panel, shown in Figure 14-8, appears.
3. **Select a file property that you want to use for the sorting process from the drop-down menu in the Sort Activity panel.**
4. **Select either Ascending or Descending as your sorting method.**
5. **Click OK to close the Sort Activity panel.**

   PhotoSuite 4 sorts the files according to the criteria you've specified.

You can also re-order thumbnails by dragging and dropping them to their new location.

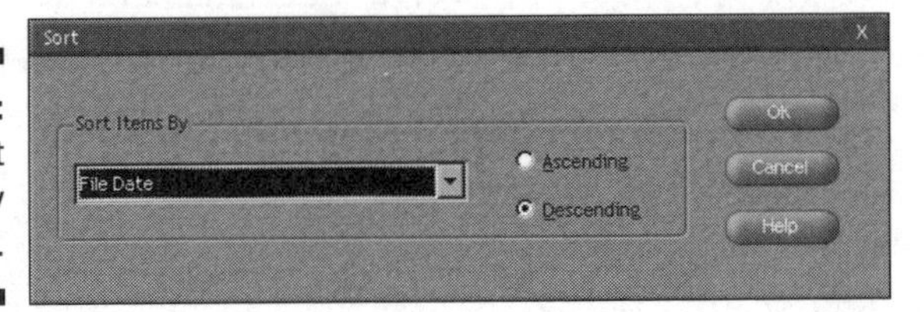

Figure 14-8: The Sort Activity panel.

Changing the thumbnails when you change the photos

When you edit a photo, its album thumbnail isn't updated automatically. To have the thumbnail reflect the changes you've made to a photo, you need to do the following:

1. **Click the Organize button on the Navigation bar.**

   The Organize screen and Activity panel appear (refer back to Figure 14-1).

2. **Click the Albums button on the Activity panel.**

   The Master Album Activity panel, containing a list of Albums maintained in the Master Album, appears.

3. **Double-click the album that contains the photo you want to update from the Master Album list.**

   Thumbnails representing all the photos contained in the album appear on your desktop.

4. **Select the thumbnail you want to update and click Update on the Activity panel.**

   PhotoSuite 4 updates the thumbnail to reflect any changes you've made to the actual photo.

Searching for a particular photo in an album

The success of any organizational system lies in how well it works when you try to find something. Fortunately, the PhotoSuite 4 album system measures up pretty well. To search for a particular photo in an album:

1. **Click the Organize button on the Navigation bar.**

   The Organize screen and Activity panel appear.

2. **Click the Search button on the Activity panel.**

   The Search Activity panel, shown in Figure 14-9, appears.

3. **In the Search In field, select the property you want to search from the drop-down menu.**

   This information narrows your search to the specified properties.

4. **Enter a value in the Search For field.**

   The value is the search criteria. For example, you might select the file date as your search property in Step 3, and then enter **June 1, 2000** as the specific value in the Search For field. This would accomplish a search for all photos bearing the date of June 1, 2000, based on a review of the dates on all the image files.

5. **Click OK to begin the search.**

   The search may take several minutes. PhotoSuite 4 either returns a photo meeting your search criteria, or lets you know that it was unable to locate an image file meeting your specifications.

Figure 14-9: The Search Activity panel.

Boring 'Em with a Slide Show

Slide shows are a great way to unveil your photos to an admiring (or politely disinterested) crowd. You can present them in chronological order or according to a theme. You can even add sound effects for real showmanship.

Slide shows have an advantage over videotape because you can allow just the right amount of time for the audience to examine and admire particular photos. You can regulate the amount of time each slide appears on-screen — something you can't do with a video without pausing it frequently.

Creating a slide show

Despite their bad rap, slide shows need not be boring. By regulating the duration that the slides appear on-screen and the length of the transitions, and by adding sound effects, you can actually create a fairly fascinating visual experience — provided that you keep the boring monologue to a minimum.

You can create a slide show either directly from an existing album or by adding photos from many different sources. Depending on which option you select, the PhotoSuite 4 interface for creating your slide show looks very different.

Creating a slide show from an album

To create a slide show from an existing album:

1. **Click the Share button on the Navigation bar.**

   The Share screen and Activity panel appear.

2. **Click the Slide Show button on the Activity.**

   Another Activity Panel appears.

3. **Click the Create from Album button on the Activity panel displayed.**

   The Create Slide Show Activity panel and screen appear, as shown in Figure 14-10.

Figure 14-10: Create a slide show from an existing album.

4. **Select an album from the drop-down menu.**

   Thumbnails for the album you've selected appear on your desktop.

5. **Select each of the specific photos you want to add, or click the Select All button to add all the photos in the album simultaneously.**

   Use the Select All button to select all the photos, or the Shift and Ctrl key simultaneously to select multiple files.

6. **Choose a default Transition from the drop-down menu.**

   A *transition* is what appears on your screen in between slides. Table 14-1, which appears later in this chapter, summarizes the different types of transitions available to you.

PhotoSuite 4 uses Cut as the default transition between each photo. (I tell you how to change the transitions individually in the section "Editing your slide show.")

7. **Click Create.**

   The New Slide Show Activity panel appears, as shown in Figure 14-11, prompting you to specify a name and other properties you've created.

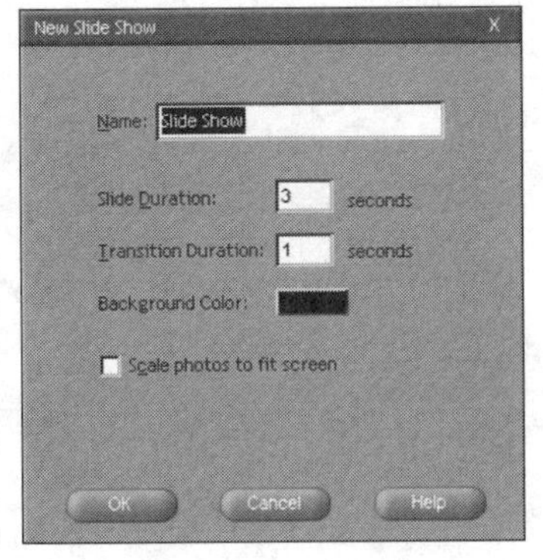

Figure 14-11: Assign Properties to a new slide show using this Activity panel.

8. **Enter a name for the Slide Show in the Name field.**

   Your slide show photos, transitions, and other settings and properties are stored in a file with this name.

9. **Enter a value in the Slide Duration field.**

   This is the number of seconds each photo slide appears on your screen.

10. **Enter a value in the Transition Duration field.**

    This is the number of seconds each transition appears on your screen in between photo slides.

11. **Click the Background Color Activity panel to select a background color for your slide show.**

    The Select Color Activity panel appears, from which you can select a color and then click OK to exit. Chapter 10, "In Color Living," tells you how to adjust and customize colors using this Activity panel.

12. **Select or deselect the Scale photos to fit screen check box.**

    If you select this option, your photos will take up the entire screen and none of the background color you selected in Step 11 appears.

13. **Click OK to save the settings you've selected in the New Slide Show Activity panel.**

    The Edit Slide Show Activity panel and screen, shown in Figure 14-12, appear.

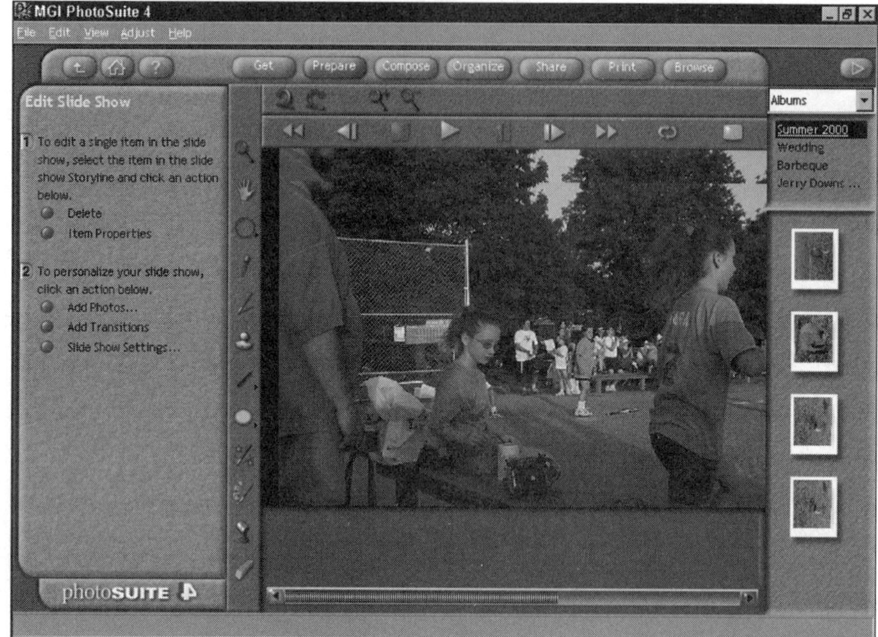

Figure 14-12: Edit slide show properties using this screen.

The Storyline, located at the bottom of screen, displays all the photos included in your slide show, in the order they appear. The Storyline also displays a symbol for each transition (see Table 14-1, later in this chapter). The number of photos in the slide show appears directly below the Storyline.

Creating a slide show from scratch

You can create a slide show from scratch by importing photos one at a time or by taking them from different albums. To create a slide show from scratch, follow these steps:

1. **Click the Share button on the Navigation bar.**

   The Share screen and Activity panel appear.

2. **Click the Slide Show button on the Activity panel.**

   Another Activity Panel appears.

3. **Click the Create from Scratch button on the Activity panel displayed.**

   The New Slide Show Activity panel appears (refer back to Figure 14-11), prompting you to specify a name and other properties for the slide show you've just created.

4. **Enter a name for the Slide Show in the Name field.**

   This is the name for the file containing your slide show photos, transitions, and other settings and properties.

5. **Enter a value in the Slide Duration field.**

   This is the number of seconds each photo slide appears on your screen.

6. **Enter a value in the Transition Duration field.**

   This is the number of seconds each transition appears on your screen in between photo slides.

7. **Click the Background Color Activity panel to select a background color for your slide show.**

   The Select Color Activity panel appears, from which you can select a color and then click OK to exit. Chapter 10 tells you how to adjust and customize colors using this Activity panel.

8. **Select or deselect the check box labeled Scale photos to fit screen.**

   If you select this option, your photos will take up the entire screen and none of the background color you selected in Step 7 appears.

9. **Click OK to save the settings you've selected in the New Slide Show Activity panel.**

   The Edit Slide Show Activity panel and screen (refer back to Figure 14-12) appear.

10. **Click the Add Photos button.**

    The Add Photos Activity panel, shown in Figure 14-13, appears, displaying source options for retrieving the photos you want to include in the slide show from your computer, scanner, or camera.

11. **Click one of the source option buttons (for example, Computer, Digital Camera, Scanner).**

    If you select Computer, an Activity panel appears that allows you to browse the drives on your computer for the photos you want to add. Simply select the photos you want and click Add. If you're adding a photo using a peripheral, such as your camera or scanner, follow the prompts that appear to add a photo.

    Chapter 5 tells you how to create and access photos using these options.

    When you've completed the process of adding a photo from your computer, scanner, or other peripheral, the Add Photos Activity panel reappears. The photo you've added appears on the Storyline located at the bottom of the screen. Photos appear in the order in which you add them. (You can rearrange the photos later using the steps I tell you about in the section "Editing your slide show.")

You can select multiple photos to add simultaneously if you're adding them from your computer. Simply select multiple files in the Activity panel that appears to enable you to browse for the photos you want; then Click Add.

12. **Click Return to exit the Add Photos Activity panel.**

    The Edit Slide Show Activity panel reappears on your screen.

13. **Click Add Transitions.**

    The Add Transitions Activity panel, shown in Figure 14-14, appears.

14. **Using your mouse, drag a transition from the Library on the left side of your screen to each transition slot on the Storyline.**

    The default transition is Cut, for which one slide is instantly replaced with the next. Table 14-1, appearing later in this chapter, summarizes the transitions types available to you.

15. **Click Return when you're through adding transitions.**

    The Edit Slide Show Activity panel reappears on your screen.

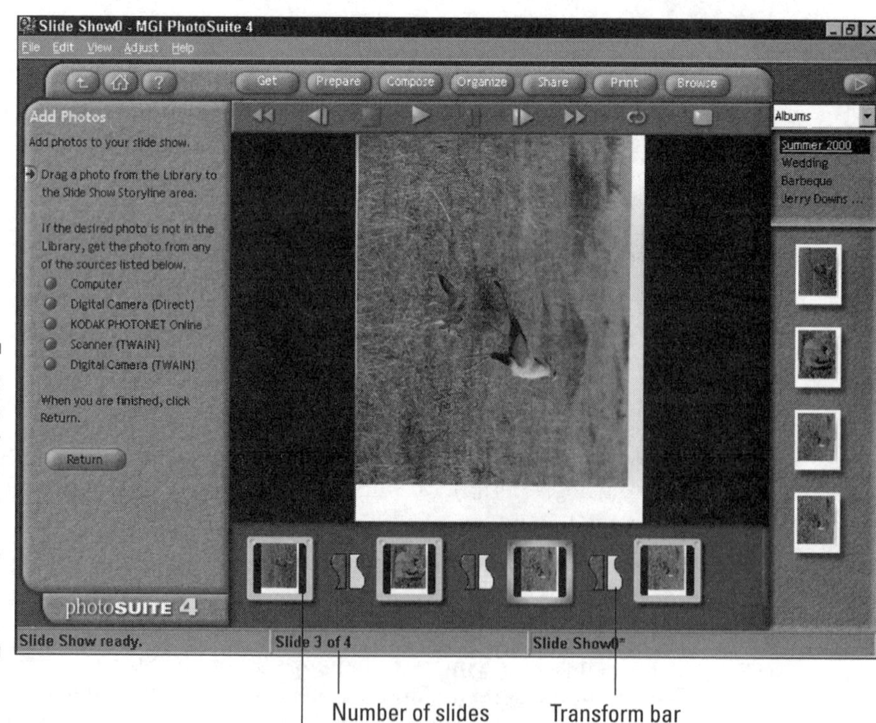

Figure 14-13: Use this Activity panel to add photos to create a slide show from scratch.

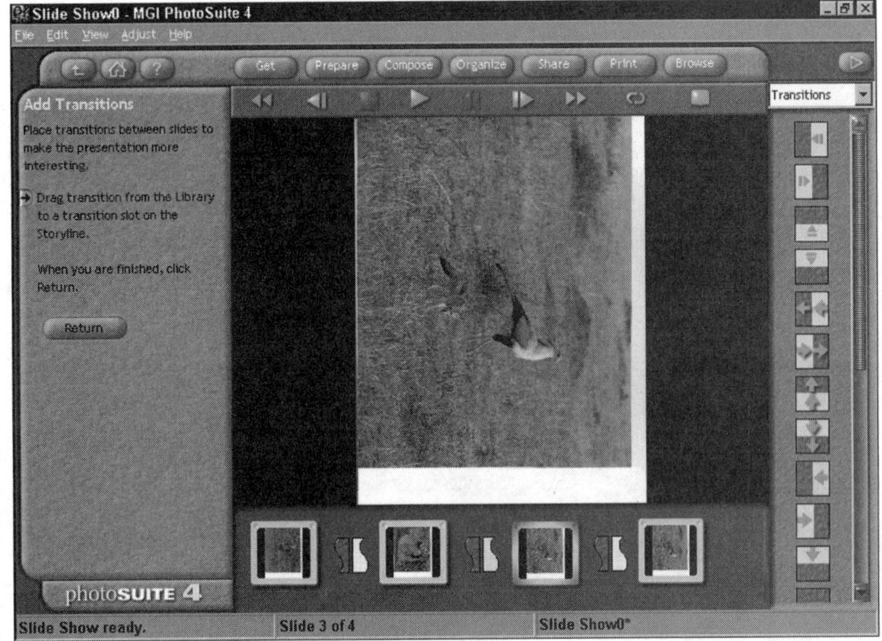

Figure 14-14: Add transitions using this Activity panel.

Editing your slide show

You're not only the director and producer with PhotoSuite 4; you're the editor.

To edit a slide show after you've created it, click the Edit and Play button on the Slide Show Activity panel (refer back to Figure 14-12). You can perform the following editing functions on this screen:

- **Delete slides and/or transitions:** Select the item in the Storyline and then click the Delete button on the Activity panel.
- **Rearrange slides and transitions:** Simply drag them to their new positions.
- **Add photos to the Storyline:** Click the Add Photos button to access the Add Photos Activity panel.
- **Add transitions between photos on the Storyline:** Click the Add Transitions button to access the Add Transitions Activity panel.

Changing slide show and photo properties

Slide show properties affect many aspects of how a slide show is seen and heard on your screen. Some settings must be modified en masse for every slide in the show. Others can be modified either for individual slides or for the whole show.

Changing properties for the whole show

In creating your slide show, you want to pay careful attention to the default settings for the Slide Show – Properties Activity panel, shown in Figure 14-15, because these are the default settings for all the photos and transitions in your slide show.

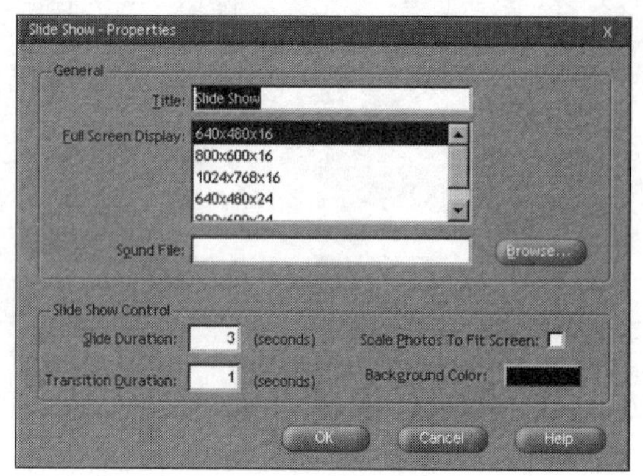

Figure 14-15: Use this Activity panel to modify the properties for your entire slide show.

To access the Slide Show Properties Activity panel:

1. **Click the Share button on the Navigation bar.**

   The Share screen and Activity panel appear.

2. **Click the Slide Show button on the Activity panel.**

   Another Activity panel appears.

3. **Click the Edit and Play button on the Activity panel displayed.**

   The Edit Slide Show Activity panel appears.

4. **Click the Slide Show Settings button.**

   The Slide Show – Properties Activity panel appears.

5. **Modify the following settings:**

   - **Title:** This is the name of your Slide Show file.
   - **Full Screen Display:** This is the size at which photos appear if you view them in Full screen mode (discussed in the section "The big premier: Playing a slide show.")

If you plan to run the slide show full-screen on your monitor, choosing a *lower* resolution enlarges the images; choosing a *higher* resolution keeps the images smaller.

- **Sound File:** You can select a sound file to play in the background for the entire slide show or just for individual files. You can even add a sound to be played for a specific file in addition to the background sound — both sound files play at one time. Click the Browse button to browse for and test the available sound files; click the Open button to add a sound file for the entire show.
- **Slide Duration:** Enter the number of seconds you want a slide to appear on your screen. You can change the duration for a single slide using the Item Properties Activity panel.
- **Transition Duration:** Enter the number of seconds you want each transition to appear on your screen.
- **Scale Photos To Fit Screen:** Select this check box if you want your photos to fit the entire screen. If you don't select it, smaller photos won't fill the screen.
- **Background Color:** Click this field to access the Select Color Activity panel, which allows you to pick a color for the background of your slide show.

6. **Click OK to exit the Slide Show Properties Activity panel when you're finished modifying the settings.**

Changing properties for just one slide

To access the Item Properties Activity panel for an individual slide, simply select and right-click the slide in the Storyline; then select Item Properties from the pop-up menu. Alternatively, you can click the Item Properties button on the Edit Properties Activity panel.

You can access and modify the following properties for an individual slide using the Activity panel shown in Figure 14-16:

- **Duration:** Enter the number of seconds you want a slide to appear on your screen. You can change the duration for a single slide using the Item Properties Activity panel.
- **Sound file:** To add a sound file for a single photo, right-click the photo and select Slide Show – Item Properties from the pop-up menu. An Item properties Activity panel appears. Click the Browse button and select a sound to accompany the particular slide by opening it.

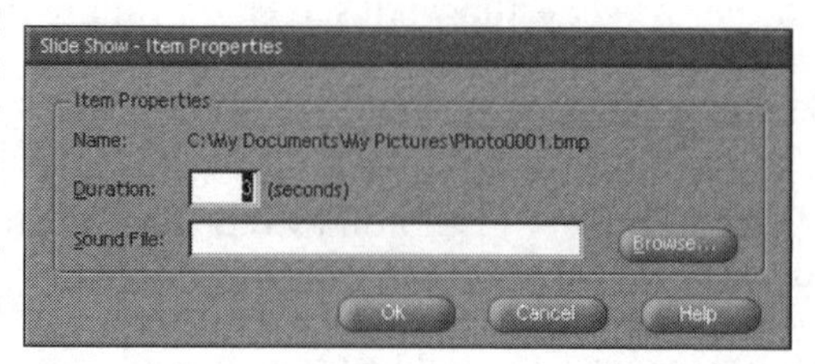

Figure 14-16: Use this Activity panel to change settings for a single slide.

The big premiere: Playing a slide show

Viewing a slide show is as easy as clicking your mouse to start it. You can sit back and enjoy the premier, or you can use the Playback controls to enhance the viewing experience.

The Playback controls appear at the top of the edit screen. To access them, click the Edit and Play button on the Slide Show control panel. Here's a list of the controls available to you:

- **First Slide:** Click this button to go back to the very first slide in the presentation at any time during the viewing of the slide show.
- **Previous Slide:** Oops! Did the slide advance before you got a good look? Click this button to go back to the preceding slide.
- **Stop:** Hold the show! You can stop the show at any time by clicking this button. The slide that was playing when you pressed this button remains on your screen.
- **Play:** Plays the show from the beginning or, if it was stopped, resumes where you left off.
- **Last Slide:** If your audience is really bored or hostile, you can click this option to advance to the very last slide of the presentation.
- **Loop:** Plays the show repeatedly in a continuous loop until someone mercifully presses the Stop or Pause button.
- **Full Screen:** Displays the show full screen on your monitor. You can't access the Playback commands while you're in this option. You need to press the Esc key on your keyboard to get out of this option and return to the standard display so that you can access the Playback commands.

Table 14-1 Types of Slide Show Transitions

Symbols	*Description*
	Wipe left (the wipe transitions give a smooth wiping effect)
	Wipe right
	Wipe up
	Wipe down
	Push left (The push effects make the photo appear pushed off the screen)
	Push right
	Push up
	Push down
	Cover left (the cover effects make the photo look obscured, as if covered)
	Cover right
	Cover top
	Cover bottom
	Cover top left
	Cover top right
	Cover bottom left
	Cover bottom right

(continued)

Table 14-1 *(continued)*

Symbols	*Description*
	Box out (A box radiates from the center and obscures the photo)
	Box in (The photo is obscured by a border that appears to move inward)
	Mosaic (A mosaic effect obscures the photo)

Making Wallpaper and Screen Savers

Some photos deserve the most prominent place of display, where they can be viewed and appreciated as much as possible. And what could be a more frequented location than your computer desktop?

PhotoSuite 4 gives you the option of immortalizing your loved ones as Windows desktop wallpaper or as screen savers. *Wallpaper* is what appears on your Windows desktop every time you turn on your computer, whereas screen savers appear when the program you're using is idle for a few minutes.

Wallpapering the desktop

To use a favorite photo as wallpaper for your Windows desktop:

1. **Open the photo you want to use as wallpaper.**

   Chapter 5 tells you how to open a photo if you need a refresher. The photo appears in your PhotoSuite 4 Work area after you've opened it.

2. **Click the Share button on the Navigation bar.**

   The Share screen and Activity panel appear.

3. **Click the Windows Desktop button on the Activity panel.**

   Another Activity panel appears.

4. **Click the Set Photo as Wallpaper button on the Activity panel displayed.**

   Your photo is now the wallpaper for your Windows desktop, and proudly appears whenever you turn on your computer.

Saving screens stylishly

To use a cherished photo as a screen saver, you must first save it to an album. Then you can access it to create the screen saver. Follow these steps:

1. **Open the photo album that contains the photo you want to use as a screen saver.**

   Earlier along in this chapter, in "Looking at photos in albums," I tell you how to open albums and access the photos they contain. (Hightail it back to that section of the chapter if you've forgotten how.)

   The photo appears in your PhotoSuite 4 Work area after you've opened it.

2. **Click the Share button on the Navigation bar.**

   The Share screen and Activity panel appear.

3. **Click the Create Album Screen Saver button on the Activity panel.**

   The Album Screen Saver Activity panel appears.

4. **Specify the following settings in the Album Screen Saver Activity panel:**

   - **Show preview:** Select this check box to see a preview of your screen saver in the Album Screen Saver Activity panel.
   - **Select Albums to play:** Select the albums that contain photos you want to use in your screen saver.
   - **How many photos to show before wipe:** Specify how many photos you want to appear on the screen before it's wiped clean. The screen saver displays the photos in the order they appear in the albums unless you select the Display Random Photos option (described later in this list).
   - **Photo size:** Adjust the photos to be displayed as a percentage of the screen size.
   - **Time interval before showing next photo:** Indicate how long you want one photo to appear on the screen before the next photo is displayed.
   - **Use transitions:** Select this box to use random transition types between photos. (You can't specify the type of transitions to be used here — PhotoSuite 4 does this.)
   - **Scale small photos up:** If you select this option, small photos are scaled up to the size specified in the Activity panel.
   - **Center photos:** Use this setting to center your photos on the screen.
   - **Display random photos:** Display photos from the album you've selected for the screen saver in random order.

5. **Click OK to exit the Screen Saver Activity panel.**

Chapter 15

Cheap Gifts and Chic Digital Accessories

In This Chapter

- Brainstorming gift ideas for miserly budgets
- Making everybody a calendar girl
- Creating fake IDs for underage nieces and nephews
- Making sports cards for your fan who has everything
- Creating gift tags, post cards, and other thinking-of-you items

If people really love you, shouldn't they be thrilled to get a likeness of you as a gift? It beats a fruitcake, right? Maybe it depends on your family — and your face.

And certainly you're not limited to creating gift items bearing your own likeness. You can give your loved ones pictures of themselves, their kids, their parents, their pets, or a person they thought they were having a discreet affair with. The possibilities are endless.

Greeting Cards That Really Greet

Hallmark may have a highly paid staff of writers, a massive marketing research department, and great greeting card artists. But there's one thing the company doesn't have — your face.

Pick a card, any card

You can insert your own likeness, or photos of anyone and anything else you choose, in card templates. Your PhotoSuite 4 CD contains the following categories of card templates:

- Birthday
- Christmas
- Easter
- Father's Day
- Miscellaneous
- Mother's Day
- Other Events
- Valentine's Day

Greeting your card

To create a really great greeting card, follow these steps:

1. **Click the Compose button on the Navigation bar.**

   The Compose screen and Activity panel appear.

2. **Click Cards and Tags on the Activity panel.**

   Another Activity panel appears.

3. **Click Greetings.**

   The Greetings Activity panel, shown in Figure 15-1, appears.

4. **Select the category of cards you want from the drop-down menu.**

   Thumbnails of the available greeting card templates for that category appear on your screen.

5. **Select the template that you want to use for your card by double-clicking it.**

   The full-size template appears on your desktop, as shown in Figure 15-2, with a cutout area surrounded by a bounding box.

6. **Drag and drop photos from the Library using your mouse, or Load the photograph that you want to use into PhotoSuite 4 from one of the other sources listed in the Activity panel (such as your computer or scanner).**

   The Library is located on the right side of the screen and contains thumbnail images of all the photos that you can drag and drop. Chapter 5, "Where Do Little Images Come From?," tells you how to load an image into PhotoSuite 4.

   The photo you've selected is automatically resized and dropped into the cutout area of the card. However, you may need to use the blue handles on the bounding box to reposition it.

If you plan to load a photo from your computer, scanner, or camera into the cutout area of the card, select the cutout by clicking it before you import the photo. Otherwise, the full-size photo is dropped on top of your calendar project and obscures the whole template with which you're working.

7. **Repeat the process to add additional photos; then click Next.**
8. **Click Return or Finish to save the photos you've added to the Greeting Card template (see Figure 15-2).**

   The Compose screen reappears on your desktop. You can add text and edit the card as you would any other project on the Compose screen. Chapter 9, "Performing Photo-Surgery," tells you how to add and edit text and add additional props to your greeting card.

9. **Save or print your project.**

   To save your project, go to the file menu and select either Save or Save As to access a Windows dialog box for saving your project. To print your project, click the Print button on the Navigation bar to access the PhotoSuite 4 printing options. (I tell you more about how to print in Chapter 13, "Graphics on the Go.")

Select card category.

Figure 15-1: The Greetings Activity panel.

Figure 15-2: A greeting card template with a photo added.

Giving Calendars for Christmas

Imagine being able to give your girlfriend, boyfriend, or spouse twelve months of *you*. One month smiling, one month scowling . . . what a gift!

With PhotoSuite 4, you can create personalized, professional-looking monthly, quarterly, and seasonal calendars using a wide selection of predefined templates. Just follow these steps:

1. **Click the Compose button on the Navigation bar.**

   The Compose screen and Activity panel appear.

2. **Click Calendars on the Activity panel.**

   Another Activity panel appears with buttons labeled 1-month, Quarterly, and Yearly.

3. **Select a calendar type from the Activity panel (for example, Yearly).**

   The Activity panel shown in Figure 15-3 appears, displaying template options for the calendar type you've selected.

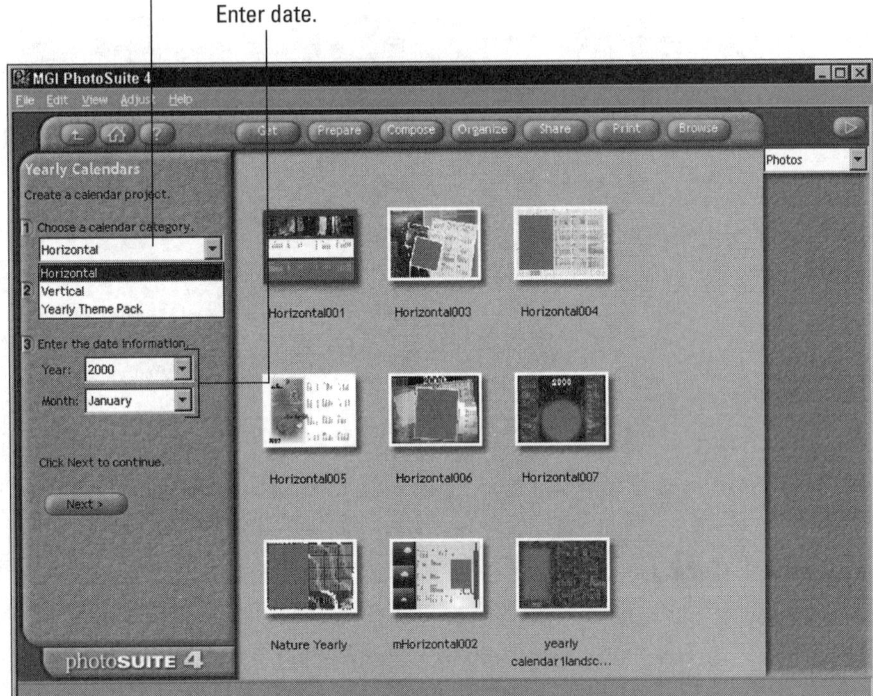

Figure 15-3: Use this Activity panel to create a yearly calendar.

4. **Select either Horizontal or Vertical (or Yearly Theme pack) from the calendar category drop-down menu.**

   Thumbnail pictures of the templates displayed for the calendar option you've selected appear on your desktop.

5. **Select the appropriate date information for your calendar.**

   For example, if you're doing a yearly calendar, indicate the year you want and the month to begin with in the Year and Date fields.

6. **Select one of the templates by clicking it.**

   The template you've selected appears, full size, on your desktop, as shown in Figure 15-4.

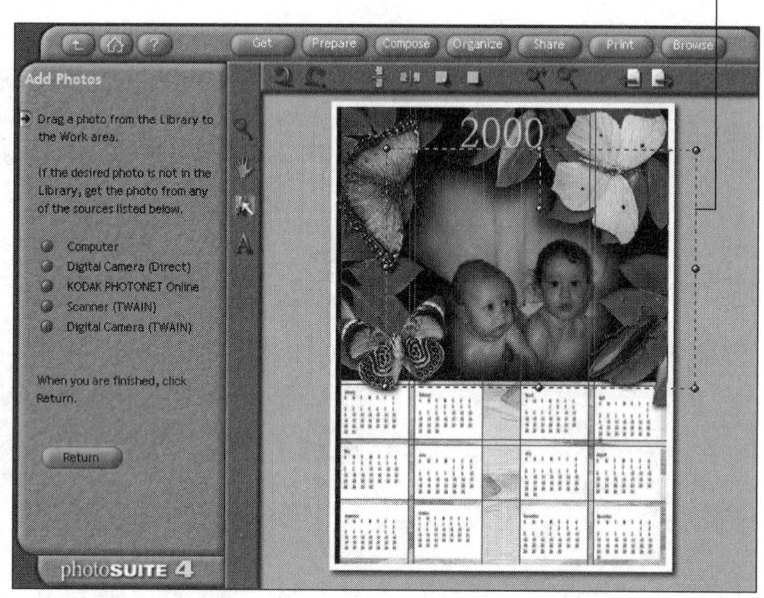

Figure 15-4: Drag and drop or import photos into the calendar template.

7. **Drag and drop or load a photo into the cutout area.**

   You can drag and drop photos from the Library using your mouse. Alternatively, click Next to load the photograph that you want to use into PhotoSuite 4 from one of the other sources listed in the Activity panel appears (such as your computer or scanner).

   The photo appears in the cutout (blank) area of the calendar, surrounded by a bounding box with blue handles.

   If you plan to load a photo from your computer, scanner, or camera into the cutout area of the calendar, select the cutout by clicking it before you import the photo. Otherwise, the full-size photo is dropped on top of your calendar project and obscures the whole template with which you're working.

8. **If necessary, resize, rotate, and reposition the photos by dragging the blue handles that appear on the bounding box around the perimeter of the photo.**

   You can also move a photo to a new position on the template or to a different cutout area simply by dragging and dropping it.

9. **Repeat the process to add additional photos; then click Next.**

10. **Click Return or Finish to save the photos you've added to the Calendar template.**

    The Compose screen reappears on your desktop. You can add text and edit the card as you would any other project on the Compose screen. Chapter 9 tells you how to add and edit text and add additional props to your greeting card.

11. **Save or print your project.**

    To save your project, go to the file menu and select either Save or Save As to access a Windows dialog box for saving your project. To print your project, click the Print button on the Navigation bar to access the PhotoSuite 4 printing options. (I tell you more about how to print in Chapter 13.)

Photos can be placed anywhere on the Calendar template — not just in the cutout area.

Adding Frames, Edges, and Borders

What could be a more perfect gift than a photo of yourself? Why, a framed photo of yourself, of course!

PhotoSuite 4 allows you to create the following complementary effects for your photo:

- **Frames and Edges:** These are templates that have the look of frame. Because they're templates, they can't be resized. Instead, you must resize your photo to fit within the frame.
- **Borders:** These are frame-like effects that fit snugly around the outer edge of any size photo.

Framing the innocent

You can access more than 100 different types of frames with PhotoSuite 4. The frames and borders included on your PhotoSuite 4 installation disk are only the tip of the iceberg. There are a lot *more* to choose from on your Content CD.

Most of the time, you want your viewing public to notice the picture, not the frame. But there are exceptions to this rule. Sometimes it's the frame that makes the picture. A good example of this are the PhotoSuite 4 Alphanumeric frames, which fit your photo into a number or letters symbol, as shown in Figure 15-5. (As you can see, I've chosen *B* for *Baby*).

Figure 15-5: Sometimes it's the frame that makes the picture.

To access and use the full array of PhotoSuite 4 frames, follow these steps:

1. **Click the Compose button on the Navigation bar.**

   The Compose screen and Activity panel appear.

2. **Click Frames & Edges on the Activity panel.**

   The Frames & Edges Activity panel box, shown in Figure 15-6, appears.

3. **Select the category of frame you want from the drop-down menu.**

   Your choices are as follows: Alphanumeric, Classic Frames, Elegant Frames, Funky Frames, Landscape Edges, Portrait Edges, and Shapes.

4. **View the frames available for each category by moving up and down the screen using the scroll bars on the right.**

   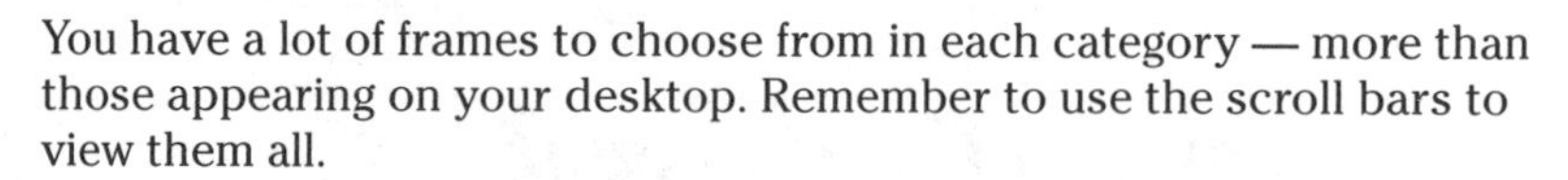
   You have a lot of frames to choose from in each category — more than those appearing on your desktop. Remember to use the scroll bars to view them all.

5. **Select the frame or border template that you want to use for your project by clicking it.**

   The full-size frame or template appears on your desktop (see Figure 15-7).

6. **Drag and drop photos from the Library using your mouse, or click Next to Load the photograph that you want to use into PhotoSuite 4 from one of the other sources listed in the Activity panel (such as your computer or scanner).**

The Library is located on the right side of the screen and contains thumbnail images of all the photos you can drag and drop. Chapter 5 tells you how to load an image into PhotoSuite 4.

The photos you've selected are automatically re-sized to fit and dropped into the center area of the frame or border.

7. **Click Return or Finish to save the photos inside your framed project.**

   The Compose screen reappears on your desktop. You can add text and edit the card as you would any other project on the Compose screen. Chapter 9 tells you how to add and edit text and add additional props to your framed project.

8. **Save or print your project.**

   To save your project, go to the file menu and select either Save or Save As to access a Windows dialog box for saving your project. To print your project, click the Print button on the Navigation bar to access the PhotoSuite 4 printing options. (I tell you more about how to print in Chapter 13.)

Select a frame or edge category.

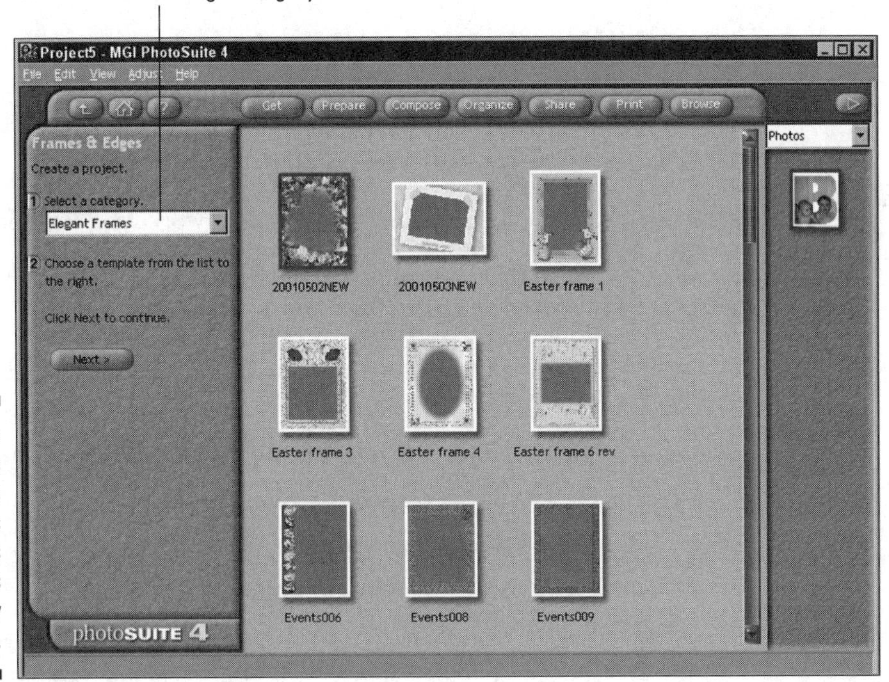

Figure 15-6: Access templates for frames and edges using this Activity panel.

Figure 15-7: Choose your frame or border template.

Bordering on insanity

Borders are a sort of one-size-fits-all type of frame. They have an advantage over frames because they shrink or expand to fit your photo when you resize it. (With frames, you have to make the photo fit the frame.)

The Border feature is available only when you're working in the Compose screen. You can begin a project on the Compose screen by clicking the Compose button on the Navigation bar and then Collage on the Activity panel. Chapter 9 tells you more about how to do this.

After you're on the Compose screen, you can bless your photo with a border by following these steps:

1. **Import a photo into PhotoSuite 4 using the Get screen.**

   See Chapter 5 if you need a refresher on how to do this.

2. **Click the Compose screen on the Navigation bar.**

   The Compose screen and Activity panel appear.

3. **Select Collages.**

   The Collage Activity panel appears with the current photo option selected.

4. **Click Next and then click Compose.**

   Another Activity panel appears.

5. **Click the Adjust Objects button on the Activity panel.**

6. **Click the Add Borders button on the Activity panel displayed and then click Add Borders on the following Activity panel.**

   The Border Activity panel, shown in Figure 15-8, appears.

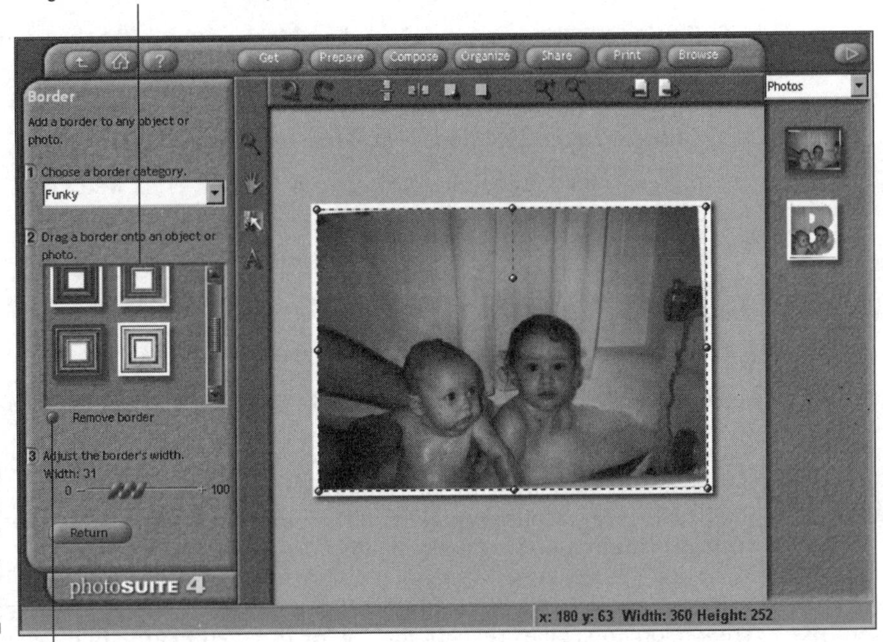

Figure 15-8: The Border Activity panel.

7. **Select a photo or object in your project.**

   The photo or object you've selected is surrounded by a bounding box with blue handles.

8. **Drag a border from the Add Borders Activity panel to the object or photo.**

   The border automatically resizes to fit the photo or object you've selected, as shown in Figure 15-9. When you resize your photo, the border automatically adjusts to fit it.

Figure 15-9: The border adjusts to fit your photo.

9. **To remove the border, select the object or photo that the border currently encloses and click the Remove button.**
10. **To Adjust the border's width, select the object or photo that the border currently encloses and use the Width slider.**
11. **When you're finished creating your border, click Return.**

Fake IDs for Any Age

Wouldn't you or your underage-for-drinking friends and relatives love to receive realistic drivers' licenses bearing their likeness and an over-21 age?

Well, you can't do it with this program — at least not with the predefined templates. PhotoSuite 4 doesn't condone the corruption of minors. In fact, the fake driver's license template in the program is more geared toward younger children playing make-believe.

You can also make fun Secret Agent IDs and fake credit cards with pictures. They're obvious fakes (except maybe for the credit cards that I've used as a second form of ID when writing a check), but lots of fun.

The ID card templates also have a few practical uses:

- You can create picture IDs for your club or organization.
- You can mass-produce the phone number of a school or camp and pin them on children on a field trip.
- You can make cute invitations.
- They're useful templates when you want to print a "Free Pass – Admit One" sort of thing.

Follow these steps to create fun IDs for the occasions that merit them:

1. **Click the Compose button on the Navigation bar.**

   The Compose screen and Activity panel appear.

2. **Click Fun Stuff on the Activity panel.**

   Another Activity panel appears.

3. **Click Fun IDs on the Activity panel.**

   Thumbnail images for 14 different fake ID templates appear on your desktop.

4. **Select one of the templates by clicking it.**

   The template you've selected appears, full size, on your deskop.

5. **Either drag and drop photos from the Library using your mouse, or click Next and load the photograph that you want to use into PhotoSuite 4 from one of the other sources listed in the Activity panel (such as your computer or scanner).**

   The photo appears in the cutout area.

   If you plan to load a photo from your computer, scanner, or camera into the cutout area of the calendar, select the cutout by clicking it before you import the photo. Otherwise, the full-size photo is dropped on top of your calendar project and obscures the whole template with which you're working.

6. **If necessary, resize, rotate, and reposition the photos by dragging the blue handles that appear on the bounding box around the perimeter of the photo (see Figure 15-10).**

   You can move a photo to a new position or different cutout area simply by dragging and dropping it.

7. **Click Return to save the photo you've added to the Fake ID template.**

   The Compose screen reappears on your desktop. You can add text and edit the Fake ID as you would any other project on the Compose screen. Chapter 9 tells you how to add and edit text and add additional props to Fake ID.

8. **Save or print your Fake ID.**

   To save your Fake ID, go to the file menu and select either Save or Save As to access a Windows dialog box for saving your project. To print your ID, click the Print button on the Navigation bar to access the PhotoSuite 4 printing options. (I tell you more about how to print in Chapter 13.)

Figure 15-10: You can select from fifteen different fun IDs.

Mugging for Magazine Covers

Whether you're creating a magazine cover for a gag or are planning on going into the publishing business, you'll be impressed with this feature. Magazine covers in PhotoSuite 4 are large templates that give you lots of creative options. You can add word balloons, props, and creative photo layouts as well as use colorizing techniques. A sample magazine cover appears in Figure 15-11.

To create a magazine cover, follow these steps:

1. **Click the Compose button on the Navigation bar.**

   The Compose screen and Activity panel appear.

2. **Click Fun Stuff on the Activity panel.**

   Another Activity panel appears.

3. **Click Magazine Covers.**

   The Magazine Covers Activity panel appears, displaying a number of thumbnails of magazine templates.

4. **Select a category of Magazine templates from the drop-down menu.**

The following categories of magazine covers are available to you:

- British Magazines
- Business
- Lifestyle
- Miscellaneous
- Science and Technology
- Sports and Leisure

When you select a category, the templates within that category appear on your screen.

5. **Select one of the templates by double clicking it.**

   The template you've selected appears, full size, on your desktop .

6. **Either drag and drop photos from the Library using your mouse or click Next to load the photograph that you want to use into PhotoSuite 4 from one of the other sources listed in the Activity panel (such as your computer or scanner).**

   The Compose screen reappears on your desktop.

7. **Click Add/Edit Text to display the options for adding and editing text.**

   Chapter 9 tells you how to add and edit text, in case you need a refresher.

8. **Click Return when you've finished adding text to your magazine cover project.**

   A thumbnail of the project appears in the Library area on the left of your computer screen.

9. **Save or print your magazine cover.**

   To save your magazine cover, go to the file menu and select either Save or Save As to access a Windows dialog box for saving your project. To print your cover, click the Print button on the Navigation bar to access the PhotoSuite 4 printing options. (for more about how to print, see Chapter 13.)

Photos can be placed anywhere on the Magazine template — not just in the cutout area.

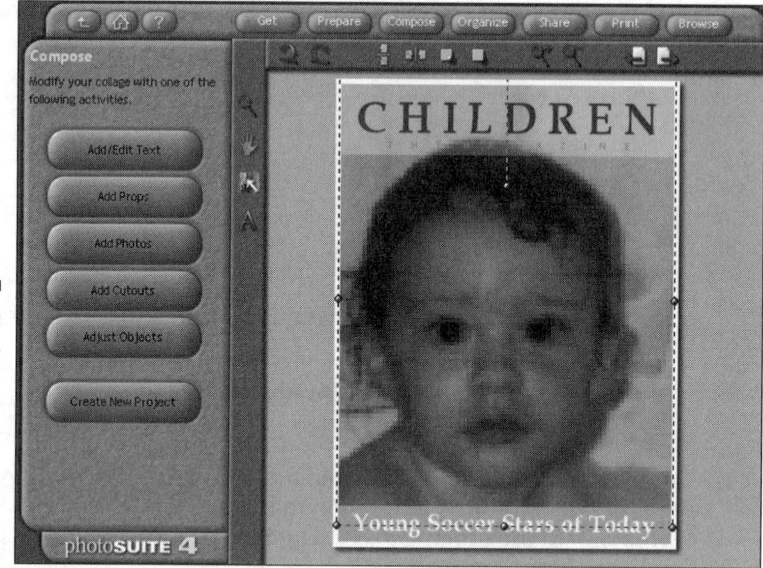

Figure 15-11: PhotoSuite 4 Magazine Cover templates offer you lots of options.

Gift Tags

Personalized gift tags are something you don't see every day, huh? You can put your own face or a tiny photo of the recipient on the tag.

Innovative gift tags, like the one shown in Figure 15-12, are easy to do. Just follow these steps:

1. **Click the Compose button on the Navigation bar.**

   The Compose screen and Activity panel appear.

2. **Click the Cards & Tags button.**

   Another Activity panel appears.

3. **Click Gift Tags.**

   The Gift Tag Activity panel box appears, with thumbnails of the various Gift Tag templates.

   Use the scroll bar on the right hand side of the screen to view all available Gift Tag templates.

4. **Select a Gift Tag template by double clicking it.**

   The full-size template opens on your desktop, as shown in Figure 15-12.

Figure 15-12: Make sure that they know who's giving the gift with this tag.

5. **Drag and drop photos from the Library using your mouse, or click Next to load the photograph that you want to use into PhotoSuite 4 from one of the other sources listed in the Activity panel (such as your computer or scanner).**

   Chapter 5 tells you how to load an image into PhotoSuite 4.

   The photo you've selected or loaded appears in the cutout area of the Gift Tag template, surrounded by a bounding box with blue handles. You can reposition and resize the photo on the Gift Tag by maneuvering the blue handles on the bounding box.

   The Compose screen reappears on your desktop.

6. **Click Add/Edit Text to display the options for adding and editing text.**

   Chapter 9 tells you how to add and edit text, in case you need a refresher.

7. **Click Return when you've finished adding text to your gift tag.**

8. **Save or print your gift tag.**

   To save your Gift Tag, go to the file menu and select either Save or Save As to access a Windows dialog box for saving your project. To print your gift tag, click the Print button on the Navigation bar to access the PhotoSuite 4 printing options. (See Chapter 13 for more on printing.)

Bookmarks

Now here's a thoughtful (and cheap) gift for your more intellectual friends and relatives. Actually PhotoSuite 4 bookmarks, like the one shown in Figure 15-13, *do* look like the ones they sell in upscale bookstores if you laminate them, and add trim or a tassel.

To create a bookmark that makes its mark, follow these steps:

1. **Click the Compose button on the Navigation bar.**

   The Compose screen and Activity panel appear.

2. **Click the Cards & Tags button.**

   Another Activity panel appears.

3. **Click Bookmarks.**

   The Bookmarks Activity panel appears with thumbnails of the various Bookmark templates.

4. **Drag and drop photos from the Library using your mouse, or click Next to load the photograph that you want to use into PhotoSuite 4 from one of the other sources listed in the Activity panel (such as your computer or scanner).**

   Chapter 5 tells you how to load an image into PhotoSuite 4.

   The photo you've selected or loaded appears in the cutout area of the Bookmark template, surrounded by a bounding box with blue handles. You can reposition and resize the photo on the Bookmark by using the blue handles on the bounding box.

5. **Click Return when you're satisfied with the result on your screen.**

6. **Save or print your bookmark.**

   To save your bookmark, go to the file menu, and select either Save or Save As to access a Windows dialog box for saving your project. To print your Bookmark, click the Print button on the Navigation bar to access the PhotoSuite 4 printing options. (I tell you more about how to print in Chapter 13.)

Figure 15-13: Make your mark with PhotoSuite 4.

Postcards, Sports Cards, and Invitations

How about a sports card with his or her own likeness for the fan who has everything? Or a personalized postcard or invitation?

It's easy to create sports cards, invitations, and postcards (like the one in Figure 15-14) using the same techniques you used to create greeting cards. To access these templates:

1. **Click the Compose button on the Navigation bar.**

   The Compose screen and Activity panel appear.

2. **Click Cards & Tags on the Activity Panel.**

   Another Activity panel appears.

3. **Click Sports Cards, Post Cards or Invitations, depending on your preference.**

   An activity panel for Sports Card, Post Card, or Invitation templates appears.

4. **Follow the same basic procedure from Step 6 on in the steps listed in the "Greeting Cards That Really Greet" section at the start of this chapter.**

Figure 15-14: Create sports cards, invitations, and postcards on the fly.

The Ultimate Wedding Gift

You can use the Collections templates to create particularly memorable gifts and projects. These templates are designed to allow you to make a stylized finished project centered on a Wedding theme.

To access the Collections templates:

1. **Click the Compose button on the Navigation bar.**

   The Compose screen and Activity panel appear.

2. **Click Collections on the Activity panel.**

   The Collections Activity panel appears.

3. **Follow the same basic procedure from Step 6 on in the steps listed in the "Greeting Cards That Really Greet" section at the start of this chapter.**

Chapter 16

PhotoSuite 4 for Fun and Profit

In This Chapter

- Creating stationery and business cards that impress
- Composing the signs of success
- Making labels and name tags
- Certifying your own merit

It seems as though everybody's got a sideline these days — some sort of business going on out of a home office or garage. Whether yours is Tupperware or bionuclear consulting, PhotoSuite 4 offers you some simple tools and templates to project your image (or to just have fun with).

Personal-Statement Stationery

Unfortunately, PhotoSuite 4 stationery can't offer you expensive watermarks or expensive embossing (yet). But it does let you include digital images, which most people find a lot more interesting to look at than a watermark.

You can select from among the following categories of stationery templates on which to add your digital images:

- **Letterhead:** PhotoSuite 4 offers you nineteen different types of professional-looking letterhead, including the template type shown in Figure 16-1.
- **Media:** Allows you make CD labels and floppy disks (this one's not exactly stationery, I guess, but this is where they decided to put it).
- **Recipes:** You can make personalized recipe cards with your picture, or maybe a photo of your tastiest dish. (I hate recipe pictures — it never turns out looking like that when I cook it.)
- **Education:** Templates for creating school notes, homework memos, and other useful items for parents, teachers, and students.

- **Notepads:** These templates contain fun and fanciful graphics that project a fairly informal image.
- **Miscellaneous:** These are mostly blank templates with carefully arranged and spaced cutout areas that make it easier for you to add your own text and graphics, using the tools explained in Chapter 9, "Performing Photo-Surgery."

Figure 16-1: Project professionalism and personality with PhotoSuite 4 stationery options.

To use the Stationery templates to come up with something professional, polished or just fun, follow these steps:

1. **Click the Compose button on the Navigation bar.**

   The Compose screen and Activity panel appear.

2. **Click Business on the Activity panel.**

   Another Activity panel appears.

3. **Click Stationery.**

   The Stationery Activity panel, shown in Figure 16-2, appears, with several thumbnail photos of stationery templates on the desktop.

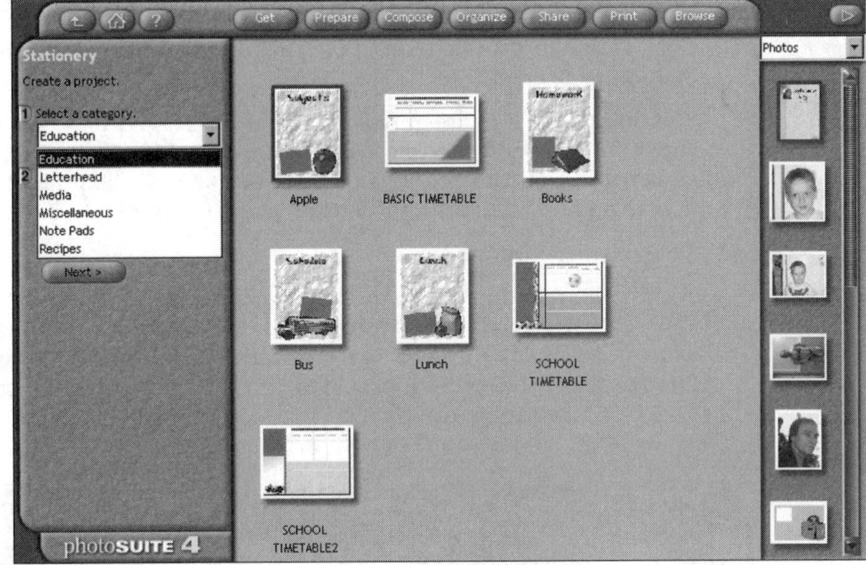

Figure 16-2: Create stationery using this Activity panel.

4. **Select a category of stationery from the drop-down menu.**

   The thumbnails of all the stationery types within the category you selected appear on the desktop.

5. **Select the template that you want to use for your stationery by clicking it.**

   The full-size stationery template appears on your desktop, as shown in Figure 16-3.

6. **Select a cutout area of the stationery to which you want to add a photo.**

   The selected cutout area is surrounded by a bounding box with blue handles.

7. **Drag and drop photos from the Library using your mouse, or click Add Photos to load the photograph that you want to use into PhotoSuite 4 from another source (such as your computer or scanner).**

   The Library is located on the right side of the screen and contains thumbnail images of all the photos you can drag and drop. Chapter 5, "Where Do Little Images Come From?," tells you how to load an image into PhotoSuite 4.

8. **Use the blue handles on the bounding box to resize and reposition the photos.**

   The Photos you've selected are automatically resized and dropped into the cutout areas of the stationery. However, you may still need to use the blue handles on the bounding box to do some adjusting and repositioning.

9. **Repeat the process to add more photos; then click Next.**
10. **Click Finish to complete and save the photo additions to your Stationery project.**

    The Compose screen re-appears on your desktop. After you've clicked Finish, you can add text and edit the stationery in other ways, as you would any other project on your Compose screen. Chapter 9 tells you how to add text and other photos or props to your stationery.
11. **Save or print your stationery.**

    To save your stationery, go to the file menu and select either Save or Save As to access a Windows dialog box for saving your project. To print your project, click the Print button on the Navigation bar to access the PhotoSuite 4 printing options. (I tell you more about how to print in Chapter 13, "Graphics on the Go.")

Figure 16-3: Import a photo into a Stationery template.

If you plan to load a photo from your computer, scanner, or camera into the cutout area of the stationery, you must first select the cutout area by clicking it. Otherwise, the full-size photo is dropped on top of your stationery project.

Promoting Your Business

What better way to promote a fledgling business than with flyers, coupons, and brochures? And what better way to give these pieces impact than with photographs of your products and yourself?

To create high-impact promotional pieces with graphics that are sure to impress any prospective client, follow these steps:

1. **Click the Compose button on the Navigation bar.**

   The Compose screen and Activity panel appear.

2. **Click Business on the Activity panel.**

   Another Activity panel appears.

3. **Click Promotions.**

   The Promotions Activity panel, shown in Figure 16-4, appears with several thumbnail photos of the templates on the desktop.

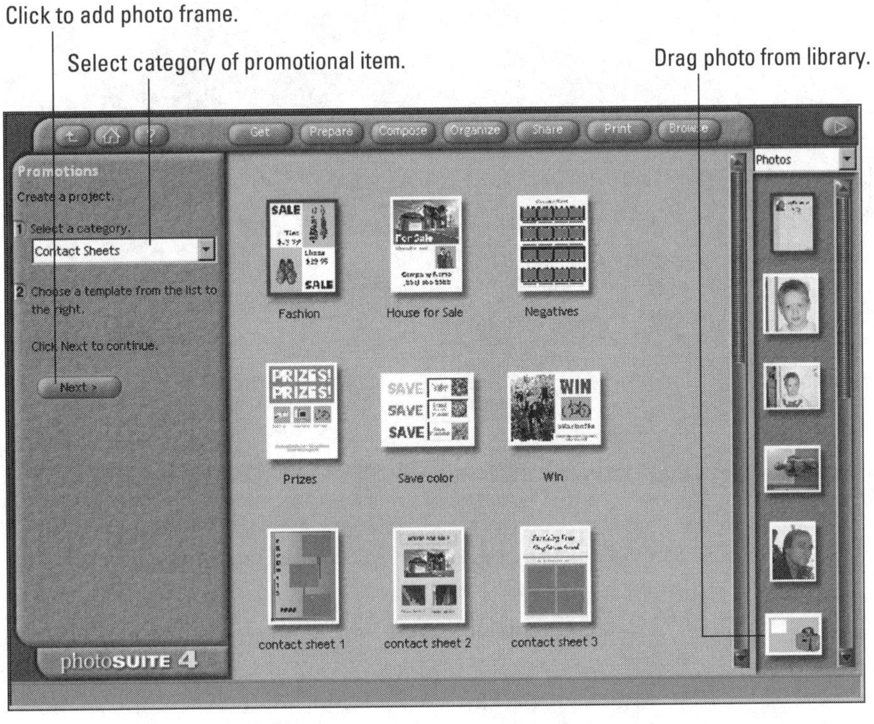

Click to add photo frame.

Select category of promotional item.

Drag photo from library.

Figure 16-4: Import a photo into a Stationery template.

4. **Select one of the following Promotions categories from the drop-down menu:**

   - Displays
   - Contact Sheets
   - Coupons
   - Flyers
   - Tickets

   Thumbnails of the templates for the category you've selected appear on your desktop.

5. **Select the project template you want to use for your stationery by double-clicking it.**

   The full-size project template appears on your desktop, as shown in Figure 16-5.

Figure 16-5: Modify your project using props, text, and so on.

6. **Select the cutout area of the template to which you want to add a photo.**

   The selected cutout area is surrounded by a bounding box with blue handles.

7. **Follow the procedure from Step 7 on in preceding section, "Personal Statement Stationery."**

If you plan to load a photo from your computer, scanner, or camera into the cutout area of the project, you must first select the cutout area by clicking it. Otherwise, the full-size photo is dropped on top of your project.

Cards That Mean Business

Professionally-printed business cards with your picture on them can be pricey. Because most business cards don't have raised lettering or embossing, you have nothing to lose and everything to gain by opting to produce them with PhotoSuite 4.

Pick a card

You can select from among the following categories of PhotoSuite 4 business cards:

- **Entertainment:** This category is for creative and artistic professions such as music, catering, and painting. I created a card for a child performer in Figure 16-6.

Figure 16-6: A business card for an aspiring rock star.

- **Sales Promotion:** This one creates cards for realtors, contractors, and other salesperson-types.
- **Services:** Here you'll find specialized cards for more than 20 different service professions, from accountant to travel agent.

- **Miscellaneous:** These are actually more service categories for a broad range of additional professions. I've created the simple business cards, such as the one shown in Figure 16-7, for an attorney using one of these templates.

Figure 16-7: A business card for an ambitious lawyer.

Making cards that call

Here's how to make cards that go calling:

1. **Click the Compose button on the Navigation bar.**

   The Compose screen and Activity panel appear.

2. **Click Business on the Activity panel.**

   Another Activity panel appears.

3. **Click Business Cards.**

   The Business Cards Activity panel, shown in Figure 16-8, appears, with several thumbnail photos of business card templates on the desktop.

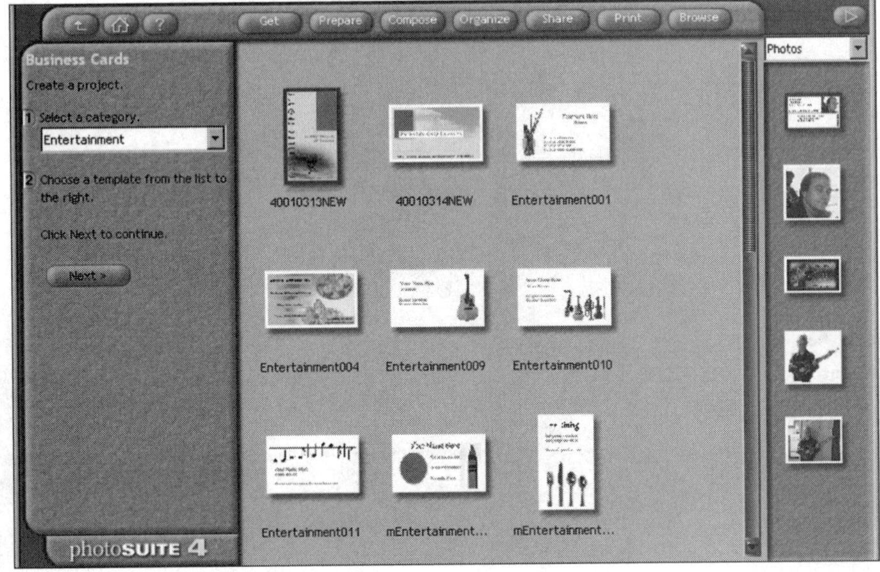

Figure 16-8: Create business cards using dozens of templates.

4. **Select a card category from the drop-down menu.**

   The thumbnails all the business card types within the category you selected appear on the desktop.

5. **Select the template that you want to use for your business card by clicking it.**

   The full-size Business Card template appears on your desktop, as shown in Figure 16-9. Some templates have a cutout area surrounded by a bounding box with blue handles.

6. **Follow the procedure from Step 7 on in the earlier section "Personal Statement Stationery."**

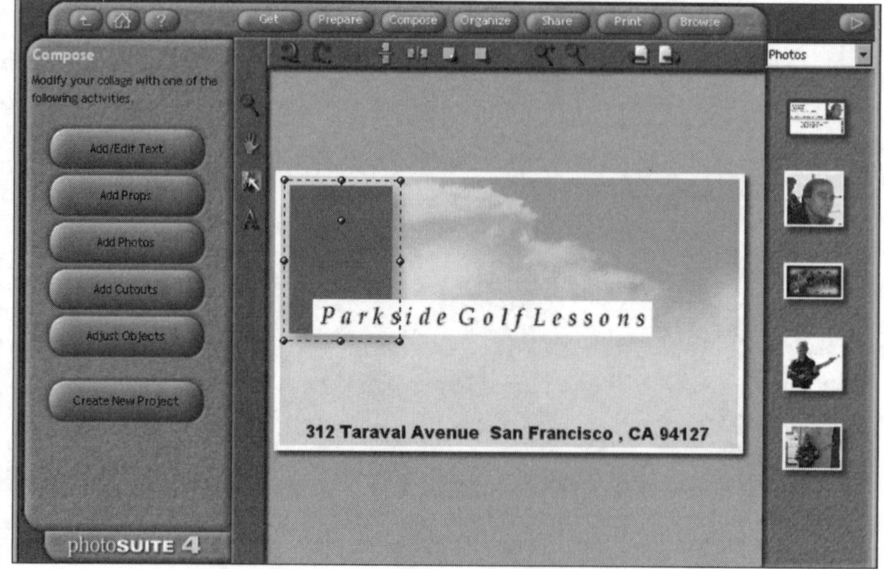

Figure 16-9: A business card ready for additions or adjustments.

Printing business cards, wallet photos, and other "multiples"

Printing business cards presents special issues, because you want to use an efficient layout and print several per page. Fortunately, PhotoSuite 4 includes an option for printing multiple images on a page.

To print several copies on a page:

1. **Open the business card, photo, or other project you want to print.**

   Chapter 5 tells you how to open a document in PhotoSuite 4, in case you've forgotten.

2. **Click the Print button on the Navigation bar.**

   An Activity panel appears.

3. **Click the Multiples button on the Activity panel.**

   The Print Multiples Activity panel and screen appear, as shown in Figure 16-10.

   There are several thumbnails of sample formats for printing multiple copies on the same page.

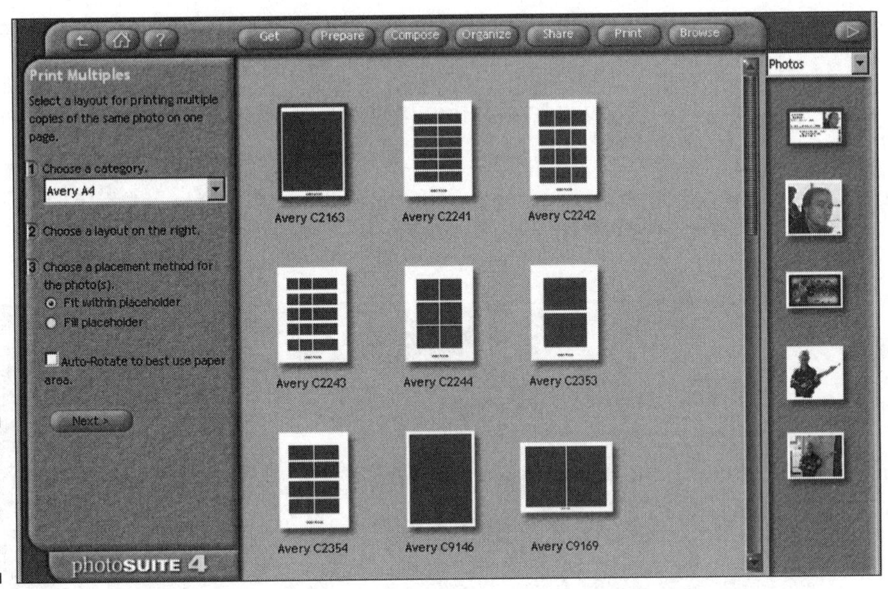

Figure 16-10: Select from these layouts.

4. **Select the layout that you want to use for printing multiple copies of the same project on the same page by double-clicking its thumbnail.**

   A Print Preview screen, such as the one shown in Figure 16-11, appears.

5. **Select the Auto-Rotate check box if you want PhotoSuite 4 to choose the optimum layout for your business cards.**

   If you select this option, PhotoSuite 4 automatically selects the most efficient orientation and layout.

6. **Select the option Fit Within Placeholder or Fill Placeholder.**

   If you select the Fit Within Placeholder, your photo is resized to fit within the template. I recommend that you always choose this option because the other option can leave you with words or text cut off.

7. **Click Next.**

   The Print Preview screen appears, as shown in Figure 16-11.

8. **Select the printer that you want to use from the drop-down menu; then choose the orientation for your paper.**

   The orientation refers to the direction of the paper — whether the longest side is horizontal or vertical.

9. **Choose the number of copies of the entire page you want to print.**

   This option allows you to select the number of copies of the layout page you want to print, not the number of individual cards or other pieces.

10. **If the Print Size option is not grayed-out, you can select the print size.**

    This option is available only for certain projects.

11. **Click Return to exit the Print Multiples Activity panel and begin printing.**

The options on the screen may vary depending on what type of project you're printing. Be sure to follow the graphically illustrated prompts.

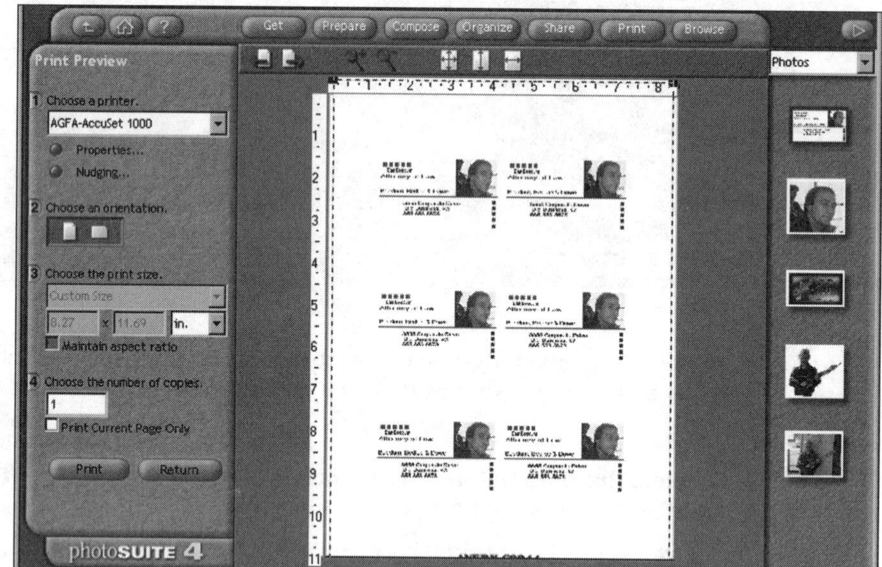

Figure 16-11: Preview your print job.

Signs That Point to Success

Signs with photos are fun to create. Currently, PhotoSuite 4 allows you to create the following types of signs:

- **Directional:** These signs that give directions — such as "Danger," "Beware of Dog," or Please Clean Up." Some of the signs point you in the right direction, with arrow templates that are superimposed on your photo for a dramatic effect, like the sign shown in Figure 16-12.
- **For Sale:** PhotoSuite 4 offers you six different types of For Sale signs to assist you in the most aggressive marketing campaign.

Figure 16-12: PhotoSuite 4 signs can point your guests in the right direction.

Here's a new twist on a classic prank. What better way to get even with someone that by creating a "Kick Me" sign bearing the person's photograph? Figure 16-13 provides an example of this sophomoric humor.

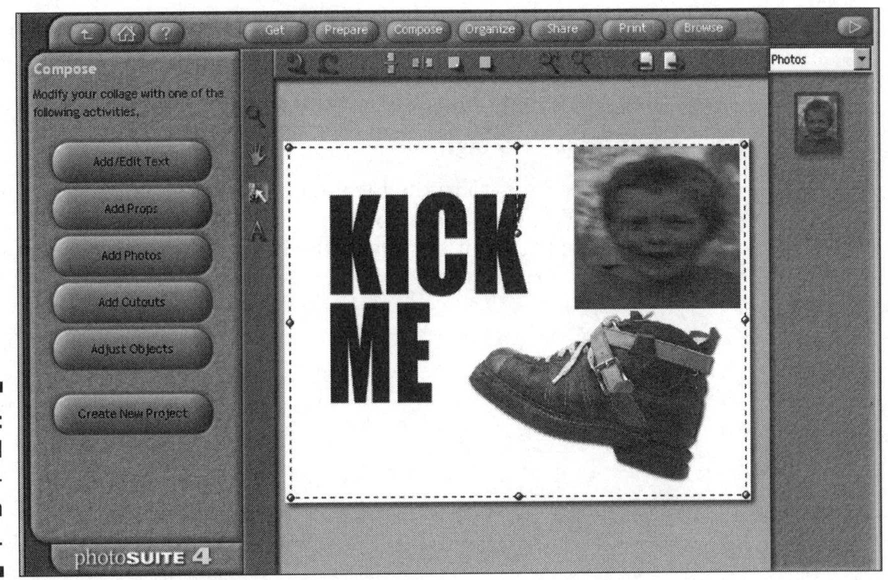

Figure 16-13: A digital enhancement of an old prank.

To create signs bearing PhotoSuite 4 digital images:

1. **Click the Compose button on the Navigation bar.**

   The Compose screen and Activity panel appear.

2. **Click Business on the Activity panel.**

   Another Activity panel appears.

3. **Click Signs.**

   The Signs Activity panel appears, with several thumbnail photos of Sign templates on the desktop.

4. **Select a Sign category (either Directional or For Sale) from the drop-down menu.**

   The thumbnails of all the Sign templates in the category you selected appear on the desktop.

5. **Select the template that you want to use for your sign by clicking it.**

   The full-size sign template appears on your desktop.

6. **Select the cutout area of the sign to which you want to add a photo.**

   The selected cutout area is surrounded by a bounding box with blue handles.

7. **Drag and drop photos from the Library or click Next to the photograph that you want to use into PhotoSuite 4 from another source (such as your computer or scanner).**

8. **Use the blue handles on the bounding box to resize and reposition the photos.**

9. **Repeat the process to add additional photos; then click Next.**

   The Compose screen re-appears on your desktop. After you've clicked Finish, you can add text and edit the sign.

10. **Save or print your sign.**

    To save your Sign, go to the file menu, and select either Save or Save As to access a Windows dialog box for saving your project. To print your project, click the Print button on the Navigation bar to access the PhotoSuite 4 printing options.

Creating Name Tags and Labels

By now, you've probably figured out that PhotoSuite 4 allows you to create business items that are highly stylized conversation pieces through digital imaging. Name tags and mailing labels provide yet another opportunity for you to get your product and face in front of your customers and prospective customers.

Labeling in PhotoSuite 4 style

You can create labels bearing a small printed image or logo in one corner, or use the opacity setting to create a shadow-like image over which you print the label information. In either case, you use commercially available blank labels that you can purchase at any office supply store.

PhotoSuite 4 offers four different categories of predefined mailing label templates that correspond to the sizes and styles of the blank labels manufactured by Kodak and Avery. These are the two major manufacturers of blank labels, and other vendors often correspond their dimensions to those offered by Kodak and Avery.

Unlike other PhotoSuite 4 templates, for which what you see on-screen is what you get when it's printed, labels are hard to view on-screen. This is because the label template may have a red or gold background on-screen although most commercial labels are white. This background makes it a little difficult when you're adjusting opacity, using the Edge Fading tool, or developing a color scheme on-screen.

To create mailing labels bearing your own graphics and text, follow these steps:

1. **Click the Compose button on the Navigation bar.**

   The Compose screen and Activity panel appear.

2. **Click Business on the Activity panel.**

   Another Activity panel appears.

3. **Click Labels.**

   The Labels screen and Activity panel appear, as shown in Figure 16-14, with several thumbnail views of sheets of labels, laid out the way they are when you purchase them commercially.

Select manufacturer.

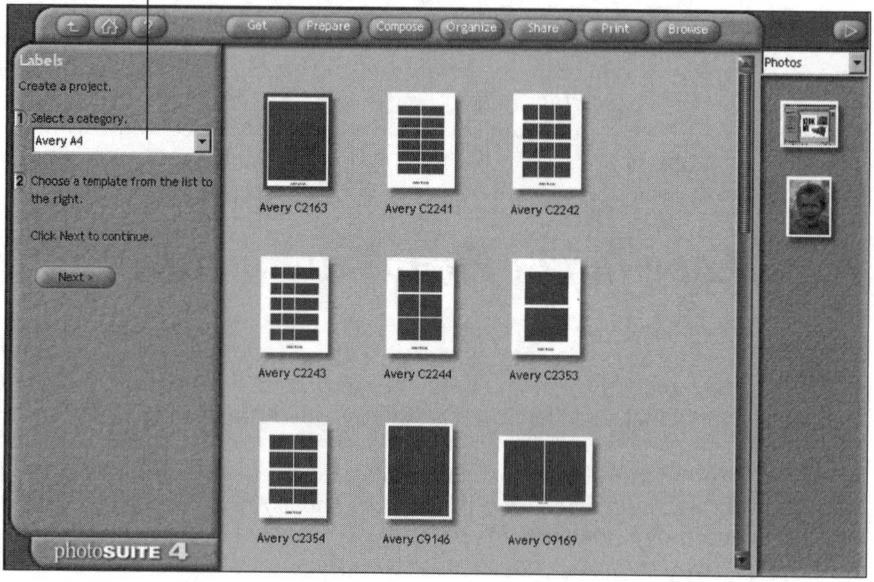

Figure 16-14: PhotoSuite 4 offers templates to match manufacturer specifications for various blank labels.

4. **Select a Label manufacturer from the drop-down menu.**

   Thumbnails of all the Label templates in the category you selected appear on the desktop. The manufacturer's style number for each label type appears under the template.

5. **Select the Label template that you want to use and double-click it.**

   The Compose screen reappears on your desktop with the full-size Label template in the Workspace, as shown in Figure 16-15.

6. **Drag and drop photos from the Library using your mouse, or click Add Photos to load the photograph that you want to use into PhotoSuite 4 from another source (such as your computer or scanner).**

7. **Use the blue handles on the bounding box to resize and reposition the photos.**

   The photos you've selected are automatically resized to fit the label and are surrounded by a bounding box with blue handles, but you may need to use the blue handles to resize and reposition the photo.

8. **Repeat the process for the remaining labels on the template.**

   You can use the same photo for each label, or different ones.

You can click the Adjust Objects button on the Activity panel on the Compose screen to access the Opacity and Edge Fading tools.

9. **Click the Print button on the Navigation bar to print your labels.**

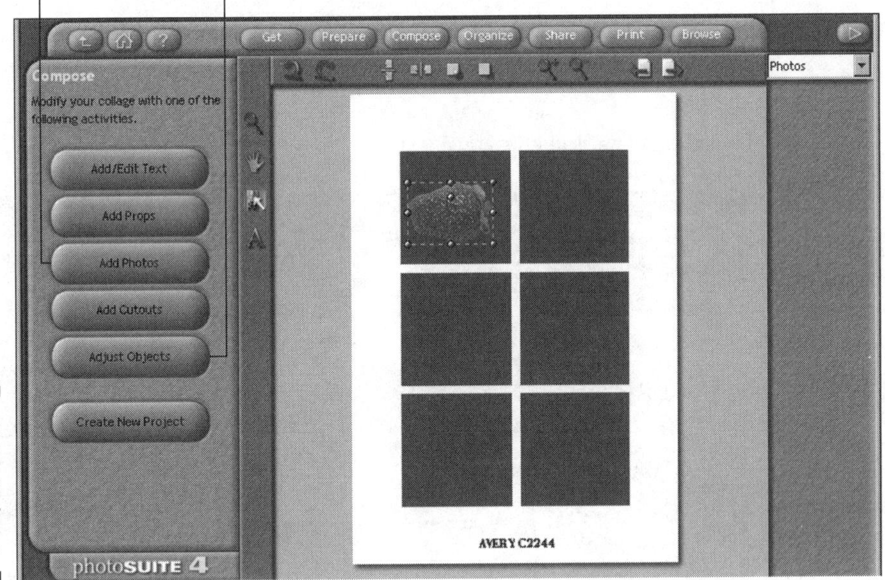

Figure 16-15: Drag and drop photos onto your labels.

The Add/Edit Text features can be cumbersome to use on the labels, which are pretty small to work with. Also, copying the text from label to label is difficult. I find it easier to use a word processing program, such as Microsoft Word, to put text on the labels after I've printed the graphics using PhotoSuite 4. I print the graphics on a sheet of labels using PhotoSuite 4 and then reinsert the sheet of labels into my printer to process the labels.

Name tagging along

Name tags with faces are sure to impress — and to provide security for an event, if necessary.

You can also have a lot of fun with the tags by using the Props menu to put the party-goers' faces on cartoon bodies, or add a party hat to the picture, as I've done in Figure 16-16.

PhotoSuite 4 provides two categories of Name Tag templates: Corporate Visitor and Party Guest. To use them, follow these steps:

1. **Click the Compose button on the Navigation bar.**

   The Compose screen and Activity panel appear.

2. **Click Business on the Activity panel.**

   Another Activity panel appears.

3. **Click Name Tags.**

   The Name Tags Activity panel, shown in Figure 16-16, appears with several thumbnail photos of Name Tag templates on the desktop.

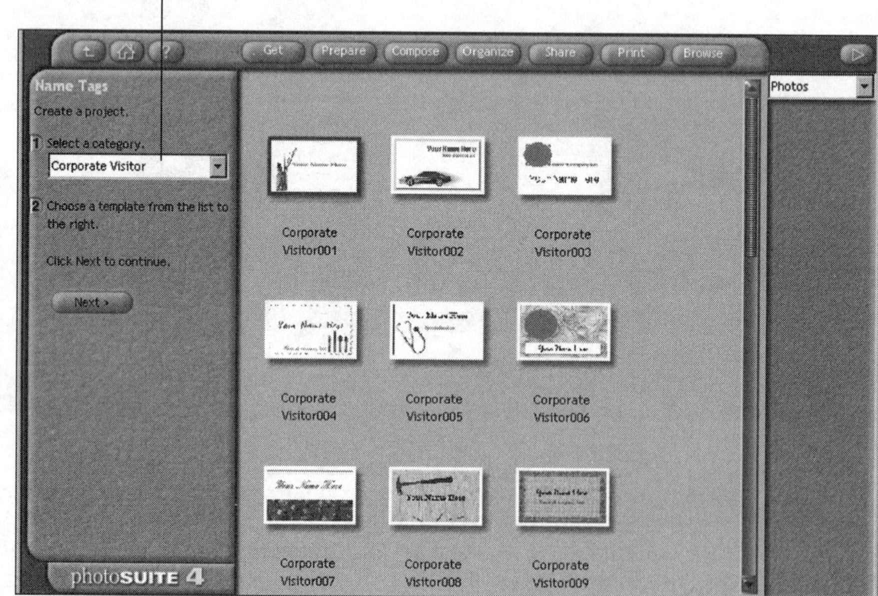

Figure 16-16: You can select Corporate Visitor or Party Guest name tags.

4. **Select either the Corporate Visitor or Party Guest name tag category from the drop-down menu.**

   Thumbnails of all the Name Tag templates in the category you selected appear on the desktop. Some of the name tags have cutout areas to insert the photo; others do not.

5. **Select the Name Tag template you want to use by double-clicking it.**

   The full-size Name Tag template appears on your desktop, as shown in Figure 16-17.

6. **If there's a cutout area on the template, drag and drop photos from the Library using your mouse, or click the Add Photos button to load the photograph that you want to use into PhotoSuite 4 from another source (such as your computer or scanner).**

7. **If necessary, resize and reposition the photo using the blue handles on the bounding box.**

   The photos you've selected are automatically resized to fit the label, and are surrounded by a bounding box with blue handles, but you may need to use the blue handles to resize and reposition the photo.

8. **Click the Add/Edit Text button to add a name or other text to your photo.**

   If you need a refresher on adding and editing text, head over to Chapter 9.

9. **When you're satisfied with what appears on your screen, save or print your name tag.**

   To save your name tag, go to the file menu and select either Save or Save As to access a Windows dialog box for saving your project. To find out how to print multiple name tags on a single page, go to the section of this chapter called "Printing business cards, wallet photos, and other 'multiples.'"

Figure 16-17: Add photos and text to a Name Tag template.

Acknowledging with Certificates

PhotoSuite 4 provides one last template under its business features that can further help you promote good will among customers and employees. The Certificate templates allow you to create certificates of achievement and acknowledgment bearing a picture of the person you want to recognize.

To certify just about anything you want for anyone you choose, follow these steps:

1. **Click the Compose button on the Navigation bar.**

   The Compose screen and Activity panel appear.

2. **Click Business on the Activity panel.**

   Another Activity panel appears.

3. **Click Certificates.**

   The Certificate Activity panel, shown in Figure 16-18, appears, with several thumbnail photos of Certificate templates on the desktop.

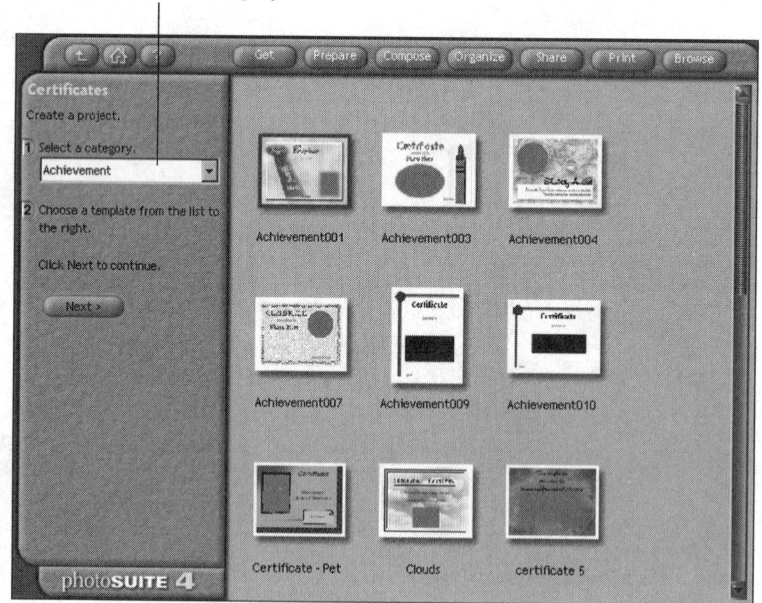

Figure 16-18: Choose your Certificate category.

4. **Select either Achievement or Acknowledgment from the drop-down menu.**

The thumbnails of all the Certificate templates in the category that you selected appear on the desktop. All but one of the Certificate templates have cutout areas to insert the photo; others do not.

5. **Select the Certificate template you want to use by clicking it.**

   The Compose screen reappears on your desktop with the full-size Certificate template in the Workspace, as shown in Figure 16-19.

6. **Add a photo to your certificate.**

   You can either drag and drop photos from the Library using your mouse, or click the Add photo button to load the photograph that you want to use into PhotoSuite 4 from another source (such as your computer or scanner). If there's no cutout, the imported photo appears on the certificate surrounded by a bounding box with blue handles.

7. **If necessary, resize and reposition the photo using the blue handles on the bounding box.**

   The photo you've selected is automatically re-sized to fit the label and is surrounded by a bounding box with blue handles, but you may need to use the blue handles to resize and reposition the photo.

8. **When you're satisfied with what appears on your screen, save or Print your certificate.**

   To save your certificate, go to the file menu and select either Save or Save As to access a Windows dialog box for saving your project. To print your project, click the Print button on the Navigation bar to access the PhotoSuite 4 printing options.

Figure 16-19: Add photos and text to a Certificate template.

Chapter 17

Photo-Drama: Stitching and Weaving Images

In This Chapter

- Putting your photos in stitches
- Finding out the secrets of successful stitching
- Weaving a photo tapestry

The PhotoSuite 4 Stitching and Tapestry features take amateur digital photography well beyond the realm of smiling kids and prize begonias.

Stitching lets you seamlessly attach up to five photos to create an Interactive Panorama, which gives the viewer the feeling of being inside the scene. (It makes me motion sick.) The Tapestry feature lets you use hundreds of thumbnail photos to create a striking surrealistic composite piece.

Stitching Photos

PhotoSuite 4's auto-stitching features allow you to effortlessly create panoramic images by attaching multiple photos. This means that if you take several photos by panning a subject (such as a horizon or skyline), you can then join them together in the editing process to create a panoramic sweep.

Threading your digital needle

The Stitching feature was developed to allow you to capture panoramic views that elude you when you're limited to a single photo. By "sewing" together several photos taken while you pan (move along) the subject area (such as a horizon), you can get a seamless, single image.

The Photo Tapestry feature works best if there's at least a 50–65 percent overlap in the subject matter of your photo. The manufacturers of the program say that you can get by with as little as 35 percent overlap, but they advise that more overlap is necessary to produce better results. This means that when you're taking pictures, you should deliberately create overlap — from one-third to two-thirds of a previous scene in the *next* scene when snapping your photos. You can join as many as 48 photos together.

Successful stitching secrets

Before you photograph for a Stitching project, the manufacturers of PhotoSuite 4 recommend that you consider and take into account the following tips to get the best results:

- **Size:** The photos you're stitching together must all be the same size.
- **Position:** All your photos must be taken from the same spot and pretty much in the same position, except for the adjustment to capture additional panned portions of the view. Try to hold your camera as level as possible, or, if possible, use a tripod.
- **Zoom level:** Be sure to take all your pictures using the same Zoom level setting on your camera.
- **Variations in subject matter:** PhotoSuite 4 needs to be able to determine where exactly to piece your photos together — sort of like a jigsaw puzzle. Your scenes should have some variations that PhotoSuite 4 can use for this purpose. For example, it's hard for the program to figure out how to piece together photos of a blue sky or open ocean, just as it would be tough for you to do a jigsaw puzzle with this subject matter.

Stitching right along

Stitching photos takes a little practice. But the results are spectacular, if you follow these steps:

1. **Click the Prepare button on the Navigation bar.**

   The Prepare screen and Activity panel appear.
2. **Click the Stitching button on the Activity panel.**

   The Stitching Activity panel, shown in Figure 17-1, appears.

3. **Choose one of the available Stitching methods.**

   The following Stitching methods are available to you:

   - **Wide:** For horizontal panoramas
   - **Tall:** For vertical scenes

4. **When you've selected a Stitching method, click Next.**

   Drag and drop the photos you want to include onto the Workspace (see Color Plate 2-4). If a photo you want to include isn't in the Library, you can import it from elsewhere on your computer or from your digital camera or scanner.

   Note: The photos you select must be in JPEG, FPX, or BMP format, and they must all have the same dimensions. The maximum number of photos you can stitch is 48.

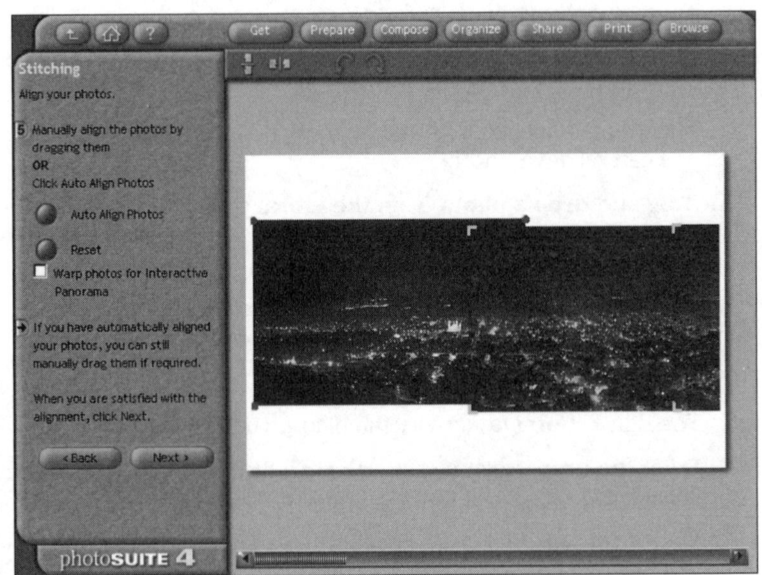

Figure 17:1: The Stitching Activity panel.

Creating an Interactive Panorama

Interactive panoramas give the photo a three-dimensional effect, as though you're inside the photo. You actually have the feeling of being wrapped inside the image. You can select from among the following interactive panorama effects:

- **Cylinder:** This works best for stitched photos. This effect gives you the sense of being inside a large cylinder with the photo wrapped around you.
- **Sphere:** Use this effect for wide vertical areas. It gives the viewer the sense of looking up at a photo that is overhead.
- **Cube:** This feature creates dramatic multifaceted effects but works only on photos that were originally created in 3D. (You need a special program for this.)

To create an Interactive Panorama:

1. **Click the Share button on the Navigation bar.**

   The Save & Share Activity panel appears.
2. **Click the Create Web Items button on the Activity panel.**

   Another Activity panel appears.
3. **Click the Interactive Panorama button and then the Create New Panorama button on the following Activity panel.**

   The Create Panorama Activity panel appears, listing sources from which you can retrieve photos.
4. **Drag and drop a photo from the Library area or obtain a photo from your computer, scanner, or camera by clicking the appropriate button.**

   Chapter 5, "Where Do Little Images Come From?," tells you more about how to import photos from various sources.
5. **Click Create New Panorama.**

   The Edit Panorama Activity panel appears.
6. **From the drop-down menu, select Cylinder, Cube, or Sphere and then click Next.**

   You've successfully created an interactive panorama. Step inside . . . .

Click the Manual Wrap button to adjust the overlap of the edges of the photo (for example, where they're attached to create the cylinder effect), if the photo doesn't appear as a smooth, continuous image.

Weaving a PhotoTapestry

PhotoTapestry recreates any photograph using thumbnail photographs drawn from a large database stored on the MGI PhotoSuite 4 CD-ROM. A color sample PhotoTapestry appears in Color Plate 2-3.

Some really excitng news is that you can create your own database of PhotoSuite 4 *tiles,* which are the thumbnails used to create a PhotoTapestry.

Tackling a Basic Tapestry

To create a PhotoTapestry:

1. **Import a photo into PhotoSuite 4 and click the Prepare button on the Navigation bar.**

   The Prepare screen and Activity panel appear.

2. **Click the PhotoTapestry button on the Activity Panel.**

   The Photo Tapestry Activity panel appears with your photo loaded, as shown in Figure 17-2.

Figure 17-2: The PhotoTapestry Activity panel with the original photo loaded.

3. **Choose a collection of thumbnail photos from those listed in the Tile Collection list box, or create your own by following the steps in the next section, "Weaving your own."**

   You must have a photo loaded into PhotoSuite 4 to access the PhotoTapestry feature.

4. **Specify the number of tiles you can use by moving the slider.**

   Using more tiles increases the realism of the photo but also increases the file size of the resulting image. Figure 17-3 is an example of an image with small tiles.

5. **Select Portrait or Landscape tiles.**

   Portrait tiles look better with photos that are higher than they are wide. Landscape tiles look better with photos that are wider than they are tall.

6. **Choose a file output size.**

   Select a small file size if the PhotoTapestry is to be viewed on a computer monitor. Select larger sizes to print enlargements of the photo.

7. **Click Create to create the PhotoTapestry; click Redo if you want to redo the Photo Tapestry using different settings.**

   The PhotoTapestry takes several minutes to be calculated.

8. **Click Return when you're finished.**

A 2MB file size is adequate for printing a 5 x 7 photo, whereas 4MB works well for printing an 8 x 10 photo.

Weaving your own

If you want to create you own Tile collection, you can do so by following these steps:

1. **Click the PhotoTapestry button on the Activity Panel.**

   The Photo Tapestry Activity panel appears with your photo loaded (refer to Figure 17-2).

2. **Click the Add Tiles button to add images stored on your computer.**

   All landscape images are cropped to a 4-to-3 horizontal-to-vertical ratio, and all portrait images are cropped to a 3-to-4 horizontal-to-vertical ratio. This means that if a photo is wider or taller than these proportions, you may lose part of it. This cropping process ensures that all photos are of identical size with no cropping bars.

3. **Select any photo and click the Remove button to delete any unwanted tiles from your collection.**

   This deletes the photo from your PhotoTapestry permanently.

4. **Click the Save Collection button when you're finished adding and deleting tiles.**

   A dialog box appears, allowing you to specify whether you want to display your photos in Portrait or Landscape orientation.

5. **Select the desired Portrait or Landscape option and then click Save.**

   You now have a customized PhotoTapestry collection you can use at any time.

To import a tile collection from a friend or from the Web, click the Add a New Tile Collection button.

You must have the PhotoSuite 4 installation CD in your computer to use the PhotoTapestry feature.

Figure 17-3: The PhotoTapestry with small tiles selected.

Part V
The Part of Tens

"...and here's me with Cindy Crawford.. And this is me with Madonna and Celine Dion..."

In this part . . .

Good things come in tens. Such as our whole decimal system. Chapter 18 tells you ten ways to take better pictures. Chapter 19 tells you about ten (actually, more than ten) different file formats that you can use to store your better pictures. And finally, Chapter 20 tells you how to troubleshoot when you are experiencing ten different types of photo-stress.

Chapter 18

Ten Tips for Taking Better Pictures

In This Chapter

- Knowing when to shoot off-center (on purpose)
- Being of steady hand and sound mind
- Knowing how far away is too far away?
- Finding out facts about flashes
- Being spontaneous, creative, and focused all at one time

PhotoSuite 4 is a bungler-friendly program that compensates for a lot of less-than-perfect technique. But even PhotoSuite 4 can't do much when you consistently cut the head off your subjects — or worse.

The better the photo you start with, the better the finished product you end up with. This chapter gives you some tips for taking decent photos using the equipment of amateurs. (I assume that you don't have lots of interchangeable lenses — just an ordinary camera with a decent flash and auto focus capability.)

Know What You're Focusing On

If your camera has an auto focus, you can't get an out-of-focus image, right? Wrong!

The best way to fuzz up an image that's supposed to be automatically focused is to accidentally aim your camera at a point that falls in between two subjects you're trying to photograph. When this happens, your camera is actually focusing on some indeterminate background point you could care less about. The subjects of your photo are blurry and out of focus. Ugh!

Alternatively, if you're using a disposable or other inexpensive camera with a fixed, nonadjustable focus, you need to read the directions on the camera package. They'll tell you what range is in focus (for example, four to eight feet). If you try to shoot out of this range, you may not get anything even remotely resembling what you see in your viewfinder.

Don't Shoot to Kill

Most of us amateurs aim the viewfinder of our cameras like the crosshairs guide of a shotgun — aiming for the bull's-eye of our subject. But this isn't the way to go. For example, you don't want to place the center dot of the viewfinder directly over center of your subject's face. If you do, you'll have lots of blank space (or background) at the top of your photo.

Of course, you can use Photo Suite 4's cropping tools to get rid of the extra background. But to save yourself extra editing effort, you should actually look at what's showing up in your viewfinder and think before positioning the markings. In this example, you probably want your subject's head to be just below the top boundary of your viewfinder, rather than at dead center.

Get on a Higher (or Lower) Plane

Pay close attention to the angle from which you're taking your shot and how it affects the subject of your photo. For example, if you're shooting small children, don't be afraid to kneel so that you're level with their sticky little faces.

You can also use the angle of your photo to create a relationship with your subject. For example, if you're taking a picture of a person standing next to a motorcycle, shooting from a position closest to the motorcycle makes it appear larger in relation to the person. If you take the same shot from an angle closer to the person, he or she appears larger. And if you decide to shoot the person sitting on top of the motorcycle, you'll have a sense of movement created by the subject being off center.

Figure Out Your Flash

Guessing about the capabilities of your camera's flash can leave you (and your subject) in the dark. Your camera's flash is designed to light up an area within a certain range. You need to consult the camera's manual for that range. You should also experiment with your flash within the range, making sure to get the results you want.

If you get too close to your subject with the flash, all you see is an overexposed glare of light. Too far, and your subjects are obscured by the darkness.

As a rule, it's easier to brighten up an underexposed photo with PhotoSuite 4 than it is to dim down an overexposed one.

Flashes are also the subject of a lot of misconceptions. A common one is that you don't use a flash outside during the daylight hours. In fact, using a fill flash to supplement natural light can eliminate harsh shadows from the subject's features and illuminate more of the detail of the scene you're trying to capture. (Chapter 4, "Imaging Equipment for All Occasions," covers flashes in more detail.

Eliminate Bogus Background

It's important to focus on your subject, but don't ignore what your subject is standing in front of. Busy backgrounds with patterned wallpaper, psychedelic curtains, and objects that appear to be growing out of the subject's head have ruined many a good shot.

Don't be shy about using PhotoSuite 4's cropping tools. These tools allow you to get rid of annoying and distracting objects that sneak into the background of your photo.

Level Out Lighting Contrasts

If you look at scene, such as a sunset on the horizon, your eyes automatically adjust for the light and dark areas. Your eyes filter (and dim down) some of the light from the sun. They "turn up" the lighting on other subjects dimmed or in the shadows. This is a wonderfully complex process carried out by the human eye that the camera has never been quite able to duplicate.

When your camera focuses on an image and adjusts for the lighting, it takes a sort of "average" reading. Some areas appear overexposed whereas others are woefully underexposed. All in the same shot!

And the funny thing is, the image may have appeared perfectly fine in your camera's viewfinder. There is no solution for this age-old photography problem (at least not with the equipment most of us have). You best bet is to avoid lighting contrasts as much as possible. Take shots in the shade and indirect sunlight whenever possible and avoid too much sunny sky in the background.

Create High-Tech Light Effects with House Lamps

It's amazing what you can do with ordinary house lamps! You can create dramatic studio effects.

The effect you get depends on the type of household lighting you're working with. If you have halogen or tungsten bulbs, your photo will have a warm, golden-brown cast.

Fluorescent lamps give you plenty of light because they're so strong. But they can also give your photo a greenish cast. To avoid having to correct the Martian glow later, try using your flash as much as possible to counteract the fluorescent lighting. If the room is very bright, you may need to dim the lights or throw a cloth over the lamp to get your flash to flare.

If you don't like the color tone that you get with your artificial lighting, you can take steps to correct and compensate for it. Chapter 10, "In Color Living," tells you how.

Keep a Steady Hand

A lot of digital cameras have an LCD viewfinder. They allow you to view the scene you're about to photograph on a television-like screen.

The problem with this type of viewfinder is that it requires you to move your camera away from your face to shoot the pictures and sometimes even to bend your arms at really weird angles. This increases the possibility that your hands may shake as you shoot the picture. The result? A blurry shot for which you may otherwise blame your auto-focus feature.

To avoid the shake-and-blur effect, you need to be aware of the problem. That way, you can concentrate on keeping your hands and arms steady when you shoot. It sometimes helps to prop your elbows on something solid. A table, a chair, or even your own torso works great.

Some digital cameras have both an LCD screen and a traditional viewfinder. If that's the case, you can turn off the fancy LCD screen and opt for the ordinary viewfinder.

Turning off the LCD viewfinder also saves on batteries.

Take Lots of Photos

Here's a secret that every photographer knows: It takes lots of disappointing photos to come up with a few really good ones.

This is because you almost never have complete control over your environment or subject. People blink. They even have the nerve to breathe.

The ability to take multiple shots in rapid succession is an area in which film cameras win out over digitals. The latter takes several seconds to save a shot to memory, during which time your subjects may have repositioned themselves. On the other hand, digital cameras allow you to delete all the photos you don't like from disk or memory, and you never have to worry about wasting film.

Be Both Patient and Spontaneous!

Carry your camera with you and then wait patiently for that elusive photo opportunity. Shots for which people are required to pose and smile rigidly are unpleasant if you're unlucky enough to be the person being photographed. They can also be really boring to view because they say nothing *about* your subject.

Photographing people while they're engaged in an activity makes them more relaxed. It also puts the subject in a sort of context for the ultimate viewers of the picture. For example, a shot of Grandma with her hands in her lap doesn't say as much about Grandma as does a photo of her knitting, cooking, gardening, or hugging a grandchild. See what I'm getting at?

Don't be afraid to scan the room for "props" to use in your photo. For example, shoot a child with a favorite toy, or grab a bunch of flowers out of the vase on the table to create a mood.

Chapter 19

Ten (Plus) Funky File Formats

In This Chapter

- Figuring out which formats you can open and save
- Knowing when it's best to compress
- Which file format best preserves image quality?
- Making sure other people can open your files

Computer files may all look alike when you view them on your desktop — identical yellow folder icons. But in reality, they're as different as the applications programs that created them. Every software program uses a native file format to save and store its data. PhotoSuite 4, for example, uses the JPEG format to store its image files.

Some formats are *proprietary*, which means that you can open and use them only if you have the particular type of software for which they were designed. Other formats are extremely gregarious, and you can easily toss them around on the World Wide Web and know that they'll get along just fine with lots of other programs.

In additon to its native JPEG file format, PhotoSuite 4 supports a smorgasbord of file formats for saving and storing images. Every supported format has its own idiosyncrasies and quirks.

TIFF

TIFF, or *Tagged Image File Format*, was developed by Microsoft and a company called Aldus. It handles grayscale, 8- and 24-bit color images. It's one of the most widely used formats and is compatible with a wide range of software programs.

The compression conundrum

A compression ratio allows you to reduce the amount of data stored in a file so that the file size is smaller and easier to transfer or work with. The higher the compression ratio, the more the file size is reduced.

Unfortunately, because compression gets rid of data, it compromises the quality of the image. The more compression, the more the image is degraded.

There are two types of compression — lossy and lossless. *Lossy* compression is the one that can really compromise the quality of your image over time. It's very aggressive in discarding image data to reduce file size. Initially, the impact of this lossy compression isn't too devastating, but over time it takes its toll. This is because every time the file is opened and closed, the file is recompressed and more data is lost.

Lossless compression only discards *redundant* data, which is data that's not actually used in producing the image. And data is not lost each time you open, close, and save the file. The disadvanatage of lossless compression is that it's much less effective in reducing file size.

Chapter 4, "Imaging Equipment for All Occasions," has an explanation of the various bit-depth ratings. These ratings tell you how much information about color your equipment or software can store, and consequently how many colors you can reproduce. For now, all you need to remember is that the 8-bit depth is the one that allows you to reproduce images having 256 colors. Sixteen-it depth gives you 32,000 colors. And still better yet, 24-it depth (called true color) stores information sufficient to produce more than 16 million colors.

TIFF is usually not the format of choice for files being transferred over the World Wide Web. This is because the files are so large.

TIFF files can be compressed using several different levels of compression, but none of the TIFF compression methods reduce file size very much. But the good thing about TIFF compression is that it doesn't degrade the quality of your images because it uses only *lossless* compression, as explained in the sidebar "The compression conundrum."

In a nutshell, you get good image quality and a compatibility with Windows and Mac applications programs using a TIFF format. The downside is that TIFF file size is unwieldy for sending graphics over the Internet.

JPEG

JPEG is short for Joint Photographic Experts Group. This group consists of folks who developed this file format primarily for use on the Internet. JPEG is PhotoSuite 4's native format.

The big advantage of this format is that it can compress data so that it fits into much smaller sizes. Smaller size means that graphics files can more easily be transferred over the Internet and take less time to download.

The disadvantage of the JPEG is it uses a lossy compression scheme. As explained in the sidebar, "The compression Conundrum," this type of compression results in data loss and degrades the image. You don't lose too much data the first time you save your shot, but each time you open and close the JPEG file, you recompress it. This means that the file size gets smaller and smaller and the image gets more degraded each time you access the file.

EXIF

EXIF, short for Exchangeable File Format, is a type of JPEG format. It's an enhanced version, sometimes called JPEG (EXIF). A lot of digital cameras use it. What makes this particular format so digital-camera friendly is its ability to store extra data pertaining to camera settings. (Generally, you care about this particular format only if it's the one your digital camera happens to use.)

GIF

GIF, or Graphic Interchange Format, is another type of format well suited for transferring files on the Internet. GIF files are always compressed. This format is limited to saving files of 256 colors or less and is largely being replaced by the PNG format discussed in the next section.

PNG

The portable graphics network, or PNG format, is an alternative to GIF. It's better for reproducing graphics than GIF because it's not limited to 256 colors. It also uses a lossless compression scheme.

As you can imagine, this format produces relatively large files because there's lots of color data and a relatively inefficient compression scheme.

Photo CD (PCD) Formats

This format was developed by Eastman Kodak specifically for storing images on disks. You can open files using this format but you can't save them in PhotoSuite 4. You can, however, download an image in PCD format, edit it in PhotoSuite 4, and save it in another format, such as TIFF.

The PCD file contains multiple copies of each image saved at different resolutions. When you open it, you can select the resolution that you want to use.

Windows Bitmap (BMP)

Windows Bitmap (BMP) is the native file format for Microsoft windows. This format is very effective for preserving the quality of images over time after multiple edit and save sessions.

Although you can use this format to save true color (24 bit) files, you can't compress them. This format doesn't allow you to compress files larger than 256 colors.

FPX

The Kodak FPX file format is specially designed to produce high quality photographs. Each FPX file contains multiple copies of the image at different resolutions.

You can use the high-resolution images to produce excellent quality photographs, using Kodak Photo Net Online, which is covered in Chapter 13, "Graphics on the Go." The lower-resolution copies work well for displaying the image on your computer screen or for printing using a standard printer.

Other File Formats Supported by PhotoSuite 4

In addition to the formats specifically discussed in this chapter, PhotoSuite 4 allows you to view and save files in a number of other formats. Table 19-1 summarizes all file formats supported by PhotoSuite 4. The table tells you the three-letter abbreviation used for the file extension (the file extension appears as part of the name of the file.) It also indicates whether you can both open and save the file using PhotoSuite 4.

Table 19-1 File Formats Supported By PhotoSuite 4

File Format	*Extensions That Appear as Part of Filename*	*Can Open File in This Format?*	*Can Save File in This Format?*
Joint Photographic Experts Group	.jog, .jpe, .jpeg	Yes	No
Portable Network Graphic	.png	Yes	No
Windows Bitmap	.bmp	Yes	No
FPX	.fpx	Yes	No
Tagged Image File Format	.tif	Yes	No
CompuServe Graphics Interchange Format	.gif	Yes	No
Gem Image	.img	Yes	No
PC Paintbrush	.pcx	Yes	No
STiNG	.stn	Yes	No
TrueVision Targa	.tga	Yes	No
Sun Raster	.ras	Yes	No
Seattle Filmworks	.sfw	Yes	No
Konica	.kqp	Yes	No
Encapsulated Postscript	.eps	Yes	No
Floppy Shot	.pic	Yes	No
Kodak PhotoCD	.pcd	Yes	No
Adobe PhotoShop	.psd	Yes	No
Windows Metafile	.wmf, .emf	Yes	No

Chapter 20

Ten Troubleshooting Tips

In This Chapter

- Accessing your digital camera and scanner with PhotoSuite 4
- Dealing with the heartbreak of botched installations
- Saving stuff from the Internet
- Emancipating e-mail that gets stuck
- Coping with crashes and lockups

Come Out ! Come Out! Accessing Your Camera or Scanner

How disappointing! You're all revved up with creative energy and your camera plays coy. Or maybe it's your scanner that gives you the slip. Try as you may, you just can't access them.

PhotoSuite 4 communicates with digital cameras and scanners through special software called a TWAIN driver, which stands for Totally Without an Interesting Name.

If PhotoSuite 4 can't access your peripheral device, it's likely that the TWAIN driver wasn't installed or maybe wasn't configured properly. You need to be sure that your camera/scanner is TWAIN compatible and that you've installed the TWAIN driver included with it.

You can test for the TWAIN driver using a program preinstalled with Windows called Kodak Imaging.

Close PhotoSuite 4 before attempting to use this program.

To access the Kodak Imaging program:

1. **Go to Start⇨Programs⇨Accessories ⇨Imaging.**
2. **After starting the Imaging program, go to File⇨Select Scanner.**

   A dialog box listing various peripheral devices appears.
3. **Select your device from the list and click Select.**
4. **Go to File⇨Scan⇨New.**

Your TWAIN interface should now appear and you can download/scan your pictures.

Wait! I Want to Open It with This Program!

If you want to open your image files with a specific program, you need to make it the *default* program for the file. If you're working with Windows (and who isn't?), the default program is Internet Explorer (IEXPLORE) for image files and Windows Media Player (MPLAYER) for video files.

To change the default file, follow these steps:

1. **Hold down the Shift key and right-click your mouse on the file.**

   A pop-up menu appears.
2. **Select Open With.**

   A dialog box appears with a list of programs.
3. **Select the program you want to be the default program for the file.**
4. **Check the box "Always use this program to open this type of file"; then click OK.**

   You need to restart Windows for the changes to take effect.

If you've already installed the program, you can select "Install additional components" from the Setup menu. You need to restart your computer for the changes to take effect.

Failure to Create Empty Document Message

Oops! If you see this message, you have an installation problem. You need to delete the MGI PhotoSuite 4 folder from your hard disk drive, reboot your computer, and run the installation again. The default location for this folder is C:\PROGRAMFILES\MGI. When you boot up after rerunning the installation program, be sure to close all unnecessary programs.

If this doesn't correct the problem, try deleting the contents of your C:\WINDOWS\TEMP folder.

Close all programs you have running before attempting to install or run the program. Make sure that you're not running any memory-protecting programs such as Virus Protection or System Monitoring Utilities (System Doctor, First Aid, PC Medic, Watchdog, crash protection, download managers, and so on). Also, disable any desktop video-enhancement programs.

The General Protection Fault Message

Do you get a message that says "General Protection Fault in MACXW4.DRV"? Does this happen when you move your mouse over the Share button?

If so, take heart. This is a known problem! I bet you have an ATI video display card and are using the Windows 98 default video drivers. To correct this issue, go to ATI's Web site and install the updated video drivers for your ATI video card. ATI's Web address is `www.atitech.com`.

Everything in life should be so simple!

Can't Save Pictures from the Web

Although PhotoSuite 4 has the capability of dragging and sending photos from Web pages into its photo library, this doesn't work on certain Web pages that use nested frames or when photos are hyperlinks. In these cases, right-click your mouse and use Save Picture As to save the photo.

Flunking the Minimum-Resolution Test

It's so exciting to get your new PhotoSuite 4 software, you can barely contain yourself during the installation process. Then, when the installation is almost complete, you get a nasty message like "PhotoSuite 4 requires a minimum screen resolution of 800 x 600 and High Color 16-bit."

If you get this message, it means that your current computer monitor settings don't meet the minimum requirements for running PhotoSuite 4.

One solution is to increase your display settings by doing the following:

1. **From the Start Menu, select Settings⇨Control Panel.**

   The Control panel dialog box appears.

2. **Double-click the Display icon.**

   The Display Properties dialog box appears.

3. **Click the Settings tab and use the Desktop Area slide bar to set the Resolution to a minimum of 800 x 600.**

4. **Use the drop-down menu to set the Color Palette to a minimum of High Color 16-BIT (65,000 color).**

   If your computer doesn't have this setting, this means that you have an incorrect display driver installed or your computer doesn't support these display settings.

Can't Send Pictures by E-Mail from PhotoSuite 4

PhotoSuite 4 automatically opens a new e-mail and attaches your photo for you directly from the program. If you can't e-mail pictures directly from PhotoSuite 4 using the Send Via E-mail command on the PhotoSuite 4 menu, it's most likely because your Windows Mail Applications Interface Program (MAPI) isn't configured properly. MAPI has to be configured before your computer can send any e-mail anywhere.

If you don't receive any prompt, or the computer freezes when you click the Send Via E-Mail option on the PhotoSuite 4 File menu, you haven't configured your system so that all your Windows applications can access the MAPI. The configuration process differs depending on the browser software you're using.

Configuring MAPI with Outlook Express 4

If you're using Microsoft Outlook Express 4 (with Internet Explorer 4), you can configure it to MAPI by following these steps:

1. **Start up Outlook Express.**
2. **Go to Tools⇨Options⇨General and select the check boxes labeled "Make Outlook Express my default simple MAPI client" and "Make Outlook Express my default MAPI client."**
3. **After selecting both options, click Apply and OK.**

   You'll need to restart your computer for the changes to take effect.

Configuring MAPI for Outlook Express 5

If you are using Microsoft Outlook Express 5 (with Internet Explorer 5), configure MAPI as follows:

1. **Start up Outlook Express.**
2. **Go to Tools⇨Options⇨General and select the check box labeled "Default Messaging Programs."**
3. **Click the "Make Default" button.**
4. **Click Apply and OK.**

   You'll need to restart your computer for the changes to take effect.

Configuring MAPI for Netscape Mail

If you're using Netscape Mail, follow these steps to configure MAPI:

1. **Start running the Netscape program.**
2. **Go to Edit⇨Preferences⇨Mail and Newsgroups.**
3. **Select the option "Use Netscape Messenger from MAPI based applications."**
4. **Click OK and restart your computer for the changes to take effect.**

Configuring MAPI for EUDORA

If you're using Eudora as your e-mail client, you need to run the file called SWMAPI.EXE, located in the Eudora program folder. Restart your computer for the changes to take effect.

Attaching images to AOL

Sorry, but you can't send e-mail directly through PhotoSuite 4 if you're an AOL user. AOL uses its own proprietary e-mail software components, which can't be accessed by PhotoSuite 4. You need to create a new e-mail as usual using the AOL email client and then attach the image file. (The AOL Help menu tells you how to send attachments.)

Catastrophic Crashing and Locking Up

What can be more annoying than your program locking up or crashing? There can be several causes for this. You can have a software conflict or obsolete video card drivers, to name a couple.

Ruling out software conflicts

The first thing you want to do is rule out a conflict between PhotoSuite 4 and another software program that may be running in the background. So close all programs (except Explorer and Systray) before you attempt to install or rerun PhotoSuite 4 after you've experienced a crash or lockup.

There are some programs that you may be running on your computer without realizing it. You need to get out of these, too. Make sure that you're not running any memory-resident programs such as Virus Protection or System Monitoring Utilities (System Doctor, First Aid, PC Medic, Watchdog, crash protection, download managers, and so on). Also make sure that you're not using any memory managers or desktop video enhancement programs. Disable these types of applications before continuing. (Your Windows Help menu tells you how to identify which programs are running.)

After you've nixed and disabled all unnecessary programs other than PhotoSuite 4, try to reboot your computer.

If you're using Windows 98 and having a problem, be sure to close the Windows Task Scheduler. You can do this by following these steps:

1. **Double-click the My Computer icon on your desktop.**

   The My Computer dialog box appears.

2. **Double-click Scheduled Tasks.**

   The Scheduled Tasks dialog box appears.

3. **Select Advanced and then click Stop Using Task Scheduler.**

4. **Now reinstall the program and try to run it again.**

Updating your video card drivers

PhotoSuite 4 makes extensive use of your computer's video card and its drivers. (A *driver* is the software that allows your computer to communicate with the video card.) It's really important to be sure that you have the correct and latest video display drivers installed.

If the video card driver is your culprit, you may get a "Protection Fault" error message. The error condition usually reports a problem with a specific .DRV (driver) file or in a beginning location of 014f: or 015f:. If you get this message and need to update your driver, the first step you should take is to upgrade your video driver. Please contact the system manufacturer for details on how to obtain and update your video driver. These days, you can download most driver updates from the Internet.

If you still encounter problems after updating your video card driver, try changing your video driver settings for more or fewer colors. You can also try to identify and exit all memory managers or RAM maximizing software and any other accessory programs that boost or enhance the video card switching.

Deactivate the hardware acceleration option

If your video display driver has an option for Hardware Acceleration, try disabling or setting it to minimum. You can find this option by doing the following:

1. **From the Start menu, go to Settings⇨Control Panel.**

   The Control Panel dialog box appears.

2. **Click the Display Properties icon.**

   The Display Properties dialog box appears.

3. **Click the Settings tab.**

   If your video display driver has a Hardware Acceleration option, deselect it.

Other things to try

Still having problems? Here are a few more things you might try:

- Perform a Windows Scandisk and Defrag to ensure that you don't have any system integrity problems. This should be done regularly to maintain maximum performance of your computer. (Your Windows Help menu tells you how to perform these operations.)
- Install the latest version of DirectX available from `www.microsoft.com`.
- Install the latest Windows Media Player available from `www.microsoft.com`.
- Try deleting the contents of your C:\WINDOWS\TEMP folder.

You Can't Open Your Album Images

If you can't open a photo in the album, it may be that you inadvertently deleted the photo.

PhotoSuite 4 albums create links to your photos when you add them to an album. The album doesn't actually save the picture in the album file. You must save the images to your hard disk to be able to access them.

RAM It!

Be sure that you have plenty of free RAM and hard disk space. When scanning with PhotoSuite 4, your computer requires at least twice the hard disk space as your scanned image. The program has a recommended minimum of 32MB of RAM to function.

Index

• A •

• B •

• C •

• D •

• G •

• H •

• I •

• J •

• K •

• L •

• M •

• N •

• O •

• P •

• R •

• S •

• T •

• X •

• Z •

Notes

Notes

Notes

Notes

Notes

Notes

Notes

FOR DUMMIES BOOK REGISTRATION

We want to hear from you!

Visit **dummies.com** to register this book and tell us how you liked it!

- Get entered in our monthly prize giveaway.
- Give us feedback about this book — tell us what you like best, what you like least, or maybe what you'd like to ask the author and us to change!
- Let us know any other *For Dummies* topics that interest you.

Your feedback helps us determine what books to publish, tells us what coverage to add as we revise our books, and lets us know whether we're meeting your needs as a *For Dummies* reader. You're our most valuable resource, and what you have to say is important to us!

Not on the Web yet? It's easy to get started with *Dummies 101®: The Internet For Windows® 98* or *The Internet For Dummies®* at local retailers everywhere.

Or let us know what you think by sending us a letter at the following address:

For Dummies Book Registration
Dummies Press
10475 Crosspoint Blvd.
Indianapolis, IN 46256

BESTSELLING
BOOK SERIES